WE AVERAGE
UNBEAUTIFUL
WATCHERS

WE AVERAGE UNBEAUTIFUL WATCHERS

Fan Narratives and the Reading of American Sports

NOAH COHAN

University of Nebraska Press | Lincoln

Acknowledgments for the use of copyrighted material appear on pages xiii–xiv, which constitute an
extension of the copyright page.

Library of Congress
Cataloging-in-Publication Data
Names: Cohan, Noah, author.
Title: We average unbeautiful watchers:
fan narratives and the reading of
American sports / Noah Cohan.
Description: Lincoln: University of Nebraska
Press, [2019] | Series: Sports, media, and
society | Includes bibliographical
references and index.
Identifiers: LCCN 2018052325
ISBN 9780803295940 (cloth: alk. paper)
ISBN 9781496216175 (epub)
ISBN 9781496216182 (mobi)
ISBN 9781496216199 (pdf)
Subjects: LCSH: Sports spectators—United States—
Psychology. | Mass media and sports—United
States. | Racism in sports—United States. | Sports—
United States—Psychological aspects. | Identity
(Psychology)—United States. | Sports in literature—
United States. | Sports journalism—United States.
Classification: LCC GV715 .C65 2019 |
DDC 306.4/83—dc23 LC record available at
https://lccn.loc.gov/2018052325

Set in Lyon Text by E. Cuddy.
Designed by L. Auten.

For Carla, Theo, and Elliot,
from your biggest fan.

CONTENTS

PREFACE

From Jackie Robinson to Muhammad Ali, Bill Russell to Mahmoud Abdul-Rauf, American athletes, especially African American athletes, have a long and storied history of political activism. And yet NFL star Colin Kaepernick's demonstrations against police brutality and antiblack violence in the fall of 2016 seemed to mark a turning point in many Americans' understanding of the interrelationship of sports and politics. Misconstrued as a symbolic attack on the nation's military forces, Kaepernick's kneeling gesture was quickly identified by then-presidential candidate Donald Trump as a means to rile up his political base with thinly veiled racist rhetoric. Demanding that Kaepernick leave the country,[1] Trump escalated his rhetoric in 2017, asserting that any demonstrating player is "a son of a bitch" who should be "fired."[2] In effect, Trump insisted that Kaepernick should "stick to sports" even as he leveraged the conservative white American public's distaste for black athletes as a political tool. Such hypocrisy led several media members to proclaim that the very notion of "stick to sports" was dead: high-profile athletic spaces could no longer be considered apolitical ones.[3]

This kind of proclamation, while perhaps well-intentioned, is short-sighted: as indicated by the longer history of athlete activism and the inherently political representation of military forces at professional games (nearly ubiquitous since 9/11), sports have long been political, especially for the players. The notion that sports could be exclusively stuck-to, then, has largely been propagated in deference to fans, many of whom have wistfully believed that sporting spaces operate independently from the urgencies of life outside the stadium. Such a belief reflects privilege born of interpretive stakes rather than participatory ones: fans make of the on-field action something largely removed from the personal motives and physical intentions of the players. Kaepernick's gesture of protest disrupted this privilege. The quarterback's message about police brutality and antiblack violence, misconstrued or not, demonstrated his prerogative to express himself on nonphysical terms that "stick to sports"-inclined fans could not escape from nor easily adapt to their liking.

Whether fans realized it or not, Kaepernick's protest forced them to reckon with their interpretive agency as readers of sports and at the same time confronted them with the incumbent limitations on such agency. The story of professional football, in other words, was disrupted such that fans were awakened to, or at least had their escapist fantasy disturbed by, their role as readers of sport. As it turns out, one of the main reasons that "stick to sports" is fundamentally nonsensical is that sports are part of the narrative fabric of our lives—they may be occasioned to provide emotional respite from a tough day at work or the death of a loved one, but that respite is still inherently woven into the rest of our lived experiences.

From that premise emerges this book, much of it written before Kaepernick's protest and Trump's rise to power, but relevant to an understanding of both. Kaepernick's admirable activism, most of it conducted outside the spotlight—especially since his blackballing by NFL ownership born of fealty to Trump—insistently calls attention to the American story of race and racism that Trump's lies deny or distort. In the narrative battle for truth that Americans must grapple with daily in the age of Trump, attention to one's own personal responsibility as an interpreter matters a great deal. But we need not limit our awareness of such a responsibility to times of discord and upheaval. An awareness of readerly interpretive agency when it comes to sports can and has benefited fans in the widest range of historical and personal contexts, just a sampling of which are considered in this book. As I will demonstrate, a narrative understanding of sports provides more than a compelling means for interpreting these games and athletes beyond the competitive "reality" of their live performance and their quantification via statistics. Recognizing the narrativity of sports, and their role as readers, also helps fans understand themselves.

Sports are real, but they are also flexible narratives subject to the interpretive imperatives of those who read and rewrite them. What's more, no less than Trump's self-interestedly flexible idea of truth and moral clarity, these fannish interpretations and modes of relation to sports narratives are worthy of comment and criticism. In this book, I pursue such comment and criticism and look hopefully to a future when a preponderance of "we average unbeautiful watchers" self-consciously choose to make of sports narratives a richer tapestry than either Kaepernick's kneel or Trump's race-baiting response would occasion on their own.[4]

ACKNOWLEDGMENTS

I'm grateful to several periodicals that published earlier versions of the work that became this book. Portions of chapter 1 appeared in similar form as "Baseball Fan Behavior as Postmodern Praxis in Don DeLillo's *Underworld*" in *Aethlon: The Journal of Sport Literature* 32, no. 2 (2015): 37–56. Parts of chapter 5 appeared in similar form as "Rewriting Sport and Self: Fan Self-Reflexivity and Bill Simmons's *The Book of Basketball*" in *Popular Communication* 11, no. 2 (2013): 130–45, published with permission from Taylor & Francis (www.tandfonline.com). Other portions of chapter 5 appeared in similar form as "New Media, Old Methods: Archiving and Close Reading the Sports Blog" in *Journal of Sport History* 44, no. 2 (2017): 275–86, published with permission from the University of Illinois Press (www.journalofsporthistory.org).

Many people and organizations helped me on the journey to finishing this book. At Washington University in St. Louis, Bill Maxwell, Iver Bernstein, Gerald Early, and Wayne Fields urged me to do a project on sports, then advised me as I wrote the version of this project that was my dissertation. There is no book, or version of me that is an academic, without their encouragement, attention, and counsel. The American culture studies program at WashU, my intellectual home in graduate school and my place of employment since 2015, has provided more support—emotional, intellectual, and professional—than I ever could have hoped for. Iver Bernstein, Heidi Kolk, Peter Benson, Terri Behr, Jennifer Gallinat, Máire Murphy, and Dave Walsh feel more like family than co-workers. I am tremendously grateful to all the members of the Sports Studies Caucus of the American Studies Association for stimulating my thinking and expanding my horizons. Among those, Amy Bass, Yago Colás, Dan Gilbert, Frank Guridy, Katherine Mooney, Dan Nathan, Theresa Runstedtler, Lucia Trimbur, and Travis Vogan deserve special thanks for their friendship and encouragement.

Thanks to the University of Nebraska Press, and Aaron Baker and Alicia Christensen in particular, for recognizing the project's potential and providing guidance in its direction. Alicia Christensen, Abby Stryker, and Natalie O'Neal demonstrated remarkable patience and kindness in putting up with my countless queries and concerns. Aaron Baker, Yago Colás, Meg Dobbins, En Li, Nick Miller, Michael O'Bryan, Philip Sewell—and surely others I'm forgetting—all read versions of this project and lent valuable wisdom. Nathaniel Friedman and Jessica Luther graciously agreed to be interviewed and provided meaningful insights into their authorship and fan experiences. I am grateful to Jared Klemp, Lauren McCoy, Michael O'Bryan, and Erik Strobl for the friendship and support they've freely given since our first day of graduate school. And thanks to John Richards and KEXP for playing the music that kept me going on long days of writing.

Last, but certainly not least, I am thankful for my family. My dad made me a sports fan. More importantly, he also inspired me to think critically about what that means. No one loves stories, or changing their details, more than my mom: I could not understand narrative, or love, without her. I am grateful to my sisters for always supportively checking my biases. To my sons, Theo and Elliot, I owe thanks for filling the world with hope and wonder. And to Carla, endlessly patient and fiercely determined, I owe every success since age twenty-two. This book, and my life, are dedicated to her.

INTRODUCTION

Here is a theory. Top athletes are compelling because they embody the comparison-based achievement we Americans revere—fast*est*, strong*est*—and because they do so in a totally unambiguous way. Questions of the best plumber or the best managerial accountant are impossible even to define, whereas the best relief pitcher, free-throw shooter, or female tennis player is, at any given time, a matter of public statistical record. Top athletes fascinate us by appealing to our twin compulsions with competitive superiority and hard data.

Plus they're beautiful: Jordan hanging in midair like a Chagall bride, Sampras laying down a touch volley at an angle that defies Euclid. And they're inspiring. There is about world-class athletes carving out exemptions from physical laws a transcendent beauty that makes manifest God in man. So actually more than one theory, then. Great athletes are profundity in motion. They enable abstractions like power and grace and control to become not only incarnate but televisable. To be a top athlete, performing, is to be that exquisite hybrid of animal and angel that we average unbeautiful watchers have such a hard time seeing in ourselves.

DAVID FOSTER WALLACE, "How Tracy Austin Broke My Heart"[1]

Frustrated with former tennis phenom Tracy Austin's "breathtakingly insipid autobiography," David Foster Wallace tried to figure out just what it was that he had expected from her in the first place.[2] In "How Tracy Austin Broke My Heart," an essay first published in the *Philadelphia Inquirer*, the not-yet-famous novelist reviewed her autobiography, *Beyond Center Court: My Story*. Using Austin's words to better understand his own status as a "rabid fan," Wallace attempted to explain why "we average unbeautiful watchers" are both so compelled by athletic genius and so disappointed in athletes' inability to explain their own profundity.[3] Regarding the latter, Wallace concluded that a lack of self-reflection among star athletes may be a requisite ingredient for achieving excellence. In a high-pressure situation, he explained, thinking about what you are doing is a sure way to ruin it. The "cruel paradox" of sports stars' excellence, then, is that "blindness and dumbness" seem to be the "essence" of their gift, leaving "we spectators, who are not divinely gifted as athletes, [as] the only ones able truly to see, articulate, and animate the gift we are denied."[4] Whatever transcendent athletic abilities Tracy Austin may possess, Wallace realized that their signification—the process of assigning meaning to competitive bodily movement—was both his gift and responsibility as a fan.

My work in this book is animated by Wallace's words. Leaving behind the question of whether excellence in athletic performance is necessarily marked by "blindness and dumbness," a notion rather more complex than Wallace recognized, I too seek to better understand how "we spectators . . . see, articulate, and animate the gift we are denied."[5] I analyze and theorize the behavior of American sports fans to understand this behavior's cultural significance beyond mere consumerism. I draw from a wide disciplinary range of scholarship on sports and fans in doing so, but mine is a work of textual analysis. I take from Wallace's example two indelible characteristics of "unbeautiful watchers" that are rarely explored in sports studies—self-reflection and authorship—and use them to argue for a reconceptualization of the way we think about American sports fans' behavior and culture.[6] Critically reading accounts of and by fans like Wallace, I demonstrate that their consumptive, receptive, and appropriative behaviors are fundamentally acts of narrative interpretation and (re-)creation.[7]

For sporting events themselves *are* narratives, though they are not often recognized as such. Marked as "real" by the competitive participation of athletes and the lack of predetermination in their outcome, sporting events nevertheless feature all of the common elements of narratives: characters, plots, and a causal trajectory from beginning, to middle, to end. And while, as philosopher Erin C. Tarver puts it, fans believe themselves to be admiring *people* . . . they are doing no such thing. Rather, fans' deeply felt attachments to the fates and achievements of people they do not know and have never met are attachments to something like the heroes of an epic narrative. Just as Odysseus's power to compel admiration in the Greeks is dependent more upon the identification with him and reiteration of Homer's narrative than on the historical facts of a person called "Odysseus," the admiration of sports heroes, in this account, tells us more about the audience than it does the person the audience is supposed to admire. Specifically, it tells us what sorts of traits they find admirable and with what sorts of characters they prefer to identify—and imagine themselves to be like.[8]

As Tarver evocatively points out, though fans may not understand their actions on narrative terms, their interaction with sport is inescapably based in storytelling: the movement of the athletic bodies on display does not amount to anything without such signification, reception, and retelling. So construed, "everyone with any interest in sport 'reads' sport in some way," as Susan Birrell and Mary McDonald put it in their influential book, *Reading Sport*.[9] I take from their work the notion that "reading" sport refers to a multimodal set of actions: it can be casual—"attending an event or talking about it to friends and colleagues"—or critical, capable of finding and analyzing "cultural meanings that circulate within particular [sports] narratives or celebrities."[10] Crucially, Birrell and McDonald recognize in the fan-reader the potential to uncover or produce "counternarratives, that is, alternate accounts . . . that have been decentered, obscured, and dismissed by hegemonic forces."[11] All fans, from the most ordinary television viewer to a literary giant like David Foster Wallace, bring to their readings of sports narrative their own interpretive priorities and possibilities. As with any cultural text, then, the power structures that permeate sports can greatly affect, but not ultimately determine, the potential meanings made by their readership. Despite their place in a real or metaphorical crowd, the team-based affiliations they may share in common, and the ostensibly limited range of on-field actions from which they make meaning, sports fans are no less idiosyncratic in their interpretations than novel readers or film watchers. Part of the reason that Wallace's "theory" of sports attraction quickly becomes "more than one theory" is that fans are not a monolithic consumerist mob.[12] Some fans do compulsively prioritize "competitive superiority and hard data," while others invest in the "transcendent beauty" of sports narratives, but these are just two options in an almost limitless range of interpretive possibilities.[13]

Where fans fall along that almost limitless range is determined largely by the personal attributes that Wallace rather dyspeptically considers "average" and "unbeautiful." Building a coherent sense of self in what literary critic Paul John Eakin calls the "narrative identity system" of modern life, humans rely on the stories we consume as well as those we gather from our personal experiences.[14] Especially when such personal "primary narratives leave [people] with a sense of alienation and inadequacy," as sociologist Robert Perinbanayagam puts it, it is the "secondary narratives" we seek out that provide the "elements with which a narrative of the self is constructed."[15] Being a sports fan is thus always an autobiographical practice: whether manifested in a text or merely in one's sense of self, sports narratives and personal identity are inextricably intertwined. Sports fans demonstrate in the manner in which the read, write, and talk about sports the vital role of these games and athletes in providing more than mere distractions from the fans' "real" lives. Instead, sports narratives provide a means by which fans can make sense of those lives.

By reading sports narratives and relating them to their own life stories, then, fans both glean meaning from athletic competitions and invariably produce new meanings of their own. Most often, those new meanings are unrecorded, even fleeting. Sometimes, however, fan narratives are recorded and have the potential to be communicated. If fans capitalize on that potential, recognizing sports as narrative and their own interpretive agency as critical readers and writers, they can even affect the way that other fans, the media, and even some athletes understand the games. By communicating the alternative aesthetic, political, or psychological ramifications they perceive in sports narratives, fans can subvert the patriarchal and corporate imperatives embedded in the broadcast and the box score. As I will demonstrate, this transformative power is particularly evident in the era of internet communication.

Followers of sport are not the only people who identify as "fans" and creatively reinterpret cultural narratives, of course. Millions of motivated fans of music, film, and television "write back" in order "to address [their] own experiences and emotions within the worlds of [their] favorite texts," as Kristina Busse puts it, and reap the benefits of their own textual production.[16] And the study of such "media" fans has a long history in academia. Yet sports fans have almost always been excluded from such considerations. For his part, fan studies pioneer Henry Jenkins—author of the seminal text *Textual Poachers*—once categorized creative and critical appropriation as the provenance of particular cult-fiction media fans that he explicitly distinguished from the followers of sport, and most scholars have followed his lead.[17] The exception that proves the rule, the athletic pursuit that *has* been studied with an overt orientation to fans' interpretation and production of narrative, is professional wrestling. But wrestling, of course, is usually considered distinct from other sports "because it distorts all the trappings of sacred 'authentic' competition," as Sam Ford asserts.[18] Wrestling's athletic exhibition is fundamentally "unreal" to everyone but the "marks"—a term for gullible spectators born from wrestling's carnival roots—because its narrative is predetermined and thus considered fictional.[19] Yet some scholars, including Cornell Sandvoss in *Fans: The Mirror of Consumption*, have demonstrated that "at the point of consumption fictional narratives and 'real life' icons are equally encountered as texts which are read and appropriated by their (fan) audience. Whether we find our object of fandom in Britney Spears, *Buffy the Vampire Slayer* or the Boston Red Sox, these are all read and negotiated as (mediated) texts by their fans."[20] Whatever the differences in the relative "reality" and cultural resonance of a cult television show like *Buffy* and a team sports entity like the Boston Red Sox, fans integrate the narratives such texts provide into their own life stories in a similar manner.

Sandvoss's view of sports fans locates them on a continuum with other kinds of fans and helpfully positions the objects of sports fandom as texts similar to, rather than distinct from, other fan objects. His inclusive framing helpfully breaks down the scholarly boundaries diagnosed by Kimberly Schimmel, C. Lee Harrington, and Denise Bielby in "Keep Your Fans to Yourself: The Disjuncture Between Sports Studies' and Pop Culture Studies' Perspectives on Fandom." As the authors of "Keep Your Fans to Yourself" note, the analysis of sports fans has largely been pursued by those trained in quantitative research, while fans of television, movies, music, and other "pop culture" phenomena have mostly attracted attention from qualitative scholarly disciplines.[21] "Far too little crossover research has occurred," Lucy Bennett and Paul Booth affirm in their influential volume, *Seeing Fans: Representations of Fandom in Media and Popular Culture*, and the resulting lack of communication and paucity of common texts limits our broader scholarly understanding of sports and media fans.[22] The consequences of this critical disjuncture are significant for a number of reasons, but they are particularly notable when considering the narrativity of sports, and they underline further the need for textual analysis in analyzing sports fan behavior.

Because the study of such behavior has largely become the provenance of academics in psychology departments and business schools, the readership and authorship of sports fans have been deemphasized. Though sports fans have been scrutinized through qualitative ethnography, a mode that produces self-reflective narratives, the terms of such reflection are established by the researcher. Some scholarship in the social sciences—like Sandvoss's own insightful study of British soccer fandom, *A Game of Two Halves: Football, Television and Globalization*—thus recognizes the identity-building aspect of sports fandom, but has rarely taken the time to consider fans' self-motivated textual production as a means of exploring that identity in depth.[23] In effect, the critical underappreciation of the narrative basis of sports contributes to an equivalent lack of scholarly attention to narratives written by and about sports fans.

In this book I address both gaps, reading and analyzing the stakes of sports fan narratives primarily by using methods adapted from literary criticism. For its part, invested as it is in understanding human experience through stories, literary study has largely ignored sports narratives despite the games' massive popularity. A few notable critical monographs exist, including Christian Messenger's two volumes on *Sport and the Spirit of Play in American Fiction*, Timothy Morris's *Making the Team: The Cultural Work of Baseball Fiction*, and Michael Oriard's *Dreaming of Heroes: American Sports Fiction, 1868–1980*. A small professional organization, the Sports Literature Association of America, publishes literary critical work in its journal, *Aethlon*. Within this already limited body of scholarship on sports literature, however, even less attention has been paid to fans. This makes some sense given that the players are the focus of most sports narratives. But while athletes may indeed drive the plot and demonstrate the metaphorical richness of many sports narratives, I contend that it is the fan-reader whose behavior is most urgently analyzed through a literary lens—both in texts easily recognizable as "literary" and those, such as films and blog posts, that are not usually the provenance of English departments. As I will show, a myriad of innovations in literary criticism—from Linda Hutcheon's postmodernist idea of historiographic metafiction, to Rita Felski's concept of readerly double consciousness, to Paul John Eakin's aforementioned notion of narrative-based identity formation, just to name a few—shed important insight into the reading practices of sports fans. Positioning sports fan narratives as a neglected literary genre with popular influence and resonance, I employ such methods to elucidate the means by which fans both construct their own identities and use sports to make sense of the world around them.

Unlike Messenger's volumes and many other works on sports literature, my study is not a survey—pointedly and intentionally. To best convey the rich possibilities of sports fan readership and authorship, each chapter closely examines only a few fan narratives as they relate to particular thematic concerns that they share in common, including historicity, mental illness, race, masculinity, and technology. Diving deep into each of the texts I have selected according to these thematic orientations, I analyze sports fandom with an eye to the particular—the individual idiosyncrasy that makes each person's connection to sports narratives distinctly her own—as well as the broader social factors that inescapably influence fans' reception and narrative production. This bifurcated approach gives each chapter its own distinct thematic argument, even as the insights gleaned from close reading contribute to my broader claims about sports fandom as fundamentally a narrative-based pursuit. In addition, I have purposefully selected fan texts that manifest aspects of their thematic concerns in the *form* in which they are expressed. From the novel to the memoir to the film to the blog post, the choice of genre in many ways reveals as much about the experience of constructing a fan identity as the content of such depictions. *How* one communicates what it means to be a sports fan matters too. As Ellen Kirkpatrick puts it, studying the manner in which fans are represented "cannot be just a case of interrogating representations as they appear on the page, it must also be about how these representations speak to the conditions of their creation and consumption."[24] The differing textual forms of the sports fan narratives I examine convey important insights into fan reception and authorship—an experience far more complicated than a stereotypical understanding of sports fans would indicate.[25]

I begin with the novel. My first chapter, "So We Fabricate: Baseball and the Unfriendly Confines of History," focuses on two novels that depict baseball fan narratives with an emphasis on history and those who write it. The form of the novel, I argue, gives renowned authors Don DeLillo and Robert Coover the opportunity to ruminate on the investigative possibilities of subjectivity in relation to the mutually agreed upon, empirically observed happenings we call "history." Yet they arrive at quite different conclusions. In the prologue to his massive social novel *Underworld*, DeLillo rewrites one of the most famous home runs in baseball history—Bobby Thomson's 1951 pennant-clinching "Shot Heard 'Round the World"—from the perspective of the fans. Reflecting on the significance of the baseball action unfolding in front of them, DeLillo's fans integrate the broad narratives of history—even before they have been formally written—into their own life stories. What's more, they understand that their personal interpretations imbue the widely accessible on-field happenings with new meaning. These fans thus become practitioners of the postmodern literary genre Linda Hutcheon calls "historiographic metafiction," in which authors situate their works within the historical record but reflexively maintain the subjective autonomy of fiction.[26] In depicting baseball fans in this way, DeLillo demonstrates that a self-reflective historicity is not the exclusive privilege of well-known writers and intellectuals, but in fact inheres in the way most people narrate and assign personal meaning to the events happening around them. In *Underworld*, the interpretive practices of American fandom elucidate postmodern theory while revealing the incorporation of experimental narrative techniques into everyday life.

While DeLillo's rendering of the fan highlights the creation of personal histories amid the roar of the crowd, Robert Coover's depiction of the solitary fan calls into question the significance of the communal experience altogether. In his intricate 1968 novel, *The Universal Baseball Association,*

Inc., J. Henry Waugh, Prop., Coover presents baseball fandom in a manner akin to the stereotypical representations of cult-media fans who follow science fiction or fantasy. In Coover's baseball association, as in popular depictions of *Star Trek* geeks, fandom is conducted by "losers" in welcomed isolation, the better to immerse oneself in an imagined world. As he becomes more and more invested in the action of the imagined baseball league he has created, Henry Waugh withdraws from his job and his few remaining friends, submerging himself so fully in the world of "the Association" that he disappears from the novel altogether. Ad absurdum, Coover demonstrates the means by which sports fans personalize and internalize the narratives they interpret. But by removing Waugh from an interpretive context in which those narratives are shared with other fans, Coover also strips away the shared observation of unscripted competition that gives sporting events the gravitas of purported reality. By pushing his account of sports experience from a record of nonfictional happenings to the opposite end of the narrative spectrum, that of purely fictional fantasy, Coover tests the limits of sports fan interpretation by removing the social experience of "making" history that provides sporting events with shared resonance.

Imagining their fan protagonists beyond the confines of history, DeLillo and Coover attempt to trouble the "reality" of sports and question the importance of the games' communal interpretation. When one's sense of reality is perpetually clouded, however, the shared meaning-making facilitated by sport is not only not obvious, but also existentially determining. In my second chapter, "It Was My Fate, My Destiny, My End, to Be a Fan: Football, Mental Illness, and the Autobiographical Novel," I examine two texts whose liminal form reflects the psychological disorientation of their fan narrators. Because they are based in part on their authors' experiences with mental illness and football fandom, Frederick Exley's *A Fan's Notes* and Matthew Quick's *The Silver Linings Playbook* are autobiographical, but they are also intentional fictions. Writing their representations of self as characters—and unreliable narrators—obsessed with athletes that their readers will recognize as "real," Exley and Quick use the form of the autobiographical novel to trouble the distinction between a routine blurring of reality that we all experience in constructing coherent identity narratives and a crippling version of it that has been deemed psychotic.

Coping with the latter, the recently institutionalized narrators, Fred Exley and Pat Peoples (Quick's representation in his text), search for a stable identity in reading sports and literary narratives on similar terms. Connecting their own life narratives to the exploits of football players and fictional characters, the two fan protagonists use Hank Baskett, Hester Prynne, Frank Gifford, and Jay Gatsby alike to make sense of their place in a society that has deemed them mentally unsound. When "society's reality" is at odds with one's own, these novels demonstrate, the similarities between the consumption of purportedly "real" sports narratives and of fictional literature are laid bare.[27] Both provide common stories that Exley and Quick/Peoples use to reconstruct their identities and reconnect with the outside world.

Positioning football games and American literature as readerly equivalents, Exley and Quick demonstrate the relevance and urgency of literary methods in analyzing sports and fan behavior. And yet, as with football, Exley's and Peoples's connections to literature are mutually predicated on analysis and emotional investment. Even as they "root" for Gifford and Prynne alike, the fan-readers reflect on and analyze their own underlying motives. In other words, they recognize that most readings of *The Scarlet Letter* or a New York Giants football game will be different than their own, and attempt to account for that difference. In part because they make no distinction between reading sports and reading literature, Exley and Quick/Peoples thus exemplify Rita Felski's notion of textual "enchantment" and the attendant readerly "double-consciousness" of analytical and emotional imperatives.[28] The author-narrators demonstrate both that motivated readings can be insightful and that they provide "a richer and more multi-faceted [experience] than literary theory has allowed."[29] While sports and media fans are often denigrated by critics for an emotional involvement so overwhelming that it renders them incapable of analysis, aficionados of high cultural forms like music, art, and literature are usually credited with analytical capacities based in aesthetic remove and emotional distance. As Felski argues and Exley and Quick demonstrate, such binaries are false; the reality of our interaction with any text is much blurrier.

Though the fictions that embellish their life stories are formally important to Exley's and Quick's representations of fandom and mental illness, most autobiographical representations of what it means to be a sports fan ground themselves in the overt pretense of portraying "real" experience. Digging deeper into the possibilities of personal narrative, I examine the genre of fan memoir in my third chapter: "Race in the Basketball Memoir: Fan Identity and the Eros of 'a Black Man's Game.'" The form of the memoir, considered distinct from the autobiography by virtue of its primary focus on a subject external to the author-narrator, usefully frames the reception mechanics of fandom.[30] Writing the self in reading another's narrative is, after all, the core activity of fans of all types, from science fiction to professional wrestling, from romance to sports. As the chapter title indicates, I analyze the life writing of fans who articulate their identity via their love for basketball, and, in doing so, are preoccupied with the sport's inescapably racialized presentation in contemporary American life. Rather than accept what critical race scholar David Leonard has called "the efforts of the NBA to obscure or mediate racial difference—to deny or minimize the existence of racism both inside and outside its arenas"—the five authors I examine each recognize, in one way or another, that race and racism inescapably inform their fan reception.[31]

The chapter examines three memoirs by white fans—Scott Raab's *The Whore of Akron*, David Shields's *Black Planet*, and Bill Simmons's *The Book of Basketball*—and two by black fans—Spike Lee's *Best Seat in the House* and John Edgar Wideman's *Hoop Roots*—chosen for their attention to the manner in which race factors into their fan behavior. Raab's, Shields's, and Simmons's books are not antiracist works by any means, but their authors attempt to understand their attraction to a game that, at the professional level, is played mostly by black players for a mostly white audience. Aware of the racial difference between themselves and the athletes who drive the basketball narrative they covet, Raab, Shields, and Simmons nevertheless put forward an erotics of fandom based on the exotification of black culture and black bodies. Lee and Wideman, by contrast, reject just the sort of white fan appropriation that Raab, Shields, and Simmons can't resist. Even so, the African American authors *also* recognize the potency and value of the game for black agency and resistance to the structures of white supremacy.

Articulating who they are via basketball fandom, the five memoirists address their own insecurities and passions not merely through the games they love, but also through their connections to its performers. And though they manifest the unreliability of memory and the fancies of their imaginations in writing memoir, Lee, Raab, Shields, Simmons, and Wideman also recognize the lived reality of the athletes they fetishize. Whatever the memoirists choose to make of athletes-as-characters in sports narratives, the performers reside—off the court, at least—on the same plane of existence.[32] Memoirs, like sports themselves, are narratives that seem to reflect reality such that their artifice is often minimized and their social relevance emphasized.

From this focus on the way fans present themselves, I pivot to consider in chapter 4 the manner in which sports fans are depicted, shamed, and disciplined by large-scale media producers. The manner in which fans are depicted on screen by the same Hollywood production companies that profit from their dedicated consumption habits is a longstanding concern in media studies, but there is little apparent consideration when it comes to sports fans. In "It's Been a Problem with Me and Women: Failed Masculinities in Depictions of Sports Fans on Film," I outline the sports narrative as a film genre and situate fan-focused works within it. I closely examine four Hollywood movies, *The Fan, Fever Pitch, Big Fan*, and the film version of *Silver Linings Playbook*, and argue that the fan's readerly relationship to sports narrative is especially difficult to depict on screen. Combined with the usual fan stereotypes, this difficulty results in a flattened caricature of the sports fan as a quintessential loser, something like what Matt Hills has called the "superfan": an in extremis pathological type designed to "reinstate fan-cultural distinction and difference in the face of so many shades of fandom."[33] Providing a backdrop for the heroic exploits of athletes or presented as a kind of shorthand for the mania brought on by the pressures of modern life, Hollywood's sports fans are usually either faceless or pathological.

On the surface, *The Fan, Fever Pitch, Big Fan*, and *Silver Linings Playbook* serve as cautionary tales about the social consequences of sports obsession. Though they arrive at vastly different conclusions regarding those consequences, each film specifically relates the protagonist's fandom to his defective manifestation of masculinity. But these fans are emasculated not merely because they are fans, but because they are self-reflective fans. By carefully considering the meanings of sport on their own terms, rather than those of conventional consumerism, these fans have misappropriated sport as a cultural touchstone of normative masculinity. This pathology does little to dampen the resonance of the fans portrayal as readers of sport, however: the very fact that *The Fan*, *Fever Pitch*, *Big Fan*, and *Silver Linings Playbook* depict fans who are driven by narrative interpretation and production means they cannot help but reveal the productive possibilities of such activities. These films, in spite of themselves, provide a glimpse of sports fandom's creative possibilities even as they pathologize their fan protagonists.

The creative possibilities of fandom need not be merely glimpsed on screen, however. In online spaces, fans of all kinds have built massively influential communities that produce astonishing amounts of creative work. Transitioning from the mass-mediated genre of film to the multimedia platforms of the internet age, my fifth and final chapter considers a widespread form of early twenty-first-century fan writing: the blog post. Juxtaposed to the forms of the printed novel, the memoir, and the film, the medium of the blog post may seem ethereal for being mediated online. Yet that attribute is in fact a determining element of its dynamism. In the chapter "Reimagined Communities: Web-Mediated Fandom and New Narrative Possibilities for Sport," I argue that internet technology, in addition to fundamentally changing the form and pervasiveness of the sports fan narrative, has enhanced its creative and critical potential. I examine three particularly notable sports blogs and examine the ways in which web interactivity influenced their notion of what it means to be a sports fan. FreeDarko, Fire Joe Morgan, and Power Forward were twenty-first-century blogs with distinct fan perspectives, analytical methods, and writing styles—not to mention different primary sports of interest—but they all shared an interest in reading sports narratives beyond the limitations of conventional media coverage. Like media fans, who produce prodigious amounts of fanfiction and other writing for their fellow fans, I show how sports fans build communities around their distinct approaches to reading and rewriting sports narratives.

Where accredited journalists once held the media megaphones, ordinary sports fans are now able to analyze, recontextualize, and personalize sports narratives for a broader audience without the assistance and approval of a newspaper editor or a book publisher. While it may be true that many of those fan narratives are not particularly well-written or insightful, those blogs that present compelling analysis—FreeDarko, Fire Joe Morgan, and Power Forward included—can and do gain significant online readerships. Integrating hyperlinks, images, videos, and social media into their writing not merely as a practical matter but as an essential one, it is no coincidence that the three blogs also read sports narratives through the lenses of art, music, politics, mathematics, feminist theory, and a myriad of other topics from "outside the sports world." Emphasizing the intertextual potential of sports narratives in part because the digital tools of the internet naturalize intertextuality, FreeDarko, Fire Joe Morgan, and Power Forward each created a body of sports literature whose form and content emphasized the richness of sports narratives and their urgency for fan-readers beyond the games themselves. Though fan considerations of sports and their narrative ramifications for personal identity long predated the web, the internet both amplified them and fostered their critical potential. Throughout the chapter, I trace the ways the blogs' authors manifested that potential through three analytical frameworks: modes of fan attachment, narrative reconceptualization, and identity politics. In each area, I argue, FreeDarko, Fire Joe Morgan, and Power Forward reoriented what it means to be a sports fan in a manner that demonstrated the distinctive influence of digital interconnectivity.

But the power of the web is not enough to liberate fandom from the normative social structures that inequitably empower heterosexual white men in modern life. In the epilogue, "Feminist Rewritings of Sports Fan Culture," I explore the feminist fan writings of Stacey May Fowles in her memoir *Baseball Life Advice: Loving the Game That Saved Me*. Embracing a game that "I was largely discouraged from loving" because it is "built for men and boys, fathers and sons," Fowles asserts that she "truly love[s] the game because it made itself hard to love and I embraced it anyway. Because of that, it belongs to me in a way nothing else does."[34] Building her book from writings first published in her "Tiny Letter," a blog-like email platform that allows Fowles to reach a dedicated group of subscribing readers, she does not hesitate to call out and condemn the hierarchical masculinist norms that shape behavior among male baseball fans and players alike. Attentive to the narrative basis for fan identification, she maintains that while fans "know so little about the players we come to love" and thus "form a connection to athletes in much the same way we come to adore the characters in our favourite books," they must nevertheless hold those same players—as well as their teams and leagues—accountable to the same standards of inclusivity and equality that they demand in their own lives outside the lines.[35] Reading *Baseball Life Advice* demonstrates the power of online fan authorship to foster a sportscape liberated from hypermasculine dictates. The "average unbeautiful watchers" of American sports are increasingly nonwhite and nonmale. By self-consciously and defiantly writing themselves into sports narratives, fans like Fowles are expanding the way that we think about the possibilities of these dynamic stories for the better.

For his part, David Foster Wallace often used sports narratives, and tennis narratives in particular, to make sense of his complex world. From "Tracy Austin," to his accounts of his own junior tennis career, to his famous essays on the brilliance of Roger Federer, to the importance of tennis for the Stice family in his masterwork, *Infinite Jest*, the notion that "great athletes are profundity in motion" was a cornerstone of Wallace's remarkable literary career.[36] No literary critic would characterize him primarily as a sportswriter, nor should they. But Wallace's desire "to get intimate with all that profundity, [to get] the Story" of sports speaks to the games' narrative richness and critical potential on par with literature, film, and other highly esteemed cultural narratives.[37] Though most athletic "geniuses-in-motion" are not "geniuses-in-reflection," nor are many fans, the ability of Wallace and other sports fans "to see, articulate, and animate the gift we are denied" is ultimately less a "cruel paradox" than an enlightening one.[38] "Unbeautiful" though most fans may be, Wallace demonstrates that the beauty inherent in sports narratives is as varied as the people watching them. Fans are not beholden to wins and losses, but rather empowered to build from those results something that performers cannot realize themselves. Boorish people will make for boorish fans, to be sure, but one need not possess Wallace's voracious intellect to "to see, articulate, and animate" sports in ways that spark critical interest and popular consequence. Examining various manifestations of their articulation and animation, I demonstrate the readerly significance of sports on intellectual as well as popular terms. In explicitly framing sports as narratives, I reclaim the games for literary consideration of their interpretive imperatives and position sports spectators within the larger frameworks for figuring fans' receptive and appropriative behaviors pioneered in media studies. "We average unbeautiful watchers" may not be the ones "carving out exemptions from physical laws a transcendent beauty that makes manifest God in man," but without self-reflective sports fans like Wallace to signal it, that beauty would not transcend or make manifest anything at all.[39]

1

SO WE FABRICATE
Baseball and the Unfriendly Confines of History

> If baseball is a Narrative, it is like others—a work of imagination
> whose deeper structures and patterns of repetition force a tale, oft-
> told, to fresh and hitherto-unforeseen meaning.
>
> A. BARTLETT GIAMATTI, *Take Time for Paradise:*
> *Americans and Their Games*[1]

Understanding fans' reception of sporting events as based in storytelling
practices has wide ramifications for our understanding of group identities
and how they are formed. Perhaps nowhere is this more apparent than
in the sport of baseball. Nicknamed the "national pastime," baseball is
commonly considered to have metaphorical importance for the self-
conception of Americans. In keeping with the expansionist iconography
of Manifest Destiny, the sport is often written into a rural nationalist
mythos of country pastures and simpler values—this despite the game's
urban origins and long association with cheating, gambling, and other
forms of iniquity.[2] Such mythographic impulses contribute to baseball's
pastoral representation in fiction. Whether nostalgic for or critical of
that pastoral idyll, however, most writers of baseball fiction focus their
imaginings on those who play the "national pastime" rather than those
who watch. They do this not only because those players are the obvious
protagonists of such a fantasy—running about in grassy fields playing a
"child's game"—but also because their actions are measurable. Though
baseball mythos may deny the industrialization that fostered the game,
the cultural resonance of the game's gauzy idyll is nevertheless buttressed
by the seemingly stark permanence of numbers on a page. Every ball,

strike, hit, run, and out is clearly articulated in the statistical record. Befitting the rhetoric of "American functionalist meritocracy," literary critic Timothy Morris asserts, "baseball offers a spectacle of the pure work of statistical meritocracy."[3] Baseball's American way of life is thus made empirical through the numerically recorded actions of baseball players. The narratives of the idyllic national pastime and its quantifiable player-heroes function both as vessels of America's self-aggrandizing nostalgia for a past never realized and as purportedly meritocratic indicators of the nation's continuing significance.

In "The Power of History," an essay published in the *New York Times Book Review*, novelist Don DeLillo ruminates on this understanding that baseball and American identity are historically linked. Explaining the origins of "Pafko at the Wall," a short story originally published in *Harper's Magazine* that would become the prologue to his 1997 opus, *Underworld*, DeLillo writes:[4]

> Front page of The New York Times. Oct. 4, 1951. A pair of mated headlines, top of the page. Same typeface, same size type. Each headline three columns wide, three lines deep.
>
> Giants capture pennant—this was the dramatic substance of the first headline.
>
> Soviets explode atomic bomb—this was the ominous threat of the second.
>
> What did I see in this juxtaposition? Two kinds of conflict, certainly, but something else, maybe many things—I could not have said at the time. Mostly, though, the power of history.[5]

Two contemporaneous events, one of the most dramatic in baseball history and one of the most significant in Cold War history, become the doubly powerful subjects of DeLillo's fiction in "Pafko." Rather than focus on the players, however, in describing Bobby Thomson's famous pennant-winning home run in "Pafko" and in *Underworld*, DeLillo focuses on the fans. The historical record of on-field events—the players' actions and statistics—carry an air of definition, he asserts, yet "against the force of history, so powerful, visible and real, the novelist poses the idiosyncratic self."[6] The idiosyncratic self is the fan, "sly, mazed, mercurial, scared half-crazy," who interprets the action in front of her in compliance with the communally recognized rules, but who is "also free and undivided," able to assign meaning to what she sees in accordance with her own set of beliefs, hopes, and more immediate stimuli.[7] Rather than secondary to the official statistical record, DeLillo asserts that the fans' idiosyncratic meaning making is "the only thing that can match the enormous dimensions of social reality."[8] Social reality, whether represented through Thomson's home run or the Soviets' mushroom cloud, functions as a dominating master narrative. But it cannot encompass or suppress humankind's infinite subjectivities. Against "history's flat, thin, tight and relentless designs," *Underworld*'s fan narratives describe a baseball-mediated mode of identity formation that is personal, contingent, quotidian, and resolutely postmodern.[9]

In realizing the potential of fiction to explore spaces within history through the fans, *Underworld* represents the postmodern genre Linda Hutcheon calls "historiographic metafiction." Distinct from historical fiction, Hutcheon's genre "works to situate itself within historical discourse without surrendering its autonomy as fiction."[10] This autonomy is maintained by self-reflection; as Kathleen Fitzpatrick puts it, historiographic metafiction "self-consciously reminds us that, while events did take place in the real empirical past, we name and constitute those events as historical facts by selection and narrative positioning."[11] DeLillo's newspaper discovery aligned Thomson's "Shot Heard 'Round the World" and the Russian nuclear test for him, but his reconstitution of the two events in *Underworld* does more than merely remind us that their meanings are neither static nor determined by their place "in the real empirical past."[12] DeLillo also demonstrates that a self-reflective historicity is not the privilege of writers and intellectuals but is inherent in the way humans prioritize and assign personal meaning to the events happening around them. That he chooses to inhabit the minds of baseball fans in depicting this process of self-reflective historicity is not coincidental. The act of "nam[ing] and constitut[ing] events as historical facts by selection and narrative positioning" is the qualifying undertaking of sports spectatorship; in the stands the actions of the players are quantified and assigned collective value even as they are perpetually afforded a distinct value in each fan's personal narrative.[13] The question "where were you when [this event] happened?" speaks to this phenomenon. Retrospectively positioning one's frame of mind in relation to a significant public event—sports-related or otherwise—is a common conversational trope. That these retrospective narratives are largely fictionalized is inevitable: as Paul John Eakin has demonstrated, the very act of recounting memories changes their shape and details.[14]

But what if fans' personal fictions were not only the product but also the source of baseball's collective narrative? Robert Coover explores this question by pushing it to its limits in his critically acclaimed second novel, *The Universal Baseball Association, Inc., J. Henry Waugh, Prop.* The eponymous Henry Waugh is not an ordinary fan: as the title indicates, he is the proprietor of the "Universal Baseball Association." Henry uses baseball statistics not only to understand the historical significance of the players in his league but also to romanticize them, writing narratives replete with green fields on sunny afternoons. The problem, or rather the spark, of the novel is that the baseball players Henry follows are unreal not only in the world of the reader but in that of the proprietor protagonist. His league is entirely imagined, the players' actions determined by the roll of three dice in Henry's living room. In a manner of speaking, rather that historiographic metafiction, Coover creates metafictional historiography: he demonstrates the necessity of self-consciously situating historical processes within the self, to bring the trappings of external order to personal uncertainty in a "world so impossibly complex, we cannot accumulate all the data needed for a complete, objective statement. . . . So we fabricate; we invent constellations that permit an illusion of order to enable us to get from here to there."[15] But by the end of *Universal Baseball Association*, Coover strips away the purported objectivity of the dice, the probabilistic mechanism that lends Henry's private sporting events their gravitas of external-determination and veneer of "reality." By pushing his account of sports experience from its conventional position as a recording of "real" events to the opposite end of the narrative spectrum, that of purely subjective fantasy, Coover demonstrates the dangers of removing the shared historicity that powers the formation of group identity surrounding sporting events.

In this chapter I examine *Underworld*'s multiple spectators and *Universal Baseball Association*'s solitary fan to demonstrate the way that sports fans signify "real" events on fictive narrative terms, and vice versa. In considering DeLillo's novel, I broaden Hutcheon's notion of historiographic metafiction beyond its ascription to postmodern literature and consider it as a personal practice in fan experience. I argue that DeLillo not only realizes the power of his narrative to give new meanings to history, but also shows us that fans realize the same power in considering how a baseball game will affect their own life narratives. As DeLillo's work resists a view of history as supreme or definitional, Coover's book presents a complementary lesson: namely, that while the individual's personal narration of shared experience is a salient and necessary aspect of fandom—and indeed of our larger lived experiences—it is dangerous if totalizing. The lush green fields of sports' utopian imaginary, in other words, can be just as reductive as the black and white text and images in an old history book.

Sport is "a medium for self-transformation," as former Major League Baseball commissioner A. Bartlett Giamatti once put it, and "participant and spectator seek that *agon*, that competition with self to make the self over, to refashion or refigure or re-form the self into a perfect self, over and over again, in sport."[16] The fan's self-transformational narrative process is never complete, just as history never ends. Henry Waugh remarks that "perfection wasn't a thing, a closed moment, a static fact, but *process*, yes, and the process was transformation."[17] Between structure and volatility, group and individual, team and opponent, objective and subjective, history and fiction, the baseball fan experience is only viable, useful, and enticing insofar as the tensions that animate its transformative process never end. DeLillo and Coover suggest that like the renewing of the baseball season every spring, sports narratives are never static for fans. As they do so, the form of the novel allows DeLillo and Coover to transcend the conventional narrative limitations of their preferred primary text, baseball, and, like media fan writers of fanfiction, explore an expanded narrative landscape.

Underworld's Metafictioners

There are three distinct groups of fans in *Underworld* that together demonstrate how DeLillo challenges the mythologized, player-centric view of baseball narrative and provides powerful metafictional possibilities for our understanding of history. In order of their introduction to the reader, the groups are: outfield fans Cotter Martin and Bill Waterson; radio broadcaster Russ Hodges and his producer, Al; and public figures Frank Sinatra, Jackie Gleason, Toots Shor, and J. Edgar Hoover. When they address the prologue, literary critics of *Underworld* tend to focus on the last fan, Hoover, because he is the lone spectator able contemporaneously and consciously to connect the Giants' pennant-winning home run to the Russian nuclear test that would accompany it on the front page of the following day's *New York Times*. But to do so is to impress a narrative preferred by critics and theorists of postmodernity—the incomprehensibility of total annihilation at a time of American prosperity—onto the limitless alternate histories and personal narratives unfolding for each spectator. This is not to say that DeLillo avoids a Hoover-centric nuclear narrative, but that he understands that "the small anonymous corners of human experience" are not subsumed by "the magnetic force of public events and the people behind them."[18] Knowledge of the mushroom cloud illuminates one fan's capacity to give meaning to the game, but that capacity should not obscure the richness and complexity of the other fans' self-narration. In this first section of the chapter, I will read the metafictions of each group of DeLillo's fans, ending with—but not prioritizing—the narratives of the FBI's "Big Name Fan."

In so doing, I claim for *Underworld*'s prologue a significance beyond the false binary constructed by anti-sport critics who would cynically position DeLillo's baseball tableau as a mere rendering of the opiate of the masses and those who nostalgically view the game through an American pastoral lens. Both historically attuned interpretive tracks, I argue, are "flat, thin, tight and relentless designs," and the genuine power of "Pafko at the Wall" lies in its refusal to endorse either one.[19] Like Bobby Thomson's home run ball, whose famous disappearance DeLillo reimagines, *Underworld*'s rendering of fans as idiosyncratic readers of baseball narratives is both highly resonant and finally impossible to locate. The novel and its depiction of sports fans give interpersonal resonance to Hutcheon's literary framework, allowing us to better understand the narrative constructions of identity that occur both inside sporting arenas and outside them.

Cotter and Bill: Race and Masculinity
Befitting the massive scope of the novel, which spans five decades and a continent, *Underworld* opens by invoking a national readership: "He

speaks in your voice, American, and there's a shine in his eye that's half-way hopeful."[20] The person who speaks for each "American" is Cotter Martin, a fourteen-year-old African American from Harlem willing to skip school and jump the turnstiles to watch his beloved Giants win a pennant. In addition to being the first character introduced, Cotter is particularly significant, some critics have argued, because he demonstrates both the obscuring capacity of popular entertainments and one of the principal injustices—racial intolerance—that they are commonly said to obscure. *Underworld*'s prologue, asserts John Duvall, "examines baseball as an aesthetic ideology that participates in masking the hidden costs of America's Cold War victory and in erasing race and class difference."[21] When Cotter "runs up a shadowed ramp and . . . sees the great open horseshoe of the grandstand and that unfolding vision of the grass," as DeLillo describes, it "seems to mean he has stepped outside his life."[22] But when he meets Bill Waterson, a white adult man with whom he is at first a friend and then a foe, such a seeming escape from grim reality is proven pure folly, Duvall argues. But such a pessimistic reading ignores the fact that DeLillo's association of "your voice," that of an anonymous, yet singular "American," with Cotter positions the reader as a distinct individual in a sweepingly broad context. It does not erase, but rather calls attention to the dichotomous fan modes Cotter Martin represents and occupies: first, that of the baseball fan so absorbed in the crowd that he feels he can leave his life behind; and second, that of an African American male whose life experience leads him to view the presence of a fellow black man—the peanut vendor—as an existential threat to his peaceful immersion in the mostly white spectators.[23] In *A Poetics of Postmodernism*, Linda Hutcheon's notion of historiographic metafiction "challenge[s] the humanist assumption of a unified self and an integrated consciousness by both installing coherent subjectivity and subverting it."[24] Via Cotter, DeLillo forcefully assigns the reader a coherent subject with which to identify, but also emphasizes that such coherence is contingent on precarious group identifications.

Cotter's experiences are thus both every American's and no one else's. His story line does not represent American racial strife smoothed over by the masses' opiates, but rather the inevitable, interpersonal, and idiosyncratic interpenetration of the two. In the first few paragraphs of

Underworld, DeLillo manages—to put it in the terms of historiographic metafiction—"to satisfy . . . a desire for 'wordly' grounding while at the same time querying the very basis of the authority of that grounding."[25] Through Cotter, DeLillo positions the reader at an event widely recognized as having historical significance, and then subverts the terms of that recognition by personalizing this reader's perspective. Cotter's narrative, like those of the other fans DeLillo personates, is about the Giants, Dodgers, and Bobby Thomson, to be sure, but it is firmly subjective in its orientation to those figures. After all, "it is fiction's role," DeLillo writes in "The Power of History," "to imagine deeply, to follow obscure urges into unreliable regions of experience—the child-memoried, existential and outside time. The novel is in the dream release, the suspension of reality that history needs to escape its own brutal confinements."[26] A "complete" record of anything is impossible; only fiction can render the idiosyncratic experiences that go undocumented in the regimes of history.

Though history and fiction may seem at odds, DeLillo does not construct a strict opposition between them. Soon after Cotter and Bill meet, the older man frames their relationship on ancestral terms: "That's the thing about baseball, Cotter. You do what they did before you. That's the connection you make. There's a whole long line. A man takes his kid to a game and thirty years later this is what they talk about when the poor old mutt's wasting away in the hospital."[27] Bill's logic speaks to Kathleen Fitzpatrick's notion of history as a "tissue of lies" constructed in lieu of the self. But Cotter's interior monologue recognizes the simplistic relational terms Bill relies on and, rather than merely refuting it, adapts it to his own distinct persona as a fan:

> Cotter likes this man's singleness of purpose, his insistence on faith and trust. It's the only force available against the power of doubt. He figures he's in the middle of getting himself befriended. It's a feeling that comes from Bill's easy voice and his sociable sweaty gymnasium bulk and the way he listens when Cotter speaks and the way he can make Cotter believe this is a long and close association they share—boon companions goes the saying. He feels a little strange, it's an unfamiliar thing, talking to Bill, but there's a sense

of something protective and enclosing that will help him absorb the loss if it should come to that.[28]

Cotter's relationship to Bill is not a mindless one, nor is it regimented by filial constructions or implicit racial hierarchies. When Bill asks, in an excerpt from the original "Pafko" that DeLillo removed from *Underworld*, "Who's better than us? I mean, we're here, aren't we? What else do we want? We have to love it, don't we?"[29] it is easy to see why Duvall asserts that DeLillo's work "double[s] as a commentary on contemporary American life and the ways it is implicated in authoritarian—indeed almost proto-fascist—urges."[30] But this assertion fails to account for Cotter's capacity to resist totalizing rhetoric.

Cotter knows, even before he and Bill fight over Thomson's home run ball, that the Giants fandom that unites them does not bind them. As it appears the Giants will go down in defeat, Cotter

> feels a mood coming on, a complicated self pity the strength going out of his arms and a voice commencing in his head that reproaches him for caring. And the awful part is that he wallows in it. He knows how to find the twisty compensation in this business of losing, being a loser, drawing it out, expanding it, making it sickly sweet, being someone carefully chosen for the role.[31]

Though he takes solace in being "miserable in the house of misery," Cotter knows that the ultimate significance of the events transpiring in front of him is his to determine.[32] In understanding how he can be "someone carefully chosen for the role" of "being a loser," Cotter recognizes that he also invests himself with that ugly term, that *he* "knows how to find the twisty compensation," not the fact of the team's losing.[33] Like the greater genre of historiographic metafiction, Cotter effectively "espouses a postmodern ideology of plurality, and recognition of difference. . . . There is no sense of cultural universality."[34] To Bill's notion that baseball's processes and results dictate behavior ("we have to love it, don't we?"), Cotter's internal monologue represents a resounding "no."[35] His narrative before Bobby Thomson's home run particularizes history and invests it with personal agency, allowing the reader to grasp the interpretive flexibility of the "reality" of a sporting event. Cotter and Bill's subsequent struggle over the ball, the prized object of historical significance, further demonstrates the unrecognized malleability of the narratives that undergird official histories, whether those histories concern a ball game or a nation.

As Thomson's home run ball lands, Russ Hodges yells himself hoarse, and J. Edgar Hoover dreamily connects the chaotic scene to the prospect of nuclear destruction, Cotter has an opportunity to fulfill that "intimate wish to be connected to the event, unendably" in a way that will powerfully demonstrate his own "selfness."[36] When the ball lands, he moves without thinking: "Next thing Cotter knows he is sidling into the aisle. . . . The game is way behind him. The crowd can have the game. He's after the baseball now and there's no time to ask himself why. They hit it in the stands, you go and get it."[37] On the one hand, Cotter's movements are unreflective, instinctual: see ball, get ball. On the other, however, they demarcate his impetus from that of "the crowd," which rhapsodizes over the National League championship the ball has won. DeLillo's description places Cotter scrambling beneath the seats, twisting arms and bending fingers until the "raised seams of the ball are pulsing in his hand."[38] When he looks up to see who has noticed, he catches "good neighbor Bill flashing a cutthroat smile" that irrevocably recontextualizes their relationship in terms of racial hostility.[39]

Followed out of the stadium and into the streets by Bill, Cotter recognizes that "if he starts running . . . what we have is a black kid running in a mainly white crowd and he's being followed by a pair of irate whites yelling thief or grief or something."[40] As they walk, Bill appeals to their bond as "budd[ies] . . . who won this game together" and recalls that his initial impression of Cotter was of "a baseball fan, . . . not some delinquent in the streets."[41] Rebuffed, Bill's implicit racial designations give way to explicit epithets in the original "Pafko," as Bill excoriates Cotter for being so "almighty nigger-ish" before issuing a faux apology in which asserts that he would "never [have] said it if you hadn't made me."[42] For Duvall the scene confirms the inability of baseball nostalgia to serve as anything but a proto-fascist falsehood: "while 'Pafko' may create a way of seeing the mirrored relation of [racial and national] binaries, it cannot transcend these binaries merely by representing them. In other words, 'Pafko' does not offer an alternative to 'us-them' thinking, even though it attempts to map the limits of such reductions."[43] Fittingly, Cotter and Bill's conversation ultimately breaks down and the quarrel becomes a footrace. Only after the two cross into "unmixed Harlem" and Bill "realize[s] where he is," does the chase end, with Cotter "running backwards, high stepping, mocking, showing Bill the baseball."[44]

Yet the epithet "nigger-ish," so obviously inflammatory in "Pafko," is nowhere to be found in the version that appears in *Underworld*. And without the word, there is no need for Bill's blame-reassigning non-apology. Which is not to say that their exchange is not racially charged, of course, merely that it is not explicitly so. Why does this difference matter? Not because *Underworld*'s version can be said to deny racism: it would be an oversimplification to assert, as Donald J. Greiner does, that "DeLillo downplays the racial tension of the 1950s that Duvall stresses and features instead the absurd comedy of a grown man pursuing a kid to grab a scuffed baseball."[45] Rather, DeLillo declines to present racial conflict as the stark binary that Duvall pessimistically imagines. Bill still attempts to manipulate the structures of white male privilege to his advantage, but he need not say the n-word for Cotter to understand that. The footrace still happens and the young African American still high-steps victoriously when he has reached a place where the power dynamics of racial inequality are reversed. In one sense, Bill calling Cotter an epithet is racism's equivalent of authorized history, a trigger that fosters oversimplified, "official" notions of race and racism. By removing it in *Underworld*, DeLillo allows the reader to see that baseball neither exclusively "mask[s]" nor exposes "race and class difference," but always contains the capacity for both in the idiosyncratic narratives of its fans.[46]

It is also notable that in escaping into Harlem with the ball, Cotter also removes it from the scope of any "official" history: he has effectively "stepped outside" of life in a different way.[47] Later in *Underworld*, Cotter's father, Manx, steals the ball from his son and sells it to another Giants fan, providing only a second-hand anecdote as authentication. By the time the larger novel's main protagonist, Nick Shay, tracks it down, the ball's historical significance is incumbent on an oral history no more certifiably "real" than *Underworld* itself. Beyond the reach of Bill Waterson's white male authority, the ball ceases to exist, at least as the "official" ball that Thomson hit. And yet, though the Thomson home run ball is lost to official history, its narrative—and that of the person who discovered it—is no less real for being unauthorized. In "The Power of History," DeLillo asserts that "language can be a form of counterhistory."[48] Since "every narrative thread in the entire novel [of *Underworld*] can be connected to the ball in some way," the ball seems to be the signifier that represents counterhistorical possibilities.[49] The effect, as Linda Hutcheon asserts in characterizing postmodern discourse at large, "is not to deny the real, but to remember that *we give meaning to* the real within . . . signifying systems."[50] When *Underworld*'s narrator opens by asserting that a young turnstile-jumper "speaks in your voice, American," DeLillo thus allows the second-person pronoun to trump the national signifier.[51] Recontextualized as agents rather than mere recipients of history, we Cotters can see that the "aesthetic ideology" of baseball may limit the terms of our engagement but not the narrative possibilities of our interpretation.[52] The sports fan always retains the capacity to read sport in her own unique way—no amount of group dominance can erase that interpretive freedom, whatever the normative stakes of the game.

Russ Hodges: Language and History

Even so, idiosyncratic interpretations of sports narrative, like those provided by Cotter and Bill, are not usually preserved beyond the vagaries of individual fans' memories. While the game they watched was televised live by NBC and covered extensively by print media, the enduring public memory of the home run (in *Underworld* and in reality) is provided by an audio recording of Russ Hodges, the radio play-by-play announcer for the New York Giants. It is for that reason, ostensibly, that DeLillo chooses to represent Hodges's "fan" perspective in *Underworld*. I use scare quotes here because, while Hodges is a spectator, his professional role at the game means that most would say he is a media member and not a fan. But as DeLillo's portrayal of the broadcaster makes clear, troubling such technical classifications is *Underworld*'s imperative. As in much other historiographic metafiction, DeLillo uses Hodges to "challenge . . . both any naïve realist conception of representation and any equally naïve textualist or formalist assertions of the total separation of art from the world."[53]

Hodges is introduced immediately after "you lose [Cotter] in the crowd," as "in the radio booth they're talking about [that] crowd," wondering "how [to] explain twenty thousand empty seats."[54] Rather than immersed in a mass of humanity that provides Cotter an escape in collective anonymity, the reader's gaze is refocused on a similar yet distinct male milieu: the press box. Just as strongly gendered as the stands, this space of "crammed maleness" is neither less crude nor less overtly racialized for its occupants' special credentials: Hodges's white male engineers exchange racist dirty jokes about Speedy Gonzalez and conduct a conversation in "black dialect."[55] And these men, while professionally invested in the Giants or Dodgers, are clearly personally attached to their teams as well. All the same, Hodges's concerns, unlike those of his booth mates, are far from ordinary.

As his tired vocal cords describe the action on the field, Hodges's inner monologue is concerned with matters of history: "he thinks everybody's who's here ought to feel lucky because something big's in the works, something's building."[56] DeLillo's Hodges measures the feeling of being at this particular game against his first-hand experience at the 1919 heavyweight boxing championship match between Jack Dempsey and Jess Willard, remembering

> what a thing that was, what a measure of the awesome . . . the greatness of the beating big Jess took in that white hot ring, the way the sweat and blood came misting off his face every time Dempsey hit him. When you see a thing like that, a thing that becomes a newsreel, you begin to feel you are a carrier of some solemn scrap of history.[57]

As Duvall reads it, this moment signifies the fact that "in the age of the electronic media . . . an event has not entered history unless it is represented by that technology."[58] Recognizing in his anecdotal account of the Dempsey-Willard fight that "the medium is the message," Hodges, "clearly an artist figure, contemplates the constructive nature of his discourse."[59] This reading is apt, but its pessimistic conclusion is unjustified. Duvall believes that Hodges's famous and thus "authorized" version of the game and Thomson's "Shot" fascistically dominates collective memory of the event, participating in the "false aura of sport [that] masks not only the politics of Cold War America but also the most fundamental reality of life, personal mortality."[60] But Hodges's remembrance of the Willard fight suggests to me just the opposite: while the attention of the newsreels may have marked the event as something everyone ought to remember,

Hodges's personal memory of small ringside details—the sweat and blood that the black and white footage couldn't represent—are "a measure of the awesome" that provide him a "solemn scrap of history" all his own.[61]

Hodges would thus recognize Cotter's fan narrative as unsubsumed, and no less significant, than his famous play-by-play account of the home run or the famous newsreel footage of Thomson mobbed by fans after the game. Nevertheless, the broadcaster must also understand the resonant power of the filmed simulacrum for an audience unable to be party to "the awesome" in person. Recalling his days in Charlotte "doing re-creations of big league games . . . the telegraph bug clacking in the background and blabbermouth Hodges inventing ninety-nine percent of the action," the announcer describes his old dream of broadcasting "real baseball . . . the thing that happens in the sun."[62] In calling those "ghost games" from telegraph dispatches,[63] Hodges recalls "construct[ing] the fiction of a distant city, making up everything but the stark facts of the evolving game";[64] for example, "inventing a kid chasing a foul ball . . . who retrieves the ball and holds it aloft . . . a priceless thing somehow, a thing that seems to recapitulate the whole history of the game every time it is thrown or hit or touched."[65] Hodges's fictional narrative of the foul ball–retrieving kid obviously conjures up DeLillo's creation of Cotter Martin. But the "fake" baseball narratives Hodges created, interspersing pure fictions among the "stark facts" to forge from the latter a more compelling narrative, finally differ little from "the thing that happens in the sun" because both narratives are necessarily selective and subjective in their construction. For Hodges and his listeners, like DeLillo and his readers, "reality" is dependent on the narrator's personal limitations and selections of detail. The differences between historiographic metafiction and history, between telegraphically mediated baseball and "real" baseball, then, are matters of degree, not kind.

While there is a big difference between providing play-by-play of a baseball game and watching it casually from the stands, both require that the observer "name and constitute . . . events as historical facts by selection and narrative positioning."[66] No matter how many millions of pitches have been thrown, home runs hit, or base runners thrown out in the past, each play resonates somewhat differently with those who watch it. As DeLillo puts it in *Underworld,*

It's the rule of confrontation, faithfully maintained, written across the face of every slackwit pitcher since there were teams named the Superbas and the Bridegrooms. The difference comes when the ball is hit. Then nothing is the same. The men are moving, coming out of their crouches, and everything submits to the pebble-skip of the ball, to rotations and backspins and airstreams. There are drag coefficients. There are trailing vortices. There are things that apply unrepeatably, muscle memory and pumping blood and jots of dust, the narrative that lives in the spaces of the official play-by-play.[67]

In a sense, no play is any different than the ones described by Hodges after receiving pages from the telegraph machine in Charlotte. Even when the statistical result of a given play is clear—a run is scored, a strike is thrown, a walk is issued—there are endless narrative descriptors swirling "in the spaces of the official play-by-play."[68] In fact, the narrative potential of those "drag coefficients" and "trailing vortices" is amplified by the seemingly "stark" nature of the "facts" that surround those spaces.[69] Baseball is so readily narrativized, so richly textured, DeLillo and Hodges suggest, because there is so much room for interpretation. Neither what Hodges sees at the Polo Grounds nor what he imagined in Charlotte are absolutely real or completely fictional, and it is possible, if not likely, that the events described in the latter fictions might coincide with the "facts" of the former at any moment in any game.

Imagining his audience huddled at the radio, Hodges remembers

how his family used to gather around the gramophone and listen to grand opera, the trilled *r*'s of old Europe. These thoughts fade and return. They are not distractions. He is alert to every movement on the field. . . . He is hunched over the mike. The field seems to open outward into nouns and verbs. All he has to do is talk.[70]

Here is history, and not *any* history, but personal recollections of his own family, an idiosyncratic history contextualized by the artistic historicity of "grand operas, the trilled *r*'s of old Europe."[71] But while these memories are present—part of his perceptions of the present moment—"they are not distractions": they do not compromise his understanding of the action on the field. Like Cotter and Bill, like Frank, Jackie, Toots, and J.

Edgar, he is always both of the crowd and apart from it. Yet he is also a narrative conduit, a practitioner of the power of language that DeLillo espouses, that which "lives in everything it touches and can be an agent of redemption, . . . that allows us to find an unconstraining otherness, a free veer from time and place and fate."[72] In seeing "the field . . . open outward into nouns and verbs," Hodges seems to understand the potential for "unconstraining otherness" in the ostensibly straightforward actions he is tasked to describe. At the same time, however, he realizes that those possibilities must flow naturally from his language: "all he has to do is talk."[73]

Crucially, the power of that language lies in its visceral expression as well as its symbolic construction of meaning. At the time of Thomson's shot,

> Russ says, "There's a long drive."
> His voice has a burst in it, a charge of expectation.
> He says, "It's gonna be."
> There's a pause all around him. Pafko racing toward the left-field corner.
> He says, "I believe."
> Pafko at the wall. Then he's looking up. . . .
> Russ feels the crowd around him, a shudder passing through the stands, and then he is shouting into the mike and there is a surge of color and motion, a crash that occurs upward, stadium-wide, hands and faces and shirts, bands of rippling men, and he is outright shouting, his voice has a power he'd thought long gone—it may life the top of his head like a cartoon rocket.
> He says, "*The Giants win the pennant.*"[74]

Perhaps more than any other moment in the novel, this one captures the dichotomous fan experience. On the one hand, Russ is of the crowd, an indistinguishable part of a stadium full of "bands of rippling men" who "feels the . . . shudder passing through the stands." On the other, his shouting is also always defined apart from this crowd: he reflects on the mike in front of him and the state of his own fragile vocal cords. And however authoritative his voice may be, it is always limited to the perceptions of the first person, to what "I believe" is happening. As the mania becomes celebration, "Russ knows he ought to settle down and let the mike pick up the sound of the swelling bedlam around him. But he can't stop shouting, there's nothing left of him but shout."[75] The collective joy that overwhelms him is the same as the one pouring out of the fans in the stands—"He says, 'The Giants win the pennant and they're going crazy'"—but it is always also subjectively his own, "a holler from the old days—it is fiddlin' time, it is mountain music on WCKY at five-thirty in the morning."[76] In passages like this, DeLillo demonstrates not merely the "inextricable interconnections of narrative and history [that make] the novel [*Underworld*] . . . 'historiographic metafiction,'" but also the fact that historiographic metafiction is created in that moment by Hodges and every other self-reflective fan in the stands.[77] The narrative that Hodges creates is more obvious for being broadcast, perhaps, but it is no more real because it could be heard on the radio. Nor, obviously, do Hodges's "official" words (as recorded by "history") provide his complete story. DeLillo may have fabricated a representation of how Hodges personally felt in that moment of collective exuberance, but it is a fact no less real than Thomson's home run that Hodges felt some unspoken things all his own. Whether or not they involved folk music in Kentucky hardly matters. That detail, like Hodges's own foul ball–retrieving boy, merely helps DeLillo's novel fill in the spaces in the play-by-play.

Having opened "the field . . . outward into nouns and verbs" that chronicled the Giants' miraculous victory, Hodges walks across the outfield after the game, reveling in the moment.[78] His producer, Al,

> points to the place in the left-field stands where the ball went in.
>
> "Mark the spot. Like where Lee surrendered to Grant or some such thing."
>
> Russ thinks this is another kind of history. He thinks they will carry something out of here that joins them all in a rare way, that binds them to a memory with protective power. . . . Isn't it possible that this midcentury moment enters the skin more lastingly than the vast shaping strategies of eminent leaders, generals steely in their sunglasses—the mapped visions that pierce our dreams? Russ wants to believe a thing like this keeps us safe in some undetermined way. . . . This is the people's history and it has flesh and breath that quicken to the force of this old safe game of ours.[79]

At the wall, where DeLillo's narrative most potently intersects with history as we know it, Hodges seems to want to bifurcate the latter, to cover over the events happening outside the stadium with the gauzy joy of Thomson's home run. It is with good reason, then, that critics have identified this moment of nostalgic inclination as DeLillo's most powerful reminder of the obscuring dangers of mass media entertainments. Hodges's hope that this "old safe game of ours" can "keep . . . us safe in some undetermined way" indeed reads as obscurative of more urgent matters when directly counterpoised against the deathly stadium hellscape imagined by the nuke-obsessed J. Edgar Hoover.[80]

But it is an oversimplification to suggest that because Hodges thinks that Thomson's home run represents a "different kind of history" from that of the Civil War or Cold War—because it "enters the skin more lastingly than the vast shaping strategies of eminent leaders"—that the game and "history" are necessarily at cross purposes.[81] It is more accurate to assert, with Donald Greiner, that "rather than stress the potential for the bomb (politics) to dwarf the magic of the home run (myth), [DeLillo] acknowledges the juxtaposition and then celebrates the social connection that the Giants-Dodgers game affirmed."[82] Thomson's home run and the Soviet Union's nuclear test should be seen as complementary factors in constructing American identities. Sports fandom is often thought to inform personal identity in merely supplementary ways, with national politics more commonly seen as definitive. But both notions oversimplify. Though the geopolitical machinations of the Cold War may have been more likely than a baseball game to have a deadly impact on bystanders, they cannot be said to deserve overwhelming authority over one's sense of identity as a consequence. Thomson's home-run-as-history can keep us safe, Hodges's thoughts suggest, not by countering or obscuring the threats of nuclear annihilation and social injustice, but rather by reminding us that those oppressive factors, real as they are, do not determine who we imagine ourselves to be. Official narratives have real consequences for sports fans, then, but they are not iron-clad or inescapable. Negotiating one's sports fan practice in relation to the historical record of sporting events is much like what media fans face when grappling with "canon," or the official narratives of the media text in question. There is plenty of narrative space beyond.

Sinatra, Gleason, Shor, and Hoover:
Celebrity, Politics, and Aesthetics

Media fandoms are also often built on fascination with celebrities, particularly when their presence in a text is unexpected. Don DeLillo explores this fascination in a sports fan context by including celebrity figures on the periphery of Thomson's shot: Frank Sinatra, Jackie Gleason, Toots Shor, and J. Edgar Hoover. Though the historical Sinatra, Gleason, and Shor were known to be friends, DeLillo's pairing of these three entertainers with FBI director J. Edgar Hoover is an odd choice, and he recognizes it:

> What's the nation's number one G-man doing with these crumbums?
> . . . Fame and secrecy are the high and low ends of the same fascination, the static crackle of some libidinous thing in the world, and Edgar responds to people who have access to this energy. He wants to be their dearly devoted friend provided their hidden lives are in his private files, all the rumors collected and indexed, the shadow facts made real.[83]

Fame powers desire, and Hoover thrills to the power of knowing and manipulating the desires of others. But his association with these men is also influenced by more conventional motivations surrounding proximity to "movie idols and celebrity athletes."[84] In fact, in the original "Pafko," DeLillo calls Hoover "a fan at heart," before mentioning his desire for friendship and knowledge of "their hidden lives."[85] Such a phrasing can be taken to convey Hoover's baseball fandom, yet DeLillo makes it clear that the FBI director cares little for the action on the field. Asked by Sinatra who he is rooting for, "a faint smile creeps across Hoover's face. 'I don't have a rooting interest. Whoever wins,' he says softly. 'That's my team.'"[86] For many sports fans, this answer would be utterly unsatisfactory and can be read as proof of Hoover's duplicitousness. When DeLillo writes that Hoover is "a fan at heart" in "Pafko," then, he means that the FBI director is a fan of the men he is with at least as much as baseball. Hoover is also clearly a fan of the homosocial interaction baseball spectatorship offers, of "smiling at the rude banter that rolls nonstop from crooner to jokesmith to saloonkeeper and back. He would rather be at the racetrack but is cheerful enough in this kind of company whatever venue."[87]

So prized is Hoover's time with these men that he feels little compulsion to leave them when he is discreetly given the news about the Russian nuclear test. After all, "no purpose [would be] served by his leaving. The White House will make the announcement in less than an hour. . . . By announcing first, we prevent the Soviets from putting their own sweet spin on the event. And we ease public anxiety to some degree. People will understand that we've maintained control of the news if not the bomb."[88] Callous and pragmatic in the face of what is potentially world-altering news, assessing nuclear proliferation in terms of narrative control, Hoover remains ensconced in his homosocial milieu. As the game progresses—as Sinatra, Gleason, and Shor comment on the game, crudely mock each other, and interact with the star-struck fans around them—"paper waves" of "happy garbage" fall around the men.[89] While Sinatra notices a page of *Life* magazine featuring a picture of "himself sitting in a nightclub in Nevada with Ava Gardner and would you check that cleavage," Hoover is diverted by the same publication's reproduction of Pieter Bruegel's macabre masterpiece "The Triumph of Death": "he studies the tumbrel filled with skulls. He stands in the aisle and looks at the naked man pursued by dogs."[90] Blurring the aisle he stands in with the destruction depicted on the pages in front of him, Hoover transposes the mania of Bruegel's orgiastic killing field onto the joyous stadium in front of him. Just as it is easy to subsume *any* individual fan narrative into a sense of the definitive communal experience, so too is it tempting for critics to subsume Sinatra, Gleason, Shor, and all the other fans within Hoover's *Life* magazine–mediated vision of nuclear holocaust, to make them, as Donald Greiner does, "Bruegel's skeletons dancing on the backs of the living."[91] Under these auspices, Bruegel's morbid art intensifies the sense of just how futile and inconsequential are the lives of the pop culture–addled masses.

As he looks around the stadium after receiving the news of the test, but before the pages of *Life* magazine float down, Hoover sees "people formed by language and climate and popular songs and breakfast foods and the jokes they tell and the cars they drive [who] have never had so much in common as this, that they are sitting in the furrow of destruction."[92] After the momentous home run is struck, as Hoover "stands in the aisle and [the fans] are all around him cheering and he has the pages in his face[,] he begins to see that the living are sinners. . . . The dead have come to empty out the wine gourds, to serve a skull on a platter to the gentlefolk at their meal. He sees gluttony, lust, and greed."[93] In the first quote, though "popular songs and breakfast foods and . . . the cars they drive" are mass mediated, they don't obscure "language and climate . . . and the jokes they tell," those esoteric characteristics that inform identity. And if the prospective nuclear war's "furrow of destruction" has imminent apocalyptic potential, as it did then and has since in every subsequent moment of human history, there's no reason to think that such a commonality limits the idiosyncrasies of identity or the capacity for critical thinking any more than common fan interests do. The second passage takes the "furrow of destruction" and renders it gruesome and pornographic, as Hoover revels in

> the meatblood colors and massed-bodies, [the] census-taking of awful ways to die. . . . Death elsewhere, Conflagration in many places, Terror universal . . . and he thinks of a lonely tower standing on the Kazakh Test Site, the tower armed with the bomb, and he can almost hear the wind blowing across the Central Asian steppes, out where the enemy lives.[94]

Transposing the mania of Bruegel's orgiastic killing field onto the joyous stadium in front of him, Hoover implies that the spectators deserve the holocaustic specter they now face, their existences cheapened by mass culture and bound to commercialized discourses of "gluttony, lust and greed."[95]

But by "directly confronting the discourse of art with the discourse of history," DeLillo effectively baits an interpretive trap.[96] He fulfills the potential of historiographic metafiction, as Hutcheon puts it, to "draw upon any signifying practice it can find operative in a society. [Historiographic metafiction] wants to challenge those discourses and yet to use them, even to milk them for all they are worth."[97] Milking the American obsession with nuclear annihilation, DeLillo also simultaneously undercuts it. "As DeLillo and Hoover both recognize," Timothy Parrish rightfully asserts, "aestheticizing cultural processes is not necessarily coincident with anaesthetizing cultural processes."[98] Which is to say that mass cultural signifiers such as Thomson's "Shot" could accompany or even temporarily overshadow the grim possibilities of the Cold War, but not "efface it from our consciousness."[99] As for Hoover, thrilling at the "genius of the bomb [and] the occasion it creates for new secrets," he wonders at the "connection between Us and Them, how many bundled links do we find in the neural labyrinth? It's not enough to hate your enemy. You have to understand how the two of you bring each other to deep completion."[100] Contradicting the binaristic terms "Us and Them"—made proper nouns to convey irony—within which he constructs consciousness, Hoover understands their relationship as nonlinear ("bundled" and "labyrinth[ian]") and ultimately complementary ("deep completion"). His juxtaposition of Brooklyn and Bruegel, of nukes and Don Newcombe, Thomson and test sites, does not speak to the occlusionary "power of history," then. It speaks to "consciousness . . . [,] extended and human truth . . . seen new."[101] Deriving meaning from the perspective DeLillo ascribes to Hoover during the game is not wrong, but defining the game through his interpretation is necessarily incomplete. When Pafko is at the wall, he is seen from thousands of angles. He can be a witness to great triumph, a forlorn symbol of disappointment, or a skeleton about to dance in nihilistic glee. Death does not triumph unless the fans in DeLillo's stadium determine that it should. From its title forward, *Underworld*'s prologue challenges the reader to assert those alternate interpretive possibilities in the face of grim circumstances—to see the baseball game beyond the nuclear war. As in Cotter's resistance to Bill's tropes of baseball masculinity, and Hodges's ability to imagine the spaces between the "stark facts" of the play-by-play, Hoover's vision of "The Triumph of Death" is a totalizing narrative neither for him nor for *Underworld*. Ultimately, in his portraits of baseball fans, DeLillo emphasizes individual autonomy and values the creative and critical narratives fans construct, even if only in their heads. His is a sanguine view, akin to Henry Jenkins's in *Textual Poachers*, of individuated fan-readers and writers with the capacity to meaningfully resist the power of history's purported master narratives.

Henry Waugh's Universal Unmaking

Yet the individual fan's ability to create his own narrative stakes, independent of those perceived by those around him, is not always considered an unalloyed good. The stereotype of the fan as an obsessive loner, out of touch with reality such that he has become delusional, even dangerous, is a pathologizing trope with a long history. Robert Coover examines the trope by creating just such a fan in his acclaimed novel *Universal Baseball Association, Inc., J. Henry Waugh, Prop.* Henry Waugh's embrace of his own baseball narratives as a self-definitional mode embodies Coover's post-modernist belief that fiction is a common mode of coping with everyday existence. "In a sense," Coover said in an interview with literary critic Frank Gado in 1973, "we are all creating fictions all the time, out of necessity. We constantly test them against the experience of life."[102] To process the enormity and mutability of external reality, in other words, we craft narrative tethers between particularly compelling or salient aspects of the self and the not-me: we "attempt . . . to merge our own lives," as Kristina Busse puts it, "with that of the fictional universes" we read and rewrite.[103]

While the physical reality of Bobby Thomson's home run tethers the alternate histories of DeLillo's historiographic metafiction in *Underworld*, however, the metafictive historiography of Coover's *Universal Baseball Association* is tied to two epochal events determined by the probabilistic outcomes of six-sided dice. The first is Damon Rutherford's "perfect game," which is followed in the next contest by Rutherford's untimely death in the batter's box, hit in the head by an offering from rival pitcher Jock Casey.[104] But rather than an example of what former Major League Baseball commissioner A. Bartlett Giamatti called "the incredible power of the random, by accident or luck, by vagaries of weather, by mental lapses or physical failure, by flaw in field or equipment, [or] by laws of physics," which impact baseball and all sports ineluctably, Rutherford's accomplishment and tragic demise depend on the "power of the random" inherent in the roll of the dice.[105] At least at the novel's beginning, Henry recognizes the importance of acceding to this power:

> Oh sure, he was free to throw away the dice, run the game by whim, but then what would be the point of it? Who would Damon Rutherford really be then? Nobody, an empty name, a play actor. Even though he'd set his own rules his own limits, and though he could change them whenever he wished, nevertheless he and his players were committed to the turns of the mindless and unpredictable—one might even say, irresponsible—dice. That was how it was. He had to accept it, or quit the game altogether.[106]

In Henry's "kitchen full of heroes and history," the dice's independence from his subjective consciousness is absolutely vital.[107] As critic Roy C. Caldwell Jr. puts it, "the true subject of Coover's novel is not the playing of baseball but the making of fiction. . . . Instead of a game, Waugh has actually devised a machine for the production of narrative."[108] This dice-powered machine ensures that the baseball action that unfolds for Henry is not determined entirely subjectively, just as the competitive performance of unpredictable human bodies powers "real" baseball's veneer of objectivity. Like the tickertape radio broadcasts DeLillo's Russ Hodges produced in North Carolina, Henry records and embellishes the game—he fills in the backstory with invented kids, if you will. But the game's baseball outcomes are determined by external information, even if that package of dice-based stimuli is not "real baseball . . . [,] the thing that happens in the sun."[109]

As Daniel Punday notes, the dice-based game that Henry creates is similar to a role-playing game (or "RPG," as they are commonly known) insofar as "he builds elaborate narratives around these random statistical events," though Henry's game is more limited in "creative agency" because of his lack of co-creators.[110] Henry is a "gamemaster," to put it in RPG parlance, but one who lacks fellow human players to help shape the direction of the narratives he creates. Unlike RPGs and fantasy sports, then, which "transform the nature of being a fan by allowing players within [the] game to act, to become agents rather than passive spectators" in a *shared* imaginary environment, Henry's game isolates him.[111] Rather than depicting widely observed physical phenomena through the lenses of several personal observers to create idiosyncratic narratives—as DeLillo does in *Underworld*—Coover's *Universal Baseball Association* limits the scope of external stimuli, rendering numerical outcomes through the mind of a singular author to create a multilayered narrative world. This difference is apparent in the two works' opening lines: while DeLillo begins by invoking the broadness of "your voice, American,"[112] Coover's *Universal Baseball Association* (or UBA, hereafter) begins with the narrow insertion of its protagonist "*in* there, *with them*! Oh yes, boys, it was on! He was sure of it! More than just another ball game now: *history!*"[113] The italicized words—"*in*," "*with*," and "*history*"—both narrow the reader's purview to the particular game in which Henry Waugh is actively invested and suggest that it bears the weight of historical significance. No less than Bobby Thomson's shot, Damon Rutherford's perfect game is marked with wide ramifications even as the reader is staked to Henry's personal insertion of self "*in*" and "*with*" the "*history*" at hand.

In this section I will use those three words—"*in*," "*with*," and "*history*"—as thematic frameworks to examine Henry Waugh's production of baseball narrative and its ramifications for how we are to understand the means by which sports fans—and indeed all humans—relate "objective" reality to the subjective narratives that help them process it. By "*in*" I mean the interrelation between the worlds that Henry produces to position himself "*in* there": the ways his lived experience affects, and is affected by, the baseball world he has created.[114] Being "*in* there" also means considering Henry's awareness of the need for balance between his lived reality and his baseball narrative, and the events that precipitate the dissolution of that awareness (and indeed of Henry himself). In examining Henry's position "*with* them," I focus on the role of interpersonal relationships in the *Universal Baseball Association*, both between Henry and his few close associates in his "real" life and between the players in his imagined league. Importantly, these social relationship spheres also blur together. "*History*," finally, is a self-reflective concern for Henry in UBA as it is for DeLillo in *Underworld* and for me in this chapter. I define it in this case as a frame for modes and methods through which Henry chronicles his league's past, records its present, and imagines its future. The attention paid to the ways in which Henry keeps records and writes backstories reflects Coover's concern with the interrelated processes of writing history and the self. In becoming "more than just another ball game," Damon Rutherford's perfect game and subsequent death in the batter's box are "history": not merely because of the events' significance, but also because they become preferred narratives that transcend the personal. Yet instead of registering widely, moving outward from the writer of history to a wider populace, the events of the UBA are transpersonal in the opposite direction: they *narrow* the frame of narrative reality. Henry disappears from the *Universal Baseball Association* because Damon Rutherford's death ultimately drowns him "*in* there, *with* them." He becomes ensconced in his fictional coping mechanism so that he cannot write history—instead, he is one with it. He has made absolute the "escape" that many fans claim to want in sports-as-non-political entertainment—immersion in a play space so complete that they aren't reminded of their "real" lives—yet for Henry that immersion in fact becomes self-destructive. Without acquiescing to or depicting any of the more conventional stereotypes of fans getting "lost" in their fandoms, Coover nevertheless effectively asserts that the meta-textual worlds created by sports fans, no less than for media fans urged to "get a life," can be damaging in their solipsistic isolation.

Being "in There": Henry Commutes to the UBA

Henry has reason to seek an escape in sports narratives: his "real" life as an accountant at "Dunkelmann, Zauber & Zifferblatt, Licensed Tax & General Accountants," does not fulfill him. His supervisor, Horace Zifferblatt, "was a militant clock-watcher, and Henry's record of late had been none too good."[115] Chronically tardy and unfocused owing to the intense drama unfolding in the UBA on his kitchen table each night, Henry has made significant accounting errors that have gotten him in trouble with his irascible boss. His only friend in the workplace, Lou Engels, worries that Henry will be fired if he doesn't clean up his act. Like so many fans, Henry seeks an escape in baseball, a transformation of his mental environs. And transform them it does: "It was autumn, but Henry felt plunged into the deepest of winters. But no, it was the middle of a baseball season, remember? Green fields and hot suns and shirtsleeved fanatics out on the bleaching boards, last to give it up and go home: he turned back to the table."[116] The passage marks Henry's mental commute to his fantasy world; through the shifting seasons, Coover portrays the differing factors that constitute "autumn" (Henry's physical reality), "winter" (his emotional state), and the "green fields and hot sun" of his imagined baseball world.[117] The closing description—"he turned back to the table"—both reminds us of Henry's bodily reality and describes the mundane physical movements (such as rolling a pair of dice) that put Henry "*in* there, *with* them."[118] As surely as he recognizes that the probabilistic nature of the dice is a vital driver of his league's narrative resonance as imagined history, Henry acknowledges that the transitions between his lived reality and his narrative enterprise are vital to the latter's continuation. He recognizes that the transition he makes in "turn[ing] back to the table" imbues the "green fields and hot sun" with their sweetness and light.[119] As Henry later ruminates,

> Sometimes, true, in the heat of a pennant chase, for example, his daytime job could be a nuisance, but over the long haul he needed that balance, that rhythmic shift from house to house, and he knew that total one-sided participation in the league would soon grow even more oppressive than his job.[120]

Henry's emphasis on "balance" makes the UBA "not so much an escape from life as it is a *part* of life, a necessary component of modern existence," as Nicholas J. Mount puts it.[121] Or, as Mark Frisch more expansively postulates,

> [Coover's] implication is that all systems, disciplines and philosophies are constructs which assist man in dealing with reality, that absolutes are virtually nonexistent and[,] as Henry realizes, that perfection is process, not stasis.[122]

In other words, commuting between lived reality and the Universal Baseball Association invigorates both realms—it is a symbiotic narrative exchange, not a utopian escape mitigated by corporeal needs.

Putting himself "*in* there," then, is an action whose power lies in its incompleteness; when Henry tips the dice to kill Jock Casey and avenge Damon Rutherford's death, he burns the bridge to reality behind him. Balance is lost and Henry subsequently disappears from the novel. But between Damon's death and Jock's, as Henry's conscious recognition of the importance of balance begins to be overwhelmed by his emotional anguish, the act of putting himself "*in* there" begins to lose its intentionality. Instead of volitionally "turn[ing] to the table" to enter the world of "green fields and hot sun," the game begins to turn to him. After Damon's death, in visits to Pete's Bar and to a florist, Henry freely discusses his league, its players and events, as if they were real. He remarks that the "odd thing about an operation like this league [was that] once you set it in motion, you were yourself somehow launched into the same orbit."[123] Henry suggests that the sense-making device that both Coover and DeLillo recognize in idiosyncratic personal fictions can function independently of volitional immersion: "the circuit wasn't closed," as Henry puts it.[124]

Like a daydream or an unreflected-upon metaphor, the UBA is "*in* there" with Henry as surely as he is "*in* there, *with* them." He has become so obsessed with his preferred narratives that he is losing his grip on reality.

"With *Them*": Henry's Blurred Fellowship

Henry's nascent mental illness, his inability to control the interjection of his narrative creations into his lived experience, becomes chronic as the novel progresses. As they sit at dinner in a local restaurant, Lou Engels asks the UBA proprietor about his personal life. Pondering the possible "great comfort, great pleasure" of companionship and family life, Henry reflects that he "had chosen the loner's life, the general pain, because . . . he couldn't help himself."[125] Further pressed on his solitary predilections and habits, Henry asserts that "I've been talking to myself all my life."[126] Out of context, these remarks would mark Henry as a lonely man by nature and inclination. As he shares these insights with Lou, however, they take on another cast.

Henry is by this point in the novel always slipping between worlds. He is with Lou but he is also ensconced in his UBA world, imagining the players carousing around him, drinking, singing, and engaging in sex acts brazen for being conducted in (an albeit imagined) public. Being "*with* them" means more than feeling immersed in the details of a compelling baseball game. For Henry, the off-the-field backstory is equally important. And, unlike the on-field action, no dice rolls are necessary to determine his players' personal lives. Henry imagines that his act of naming the players marks their destinies. "Name a man and you make him what he is," Henry ruminates, "of course, he can develop. And in ways you don't expect. Or something can go wrong. Lot of nicknames invented as a result of Rookie-year surprises. But the basic stuff is already there. In the name. Or rather: in the naming."[127] In naming his characters, Henry thus defines them in ways the dice can't. Granting his players monikers like "Jock," "Brock," and "Long Lew," it shouldn't surprise anyone that Henry's UBA off-the-field backstories prioritize stereotypical rituals of masculine homosocial intimacy: drink, song, and the denigration and sexual domination of women. Henry marks himself as bearing the "general pain" of his solitary existence and thus his outward failure in the terms of heteronormative patriarchy, but the notion that he "couldn't help himself" in choosing to be a loner is not primarily a marker of weakness or psychosis. Rather, it is an indicator of Henry's preference for a homosocial male dreamscape over attempts at real female companionship or family life. Reveling in Damon Rutherford's perfect game and imagining that his local bar, "Pete's," is "Jake's," the bar favored by the UBA players, Henry describes

> Brock the Great reeling boisterously down the street, arm in arm with Willie O'Leary and Frosty Young, those wonderful guys—and who should they meet up with but sleepy-eyed Mose Stanford and Gabe Burdette and crazy rubber-legged Jaybird Wall. Yes, and they were singing, singing the *old* songs, "Pitchin', Catchin', Swingin'" and "The Happy Days of Youth," and oh! it was happiness! and goddamn it! it was fellowship! and boys oh boys! it was significance![128]

Thus, while Henry might have no "real" friends save for Lou, male bonding and nostalgia—the "main vice[s]" of his imagined bar narrative—abound in the world he has created. "The narrative that lives in the spaces of the official play-by-play," as DeLillo puts it, has for Henry become preferable to the day-to-day possibilities of his lived experience.[129] Henry "couldn't help himself" not merely because he is naturally inept in social spheres, but also because the reward offered seems to pale in comparison to his imagined bounty of male intimacy.

Crucial to Henry's preference for homosocial relationships is a manipulation of women and a disregard for their equality as empowered human subjects. Sex with women figures into both Henry's physical life and his UBA fantasy of male intimacy, but it is merely transactional, a means to male empowerment. The primary romantic encounter of Henry's in the novel involves intercourse—verbal and sexual—with Hettie, a local "b-girl," immediately after Damon Rutherford's perfect game. Hettie is not a fan of real baseball, so she listens to Henry's accounts of the UBA and takes them at face value. This allows Henry not only to discuss his imagined league as if it is real, but also to submerge himself deeper in its universe. As they have sex, Henry asks Hettie to call him Damon and imagines his progress during coitus through clichéd slang baseball terms:

> "*Play ball!*" cried the umpire. And the catcher, stripped of mask and guard, revealed as the pitcher Damon Rutherford, whipped the uni-

form off the first lady ballplayer in Association history, and then, helping and hindering all at once, pushing and pulling, they ran the bases, pounded into first, slid into second heels high, somersaulted over third, shot home standing up, then into the box once more, swing away, and run them all again, and "Damon!" she cried, and "Damon!"[130]

Later in the novel, Hettie becomes aware that Henry's baseball ramblings are pure fiction, calling him a "complete nut."[131] Though she still seeks his companionship, Henry loses interest in her. The narrative pleasures the unwitting Hettie had provided Henry are far more rewarding than the personal or even sexual ones.

The objectification of women is even more pronounced in the UBA narrative. The only prominent female character in Henry's diegetic world is Fanny McCaffree. Her fame, recounted in song by drunken ball players, stems from her status as the league's most famous rape victim. Set upon by the phallicly named Long Lew Lydell in the dugout before a game, Fanny suffers a public sexual assault at which the observers "all laughed to watch it rip."[132] Even more horrifying, Fanny is subsequently married to her rapist, in a union marked as significant to the UBA because her father, Fenn McCaffree, is the league's commissioner and Lydell fancies himself a successor.[133] Fanny McCaffree's metonymic status for women as sexual objects is thus doubly important in the homosocial dreamscape that Henry cherishes. Fanny's victimization presents a glimpse of Henry's acculturation to the norms of a particularly toxic and rapacious form of masculinity; in being violated, she unites the official male preserve of political power with the mythos of male bonding. As Chancellor McCaffree notes, alcohol-sodden, song-filled male "gatherings . . . always did something to the ones who came. Changed their politics, altered their view of reality, transformed them in subtle but often surprising and upsetting ways."[134] Lonely—on both sexual and platonic terms—and disillusioned, Henry employs the UBA noxiously to address the inadequacies he perceives in his seemingly aimless reality. Though Henry is clearly disturbed, it is worth noting that seeking in sports a manifestation of the sex or violence one craves in lived experience is hardly abnormal. One need merely think of the sexually explicit presentation of female cheerleaders as sideline accessories in American football, or the brutal violence of the same game, to see the way in which these sporting events cater to a hypermasculine sense of homosocial camaraderie among male fans.

Henry ultimately aims to unite his feelings of UBA fellowship with his "real" friendship with Lou Engels, since he "longed not only to talk about his game, but to have somebody to play it with him."[135] But by the time Lou finally enters the inner sanctum of Henry's apartment, the proprietor has already begun losing his grip, "destroying the association" by determining that the Knickerbockers—the team of Jock Casey and thus the team responsible for the death of Damon Rutherford—must lose every game.[136] The two men share pizza and beer before beginning to play, and it quickly becomes clear to Henry that Lou, like the greasy pie, is sloppy: he shows "disinterested ignorance" rather than mere "inexperience" in learning the precise and complicated gameplay that Henry has fabricated.[137] Disregarding the fact that Henry's teams are bound by season-long story lines and thus long-term strategic priorities, Lou hastily decides to pitch his "ace" (on short rest) and start slumping players in opposition to the dictates of Henry's narratives. Feeling that "the whole thing was fast becoming pointless,"[138] Henry cannot immerse himself in his UBA world as he normally would:

> He sat, took up the dice. He tried to get his mind down into the game, but Lou's bulky presence seemed to blank him out, and all he saw was paper. He didn't seem to be playing with Lou, but through him, and the way through was dense and hostile.[139]

Understanding their relationship on "real" terms, Lou is less a wall blocking access to the UBA than a revolving door. He continually giggles at the quirky intricacies of Henry's story lines—rendering the proprietor self-conscious—and persistently chats about an old movie, implying that Hollywood's narrative landscape is more real to him than Henry's. Perturbed, Henry soldiers on, building the game to a crescendo until Lou, standing up to go home because of the late hour and urging Henry not to be late to work again tomorrow, knocks a beer over on the tabletop.

Like Bruegel's "The Triumph of Death" superimposed over the Polo Grounds in Hoover's mind's eye in *Underworld*, the thin layer of suds that soaks Henry's play sheets augurs destructive and imaginative possibility:

It's all over, he realized miserably, finished. The Universal Baseball Association, proprietor left for parts unknown. A shudder raked through him as he sighed, and he felt ill. . . . Great moments form the past came floating to mind, mighty old-timers took their swings and fabulous aces reared back and sizzled them in. . . . Should he keep it around, or . . . ? No, better burn it, once and for all, records, rules, Books, everything. If that stuff was lying around he'd never feel free of it. He found a paper shopping bag under the sink, gathered up a stack of scoresheets and dumped them in, reached for that of the night's game. He saw the dice, still reading 2-6-6, and—almost instinctively—reached forward and tipped the two over to a third six. Gave York and Wilson back- to-back homers and moved the game over to the Extraordinary Occurrences Chart. Easy as that.[140]

With Lou Engels departing Henry's apartment in disgrace, the proprietor's desires for camaraderie are long forgotten. Rather than the bawdy intimacies of the homosocial type Henry's players enjoy in his UBA imaginings, Lou has provided him with a catastrophic possibility akin to Hoover's Bruegelian insights. The probabilistic determinations of the dice, their possible outcomes outlined in the beer-sodden charts that he discards, are no longer available to Henry. Thus departed also is any notion of the possible objectivity of history. But "the narrative that lives in the spaces of the official play-by-play" is undamaged, and, with the flick of Henry's finger and the consequential death of Jock Casey, forever transformed.[141]

History: Metricized Reality and Narrative Possibility

Henry's tipping of the dice is world-altering for the UBA. Even at the novel's outset, their six-sided status as insensate arbiters—"heedless of history yet makers of it"—is pronounced.[142] And though Henry recounts to Lou that he enjoyed the crowds at baseball games—they made "ball stadiums and not European churches . . . the real American holy places"—he stopped attending because he found the real game far less edifying than the scorecard it produces.[143] "[T]o tell the truth," Henry admits, "real baseball bored him—[he preferred] the records, the statistics, the peculiar balances between individual and team, offense and defense, strategy and luck, accident and pattern, power and intelligence."[144] Henry understands that these necessary numbers only tell part of the story, and his ledgers record UBA history in stylized accounts that "varied from the extreme economy of factual data to the overblown idiom of the sportswriter, from the scientific objectivity of theoreticians to the literary speculations of essayists and anecdotalist[s]."[145] Even before the spilled beer destroyed his baseball world like Noah's flood, then, Henry understood and relished the narrative flexibility he found among the numbers. Like any fan, Henry's process of signification was incumbent on the overlap between his personal narrative, the sporting events with which he was presented, and his consequent emotions. The result is something much like DeLillo's "unconstraining otherness, a free veer from time and place and fate."[146]

Or, in the judgment of Ricardo Miguel-Alfonso, what Henry values most about the Universal Baseball Association is its "synthesis of binary oppositions," its status as a "fusion between the folk, mythical and religious, on the one hand, and the scientific, mathematical sides of the game, on the other."[147] In a certain sense, the UBA *is* history, in its truest, messiest sense: data- and narrative-driven, humanistic and scientific, numbers and dreamscape. Henry's authorship of the UBA thus reveals both a self-reflective fan aware of his idiosyncratic and imaginative role—a metafictioner, if you will—and an empiricist intellectual concerned not merely with *what* history is recorded but *how* it is recorded: a historiographer, in other words. As such, Henry reflects Coover's existential concern that because

> human existence is so brief [and] the world is so impossibly complex, we cannot accumulate all the data needed for a complete, objective statement. To hope to behave as though this were possible is to invite paralysis through crushing despair. And so we fabricate; we invent constellations that permit an illusion of order to enable us to get from here to there.[148]

Unlike the real baseball interpreted and narrativized to permit "an illusion of order" in *Underworld*, however, Henry's history is set in motion not by collective human action but by a sole godhead. However heedless the dice may be of the history they make, someone has to roll them.[149]

The "idiosyncratic self" that DeLillo's "Power of History" asserts is the realm and responsibility of the novelist is in Coover's novel also always arbiter of that history. Ultimately, Henry loses sight of the fact that his idiosyncratic "language [is] a form of counterhistory."[150] He usurps the objectivity of the dice, and merges history with himself.

The potential for this annihilation of the separation between me and not-me, of history subsumed to the self, is signaled earlier in the novel. Crammed on a bus with Lou, Henry notes that "the paper spoke blackly of bombs, births, wars, weddings, infiltrations, and social events" and asserts that "you can take history or leave it, but if you take it you have to accept certain assumptions or ground rules about what's left in and what's left out. . . . History. Amazing, how we love it. And did you ever stop to think that without numbers or measurements, there probably wouldn't be any history?"[151] In this banal moment, Henry reflexively recognizes the power of records, of purportedly objective measurements, to counterbalance the innate uncertainty of subjective human experience. "The interdependence of imagination and actuality," as Brenda Wineapple puts it, "assumes their separation. One realm must not be totally submerged to the other. . . . We need our fictions to cope with life and we need experience to keep our fictions vital."[152] The newspaper, with its "casualty lists, territory footage won and lost, bounded sets with strategies and payoff functions, supply and communication routes disrupted or restored, tonnage totals, and deaths, downed planes, and prisoners socked away like a hoard of calculable runs scored," provides "numbers and measurements" meant to assure the reader that "what's left in" is reality.[153] But Henry is not so naïve. He recognizes the "snapping of the paper" takes "the world to heart and mind, or some world anyway."[154] We choose the newspaper's measurements of "reality," in other words, over the world "left out," the one not metricized by hits or casualty lists.[155] Henry ultimately rejects this choice in the world of the UBA. Despite the "intransigent will" of the "collective history-maddened eye" that looms over his league, Henry tips the dice and embraces what is left out by numbers and measurements. In the process, the need to separate Henry from the world of imagination he has chosen is lost.[156] In Henry's case, "one realm" genuinely has been "totally submerged by the other."[157]

After Henry disappears, Coover's novel jumps forward 150 years in UBA history to a time in which the history that the dice created has become religious mythography. Henry is nowhere and everywhere, and "all that counts is . . . here's the boys and there's the crowd, the sun, the noise."[158] Despite the sunny tableau, the ending of *The Universal Baseball Association* is dark. For one thing, Henry's disappearance and implied apotheosis suggests mental illness: he forgets, in effect, that he is the one giving meaning to the real. Or, as "Professor Costen Migod McCamish," an academic critic of Coover's own making, puts it in the final chapter: one "come[s] to the conclusion that God exists and he is a nut."[159] But the communal fan experience depicted in Coover's post-Henry section is even more chilling. Future ballplayers perform the roles of Damon Rutherford and Jock Casey in rituals that re-create their deaths via beanball—the martyrs' names screamed by rabid crowds as human sacrifice is carried out in the imagined stadium. Here baseball fans are mindless members of the blood-thirsty mob, just as DeLillo's Hoover imagines them in transposing "The Triumph of Death" over the Polo Grounds. Balancing self and other, history and fiction, the Universal Baseball Association and *The Universal Baseball Association*, is an act that cannot be sustained. We must either lose ourselves in the crowd or lose the crowd in ourselves.

Ultimately, then, Coover and DeLillo present conflicting visions of fan interpretation and narration. Both depict the manner in which baseball fans define themselves against history, but come to different conclusions about the possibilities engendered by the "sly, mazed, mercurial, scared half-crazy" nature of the "idiosyncratic self" and the baseball stories it produces.[160] DeLillo finds cause for optimism in the fans' resistance to the "power of history." In the face of cultural intolerance and the omnipresent threat of worldwide destruction, DeLillo's fans use baseball to write American stories all their own. Coover, by contrast, sees the threat to fandom emanating not from without, but within. He finally imagines baseball fan behavior *in extremis* as pathological. He characterizes Henry's behavior as delusional in much the same way that fans of all kinds—but especially fans of "cult" media texts like *Star Trek*—have been considered delusional, so enamored of their preferred text that they have lost grip on reality. For Coover, when the sports fan becomes more writer than reader, he cannot help but build himself a prison of the mind. But this pessimistic viewpoint undervalues the communal appeal of sport, and especially of baseball. Group identity is a powerful driver of fan identification, even as fans write their own stories, and Henry Waugh's failure to connect with those around him and share the fan experience puts him on the path to ultimate solipsism. What's more, when it comes to actual mental illness, that same potential for interpersonal identification can allow sports fandom to function as an important road of return to wellness, as we'll see in the next chapter.

2

IT WAS MY FATE, MY DESTINY, MY END, TO BE A FAN

Football, Mental Illness, and the Autobiographical Novel

> If he himself is not to be victimized, then the strong poet must "rescue" the beloved Muse from his precursors. Of course, he "overestimates" the Muse, seeing her as unique and irreplaceable, for how else can he be assured that he is unique and irreplaceable?
>
> HAROLD BLOOM, The Anxiety of Influence[1]

While baseball's green fields idyll can be said to foster a particular mode of pastoral nationalist group identification among fans, albeit one that Don DeLillo and Robert Coover take pains to complicate, football's violent action is often characterized as inducing a more rabid mode of interpersonal fan behavior. Such mania can and has led critics like Christopher Lasch to assert that fandom is a major driver of mental illness. In *The Culture of Narcissism*, Lasch posits that fan identification "intensif[ies] narcissistic dreams of fame and glory, encourage[s] the common man to identify himself with the stars and to hate the 'herd,' and make[s] it more and more difficult for him to accept the banality of everyday existence."[2] To back up this claim, Lasch turns to a literary source, Frederick Exley's *A Fan's Notes*, whose author he considers representative of a cadre of "confessional writers [who] walk a fine line between self-analysis and self-indulgence."[3] Lasch posits that the mentally ill Exley "depicts himself or his narrator—as usual, the distinction is unclear—as a yawning void, an insatiable hunger, an emptiness waiting to be filled with the rich experiences reserved for the chosen few."[4] The only way for Exley to fill that void, to sustain "the illusion that [he] could escape the bleak anonymity of life," is to be a fan, a sports fan, and, above all, a fan of New York Giants football star Frank Gifford.[5] Lasch makes the thrice-institutionalized Exley the paragon of mass media fandom, dubbing him a "new Narcissus."[6] Just as vital to this designation as Exley's sports fanaticism, however, is his work's ambiguous genre: his self-described "fictional memoir" meets Lasch's confessional criteria, blurring the line between autobiography and fiction by positioning its author-narrator as both intrinsically self-revelatory and unreliable.[7] The indeterminate form of *A Fan's Notes* thus represents "the narcissist's [propensity to] pseudo-insight into his own condition, usually expressed in psychiatric clichés, [and] serves him as a means of deflecting criticism and disclaiming responsibility for his actions."[8] Egocentric and prone to fantasy, Exley as author-narrator incarnates for Lasch the postmodern American's blurred sense of reality and need for external validation.

But Exley's fanatical narcissism also conflicts with another prominent stereotype by which sports fandom is stigmatized as mental illness. Exley's impressive intellect, literary acumen, and propensity to self-reflection belie the notion that sports are, as John Gerdy puts it, "what we talk about when we want to avoid thinking or talking about anything meaningful or important."[9] Characterizing sports fandom in terms of addiction—where "like crack addicts sitting around their pipe in a dream state waiting for the next 'hit,' we sit in front of our televisions, unresponsive to the world around us"—Gerdy better describes the chemical exacerbator of Exley's mental illness, alcohol, than his desire to associate his life and Frank Gifford's.[10] Other critics of spectator sports, like David P. Barash, have found fans "lacking a firm grip on reality" in a similar vein, which is to say as a form of illness that involves "a surrender of personal identity," rather than an obsession with it, á la Christopher Lasch.[11] To explore this distinct-yet-related stigma, as well as Lasch's claim that Exley's work typifies a connection between narcissistic content, authorial unreliability, and blurred genre, in this chapter I will examine *A Fan's Notes* alongside a more recent work that similarly considers American football fandom, identity, and mental illness: Matthew Quick's 2008 novel, *The Silver Linings Playbook*.

Quick's debut novel, like Exley's, is narrated by a recently institutionalized football fan whose connection to the sport is ineluctably tied to a particular player. Though Quick's narrator-protagonist, Pat Peoples, does not share the author's name, the character's experiences with football fandom and mental illness are partly based on Quick's own experiences.[12] This similarity between author and character is not so pervasive that it influences the form of *The Silver Linings Playbook*—as it does in *A Fan's Notes*—but Quick indeed blurs the novel's formal reality by presenting Peoples via diary entries that attempt to fill the massive gaps in his memory. Unlike Exley, Peoples's psychological and physiological damage is such that his thirty-five-year-old brain has been "knocked . . . back into teenager mode" and *The Silver Linings Playbook*'s ostensibly naïve narration often makes it sound more like young adult fiction than the art novel to which *A Fan's Notes* baldly aspires.[13] Yet Peoples, like Exley, turns to both football and literature to make sense of his fractured life and the events that led to his institutionalization. Rather than categorizing the novels they read as somehow distinct from or opposed to the narratives they covet on the football field, both narrator-protagonists mesh their literary influences with sporting interests when attempting to make sense of their own life narratives.

Reading the protagonists' sporting and literary fandoms as complementary modes of textual interpretation, I argue that the generic flexibility of *A Fan's Notes* and *The Silver Linings Playbook* allows their authors to represent the readerly complexity and interpretive flexibility of fans. Exley's and Quick's works manifest Garry Crawford's assertion that "being a fan . . . is not an isolated incident or coherent 'thing,' it is an identity and as such is a highly complex social construction, which is neither wholly imposed, ascribed, achieved nor chosen."[14] Sometimes some fans are, as Barash and Gerdy assume, passive consumerist dupes, and others pseudo-psychologizing narcissists in the vein outlined by Lasch. But as Pat Peoples and Frederick Exley demonstrate, mental illness and sports fandom are not definitionally or coterminally linked. Sports don't blur reality—reality is always already blurred. Along with literature, sporting narratives are one place where the self-determining possibilities of that blurring are most apparent. In drawing a parallel between the receptive practices of sports fandom and literary interpretation, Exley's and Quick's works show us that, distinct as a live sporting event and a work of literature may seem, our readerly interactions with each are subject to similar impulses, no matter the cultural pretenses. The distinctions that are thought to separate media fans and sports fans, at least in academic considerations, are nonsensical when it comes to the omnivorous ethos of fan reception and interpretation pursued by Exley and Peoples.

"To Eliminate Our Realities and Substitute Those of Society": Fandom and Institutionalization

Regarded as a critical success, Exley's *A Fan's Notes* received the William Faulkner Award for the best first novel of 1968, as well as the National Institute of Arts and Letters Rosenthal Award for "that work which, though not a commercial success, is a considerable literary achievement."[15] The novel has enjoyed modest success since then, selling, as Exley biographer Jonathan Yardley puts it, "steadily if not spectacularly" in paperback.[16] But the work has been largely ignored by literary critics, and what scant attention it has received has tended to be overwhelmed by an association of football with a national paradigm of cultural corruption and individual alienation.[17] Exley himself blames America at large for his "inability to function properly in society," but football itself is not a pariah.[18] Rather, it is his "anodyne" and "intellectual stimulation."[19] Exley's obsession with Frank Gifford and the New York Giants is not a psychotic source of unreality, he posits, but a form of treatment: when Exley is committed, he asserts that the staff at the mental institution "found it simpler to eliminate our realities and substitute those of society," to make acute "the sense of one's anonymity, the loss of self."[20] Faced with such anonymity, Exley asserts that Gifford came to "represent to me the possible ... sustained for me the illusion that I could escape the bleak anonymity of life."[21] At one point in the novel, after enlisting a friend—his future wife Patience—to check him out of the mental hospital in order to watch the Giants game, Exley is asked if he should envy and hate Gifford rather than love him. He responds with "great incredulity. 'But you don't understand at all. Not at all! He may be the only fame I'll ever have!'"[22] Rather than facilitate the "surrender of personal identity" as Barash fears, fandom is a tether to the self for Exley.[23] It functions, as Erin Tarver puts it in applying Foucauldian principles to sports fandom, as a "subjectivizing practice ... , [a] means by which individuals both subordinate themselves to a discipline and, by virtue of it, achieve a sense of their own identities."[24] So long as Gifford "possessed the legs and the hands and the agility, the tools of his art," Exley feels as though he can recapture the lost "tools of mine, writing."[25] But Exley's association with Gifford is about more than authorial inspiration: it is always also about a psychic need to live up to the notoriety of his father, Earl Exley.

One of the greatest football players in the history of Watertown, NY, Earl was a local celebrity, a man so beloved he could not walk down the street without encountering admirers. "Like most athletes he lived amidst the large deeds and ephemeral glories of the past," Fred Exley asserts, and Earl valued the adulation of the crowd above all.[26] The consequence, for the younger Exley, is a sense that "the crowd [came] between my father and me," inhibiting intimacy in large part because his own athletic abilities were not on par.[27] Subsequently traumatized by his father's premature death, Exley imagines that "had [he] found the words to tell me why he so needed The Crowd, I might have saved my soul and now be . . . sublimely content."[28] Instead, Exley "suffered . . . the singular notion that fame was an heirloom passed on from my father," and desperately seeks "to have [his] name whispered in reverential tones."[29] The game of football inescapably impacts Exley's unfulfilled filial relationship. As Yardley puts it, "on the football field, or, later, in the stands or in a bar with the television set showing a game, Fred was in the company of his father."[30] Joining "The Crowd" his father cherished, but unable to command it with an athletic performance, Exley is driven to seek its adulation elsewhere.

Given such personal trauma, Exley's performance of fan behavior is easily figured as a manifestation of his psychosis. The notion of the fan as "fanatic," a rabid zealot of biased support for one team or another, fits Exley's description of himself at the onset of *A Fan's Notes*. Drunk and running around a bar, Exley dramatically mimics the New York Giants players' movements among the barstools. An object of spectatorship for other patrons, Exley describes their interest as "the morbid fascination which compels one to stare at a madman."[31] But he doesn't mind such fascination. In fact, Exley seems to relish making others uncomfortable, including *A Fan's Notes'* readership: he unflinchingly depicts the uglier side of his nature, exhibiting misogyny, racism, and homophobia in writing his "fictional memoir."[32] As Yardley puts it, "*A Fan's Notes* is not for the fastidious."[33] In several instances, the Exleyan fan account is inglorious and offensive in a way that merits the condemnation of Barash, Gerdy, and other antisport critics. But Exley also notably embraces the ugliness of his character in opposition to a mental health industry that embraced shock therapy and lobotomy, that would "scrape away all grief, all rage, all violence, all the things that make us Man, leaving one great hulk of loonily smiling protoplasm. . . . Yes, I was insane. Still, I did not despise my oddness, my deviations, those things which made me, after all, me. I wanted to preserve those things."[34] Faced with medically sanctioned mental oblivion, football fandom and the dream of fame that Gifford provides do not excuse Exley's behavior, but they are similarly figured as defense mechanisms that he uses to preserve some semblance of idiosyncratic self-knowledge.

In *The Silver Linings Playbook*, Pat Peoples faces similar quandaries about the nature and distinctiveness of his identity in the face of institutionalization and psychiatric therapy. Unable to remember the previous four years of his life as well as the incident that led to his institutionalization, Peoples knows merely that the developments have resulted in legally mandated "apart time" from his ex-wife, Nikki.[35] Released from the "bad place" at his mother's behest over the objections of his physicians, Peoples spends the novel attempting to figure out a way to reconcile with Nikki while living with his parents in Collingswood, New Jersey—a suburb of Philadelphia.[36] Unlike Exley, whose time with family members in *A Fan's Notes* is largely spent in self-imposed sedentary incapacity (with the exception of football Sundays, when he paces manically around the living room), Peoples spends his days in constant motion, exercising obsessively in the hope that his improved physical appearance will allow him to win Nikki back. His routine is, at least initially, interrupted by just two activities: visiting his therapist and rooting for the Philadelphia Eagles football team.[37]

The latter activity forms the core of family life in the Peoples household, at least for the males, and it provides Pat a means of updating his identity even as he attempts to remember the person he used to be. He associates himself, like Exley, with a particular player on his chosen team: in this case, Eagles wide receiver Hank Baskett. Though the associative animus is initiated by consumerism—Pat's brother Jake buys him the jersey in order to welcome him back—Pat quickly begins to feel "as if my future were somehow linked to the Eagles' rookie wide receiver."[38] Like Exley, whose connection to Gifford is biographically oriented in that both men attended the University of Southern California and moved to New York shortly thereafter, Peoples sees in the undrafted, unheralded player an underdog like himself. And, like Exley with Gifford, when Baskett plays well, Peoples correlates the player's successes to his own. He even receives public credit from other fans for Baskett's success, getting high-fives in the stadium and hearing from his manic father that "Baskett healed the family" after an Eagles victory.[39] This public association between player and fan is extended in less successful times as well. Peoples, in keeping a promise to his friend and eventual romantic interest, Tiffany, does not watch any Eagles games until the dance competition for which they are training has concluded. During his absence, the Eagles fail to win any games and Baskett struggles. Peoples's family, friends, and even his therapist, Cliff, bemoan his absence and cheer him on in the dance competition, in large part because they hope the culminating event will end the "Pat Peoples curse" on the team.[40] As if confirming the merit of this superstitious belief, when Peoples returns to cheering for the Eagles, the team goes on a winning streak and makes the playoffs as Baskett thrives.

In addition to filling the void in his identity caused by memory loss, Eagles fandom provides Peoples a path to acceptance from his skeptical father, Patrick Sr. He describes watching the Eagles game and "glanc[ing] over at my father from time to time, making sure he sees me cheering, because I know he is only willing to sit in the same room with his mentally deranged son as long as I am rooting for the Birds with everything I got."[41] Yet Peoples also recognizes that this standard for intimacy predates his institutionalization, that "all the time I have ever spent with [my brother] Jake or him has always revolved around sports [and that] this is all he can really afford emotionally."[42] Like Exley, then, Peoples's relationship to his father is predicated on the younger male's identity as a fan. Unlike Exley, however, Peoples cheers alongside his father in the crowd rather than watching him earn adulation from it. Still, Peoples's fan identity is sublimated to his father insofar as the elder Peoples can claim a measure of authenticity reserved for the truly fanatical. Insulted by a fan of the Dallas Cowboys many years earlier,

Dad lost it, attacked the Dallas fan, and beat him within an inch of his life. My father was actually arrested, convicted of aggravated assault, and incarcerated for three months. If my uncle hadn't made the mortgage payments, we would have lost the house. Dad did lose his season ticket and has not been to an Eagles game since. Jake says we could get Dad in, since no one actually checks IDs at the gate, but Dad won't go back, saying, "As long as they let the opposing fans in our house, I can't trust myself."[43]

Here is a fan for whom, as Allen Guttmann puts it, "the identification with those who seem to represent them is clearly pathological."[44] Patrick Peoples seems to confirm the notion that the ostensibly "deindividuated" spectator easily becomes a part of the violent "mob-mind" that social psychologist George Elliot Howard warned of in 1912's "Social Psychology of the Spectator."[45] For the elder Peoples, the individual consequences of this partisan violence separate him from the stadium crowd that ostensibly inculcated it, but do not lessen his passion for the team nor mitigate the malignant mode of socialization it seems to have fostered in him. He breaks a television after a particularly painful Eagles loss, treats his family poorly when the team is struggling, and, when Pat goes missing late in the novel, refuses to join the search for his son because the game is on. The question as to whether Pat Peoples Jr. or his father is the "mentally deranged" one occurs to the former as they watch a game: "'Scream your goddam lungs out, because you're the twelfth man!' Dad says. The way he talks at me—never really pausing long enough for me to say anything— makes him sound crazy, I know, even though most people think I am the crazy person in the family."[46]

The specter of his father's violent reputation influences Peoples beyond the social dynamics of the family. In grappling with the reasons for his institutionalization, which he cannot remember, Peoples recognizes that his own propensity to violent outbursts is also predicated on specific triggers. One such trigger is the music of Kenny G, which, heard while in the waiting room at his therapist's office, provokes him "out of [his] seat . . . screaming, kicking chairs, flipping the coffee table."[47] Peoples's therapist, Cliff, characterizes his reaction in terms of fan reception: "The Kenny G song really got to you. I can't say I'm a fan either."[48] Attempting to help

Pat recover memories of the traumatic incident that he associates with G's music (which the therapist knows to be violent), Cliff thus recognizes fan and antifan identification as significant psychological epistemologies. This understanding extends to Eagles fandom as well, as the Indian American psychiatrist reveals himself to be a fellow avid fan and member of the "Asian Invasion," a group of South Asian Eagles fans who tailgate at every game.[49] Communing with Cliff and his fan cohort in that tailgate setting later in the novel, Peoples recognizes the potential positive social benefits of fandom, thinking of the racially diverse group that "all it really takes for different people to get along is a common rooting interest and a few beers."[50] Cliff thus provides for Peoples a more positive model for fan behavior.

Even so, the site of the tailgate is also one in which the sins of the father are revisited by the son. Confronted by a Giants fan looking for trouble, Peoples, his brother Jake, and their friends initially rebuff the interloper with insults. Though Peoples feels bad on behalf of a "little boy with [the trespasser fan, Steve,] who is also wearing a Giants jersey," he admits "it feels sort of thrilling to be part of this mob—united in our hatred of the opposing team's fans."[51] When that Giants fan escalates the conflict and "throws Jake to the ground," Peoples's rage is triggered

> and before I can stop myself, I'm moving forward like a Mack truck. I catch Steve's cheek with a left, and then my right connects with the south side of his chin, lifting him off the ground. I watch him float through the air as if he were allowing his body to fall backward into a pool. His back hits the concrete, his feet and hands twitch once, and then he's not moving, the crowd is silent, and I begin to feel so awful—so guilty.
> Someone yells, "Call an ambulance!"
> Another yells, "Tell 'em to bring a blue-and-red body bag!"
> "I'm sorry," I whisper, because I find it hard to speak. "I'm so sorry."
> And then I am running again.[52]

Though Peoples avoids being caught by the authorities, the gravity of his actions continues to weigh on him long afterward. Jake argues that his brother is a hero for defending him, but Peoples doesn't "feel proud at all. I feel guilty. I should be locked up again in the bad place."[53] The consequences of being reinstitutionalized in the mental hospital are ano-nymizing for Peoples as they are for Exley: "I know I really shouldn't have hit that Giants fan, and now I'm crying again because I'm such a fucking waste—such a fucking non-person."[54] Though he cannot remem-ber the details of what happened, Peoples knows that violence led to his institutionalization, and that the wiping clean of that prior improper identity—nonpersonage—is associated with the rehabilitation that takes place there. Rather than attempt to preserve the "deviations, those things which made me . . . me," as Exley puts it, Peoples seeks to remember them.[55] In both cases, however, the narrative details of personal identity are closely associated with on-field events.

Though he cannot return to the parking lot if he wants to avoid being arrested for assaulting the Giants fan, Peoples enters the stadium at his brother's encouragement and watches the game. The Eagles take an early lead and Baskett pulls in an important catch, but the Giants make an improbable comeback and win the contest. For Peoples, then, the game's sequence of events seems to mirror his own traumatic failings in the parking lot. On returning home, this connection is transferred to his subconscious:

> In my dreams the fight happens again and again, only instead of the Giants fan bringing a kid to the game, the Giants fan brings Nikki, and she too is wearing a Giants jersey. Every time I knock the big guy out, Nikki . . . kisses his forehead and then looks up at me [and] says, "You're an animal Pat. And I will never love you again."[56]

The Giants' victory comes to represent Nikki's rejection of Pat for violence he "can't control" or understand.[57] The same holds true for Exley at the climax of *A Fan's Notes*. The inescapable narrative connection between on-the-field defeat and personal failure, between the sanctioned competitive violence of football players and the unauthorized criminal violence of the fan, between frenzied mental instability and attendant self-analysis, are evident.

With the Giants in the hunt for the 1960 NFL championship, Gifford and Exley enter Yankee Stadium for a game against the Eagles. Playing in the twilight of his career, Gifford begins to excel, his quarterback throwing the ball "to some memory of the ball player [Gifford] once had been."[58] Exley exults that "the crowd was wild. The crowd was maniacal. The crowd was his."[59] In this moment, Exley's connection to Gifford yields the adulation he craves from the crowd he fears. At the apex of Exley's joy, however, he detects the crushing force of Chuck Bednarik, the Eagles' All-Pro linebacker, bearing down on Gifford. "Quite suddenly," Exley observes, "I knew [what] was going to happen; and accepting, with the fatalistic horror of a man anchored by fear to a curb and watching a tractor trailer bear down on a blind man, I stood breathlessly and waited."[60] Exley is forcefully reminded of his role as a helpless spectator when, in one of the most famously vicious hits in NFL history, Gifford is brought "to the soft green turf with a sickening thud," his body rendered "a small, broken, blue-and-silver mannikin" that is subsequently carried from the field on a stretcher.[61] Despite the emotional trauma he suffers at this violent encounter, Exley's critical faculties remain with him. He describes the scene as "in a way . . . beautiful to behold. For what seemed an eternity both Gifford and the ball had seemed to float, weightless above the field, as if they were performing for the crowd on the trampoline."[62]

In the aftermath of what appeared to be a career-ending, if not life-threatening, injury to Gifford, Exley "seek[s] out a less subtle defeat" of his own.[63] He starts a fight with a passing pair of men, of differing races and presumed to be homosexual, for whom he exhibits contrived bigotry in order to instigate violence. "In that limp and broken body against the green turf of the stadium," Exley asserts, "I had had a glimpse of my own mortality. As much as anything else, that fist fight was a futile rage against the inevitability of that mortality."[64] Though he has captured the aesthetic potential of Gifford's violent athletic demise,[65] Exley's ultimate reaction to the event is to push his emotional response to the ugliest potential combination of fan zealotry and his own mental illness, screaming "nigger fucker" at a stranger for the sake of provoking him: "it was a lament, this fight, a lament for a conspiracy . . . against anonymity begun so many season before and ended that very day; so that even as I took this black man's blows I could see that broken, blue-and-silver figure, stretcher-borne."[66] Concluding that, like Gifford, he has been broken and cannot possibly recover, Exley is content with futile rage, choosing an outward expression of bigoted, violent fan behavior even as he portrays himself as capable of historicizing Gifford's defeat and his own. In this moment, Exley resigns himself to the fact that "it was my fate, my destiny, my end, to be a fan": in effect, to be only one voice in a cacophony of amateur appreciators, never a recognized performer like his father, the football star.[67] But in doing so, Exley also demonstrates the critical complexity of fan behavior. He shows that fans, like readers of the broadest range of cultural texts, whether aesthetically oriented or not, have multiple motivations and reactive registers. His art, finally, is born of the bleachers whose reason and creative capacity he questions. It is his fate to articulate the complicated stakes and blurred reality of fandom with equal measures of artistry and ugliness. *A Fan's Notes* ends with Exley "ready to do battle . . . running: obsessively running," like Peoples, from his personal failure.[68] Despite three institutionalizations, he cannot reconcile his reality to "this new, this incomprehensible America."[69] It would seem that football fandom, synecdochally represented by Gifford's broken body, has failed positively to reshape "society's reality" for Exley.[70] A broader consideration of that fandom's impact in relationship to his literary aspirations tells another story, however.

"Life Often Ends Badly . . . Literature Tries to Document This Reality": Fandom and Literature

The idea that sporting events are narrative entertainments makes sense when they are directly compared to popular media serials: it's not that difficult to see the similarities between a media fan and the favorite cult TV show to which he returns weekly, for example, and a sports fan's ritualistic consumption and interpretation of a regularly scheduled football game. But sports' inherent narrativity is rather more difficult to analogize to high-brow or canonical literature, on the basis of cultural cachet and intellectual esteem if nothing else. In "Toward a New Male Identity: Literature and Sports," critic Ross J. Pudaloff asserts that "superficially, there would appear to exist an inverse relationship between writing and reading and modern sports, a distinction between solitary, reflective, withdrawn and culturally feminized activities and mass-based, socially approved, aggressive, and masculine ones."[71] Yet, even as the weekly rhythms of their lives are determined by football fandom, Peoples and Exley are perpetually motivated by literary appreciation. As with football, both are attuned to the resonances of literature in relationship to their own life narrative. Treating sports and literary narratives similarly, Exley and Peoples affirm Pudaloff's notion that "literature and sports are . . . linked because both discover and value the presence of fantasy and desire at the center of the social and ordinary world."[72] Uncertain about what constitutes reality, Exley and Peoples seek escapist fantasy in consuming the two seemingly distinct narrative forms. Even so, Peoples's association with Hank Baskett and Exley's imagined connection to Frank Gifford also impact their otherwise unpalatable realities in meaningful ways. By constructing their own identities both *in* the diegetic landscape of *A Fan's Notes* and *The Silver Linings Playbook* and *through* the act of writing their stories, the narrator-authors demonstrate the agency of fans and readers to appropriate the elements of their passion, use them to create identity on the page, and disseminate that self-expression such that it impacts lived experience.

Fans of rival football teams in the Giants and Eagles, albeit at different times in football history, Exley's and Peoples's efforts to forge new realities through immersion in the literary are likewise distinct in both method and motivation. Exley's connection to literature is predicated on his university experience—he asserts that he "quite naturally became an English major" at USC because "The Books, The Novels and The Poems [provided] pat reassurances that other men had experienced rejection and pain and loss"—as well as his aspiring authorship of "The Big Book," a prospective work he calls his "literary fantasy."[73] For Peoples, on the other hand, the aspiration is informal, rehabilitative, and social: "to read all the novels on [Nikki's] American literature class syllabus, just to make her proud [and to] be able to converse with her swanky literary friends."[74] While Exley hopes "The Books, The Novels and The Poems" will help elevate him from "The Crowd" to Giffordian fame in the social sphere of the literati, Peoples desires to reshape his mind, like his body, to please the woman he loves but with whom he is denied reconciliation. The two men approach literature from distinct backgrounds and with different motivations, then, but they both find in its pages—as on the football field—the inspiration to reshape their unpalatable lives.

Because Peoples's roadmap is his ex-wife's high school American literature syllabus, his literary rehabilitation features a predictable list of famous titles. And equally predictably, given his mental state, Peoples's reactions to *The Great Gatsby*, *A Farewell to Arms*, *The Scarlet Letter*, *The Catcher in the Rye*, and *The Bell Jar* are not oriented to historical or literary frameworks, but to a childlike measurement of his own sympathy for the protagonists. Peoples relates himself directly to the characters on the page in part because he sees himself as a character on the big screen. He thinks of his "own life [as a] movie" and takes solace in his belief that despite his troubles "it's almost time for the happy ending, when Nikki will come back."[75] Conceptualizing his life on melodramatic terms inspires Peoples to see the "silver lining" in his situation, and he seeks the same ultimate optimism in measuring the narrative priorities of the literature he reads. This leads to frustration at "how Gatsby loves Daisy so much but can't ever be with her no matter how hard he tries" and disappointment that "Fitzgerald never took the time to look up at the clouds during sunset."[76] Authorial ascriptions of this type persist: Peoples's anger at the unhappy demise of Catherine in *A Farewell to Arms* leads him to vow never to "read another one of [Ernest Hemingway's] books. And if he were still alive, I would write him a letter right now and threaten to strangle him dead with my bare hands just for being so glum. No wonder he put a gun to his head."[77] Transferring his own potential for violent psychosis to the page in his threat to the famous(ly) dead author, Peoples also blames one of the actual victims of that psychosis, his ex-wife Nikki, for "teach[ing] this book to children. . . . Why not just tell high school students that their struggle to improve themselves is all for nothing?"[78]

Unhappy endings, familiar as they may be in individual sporting outcomes, are bothersome to Peoples in literature for their finality. Thus a novel like Nathaniel Hawthorne's *The Scarlet Letter*, difficult though it may be for Hester Prynne, is redeemed because its unhappiness comes before the end. Hester gets to live "a fulfilled life and [get] to see her daughter grow up and marry well," Peoples asserts, because "she believed in silver linings [and] stuck to her guns" when faced with "that nasty throng of bearded men in hats."[79] Mapping his own "struggle to improve" himself onto the plot arcs of each novel, Peoples sees their final outcomes in football's binary terms of wins and losses and rejects those narratives that would suggest that his narrative could, at least when it comes to Nikki, already have ended unhappily.[80] Even when presented with evidence of just such finality, Peoples still rejects the possibility of such a conclusion.

At long last remembering viciously beating the man with whom he caught his wife cheating, Peoples subsequently learns that the letters he thought he was receiving from Nikki were in fact the fabrications of Tiffany, his equally mentally ill dance partner. In truth, Nikki has not been in touch, and will never reconcile with him. And yet Peoples defiantly asserts that his "movie isn't over," citing the way "moviemakers trick the audience with a false bad ending, and just when you think the movie is going to end badly, something dramatic happens, which leads to the happy ending."[81] Urging him to move on from Nikki and start a new life with Tiffany, Cliff attempts to impose what Exley would call "society's realities,"[82] assuring Peoples that "life is not a movie. You're an Eagles fan. After watching so many NFL seasons without a Super Bowl, you should know that real life often ends poorly."[83] Tiffany herself, impersonating Nikki in a letter, does the same, contextualizing failure on literary terms:

> I'll tell you the same thing I tell my students when they complain about the depressing nature of American literature: life is not a PG feel-good movie. Real life often ends badly, like our marriage did, Pat. And literature tries to document this reality, while showing us it is still possible for people to endure nobly.[84]

Documenting that noble possibility in authoring the literary chronicle of his own life, Peoples nevertheless rejects this literary metaphor, just as he does Cliff's football version, because he finds it "defeated by pessimism."[85] Instead, he chooses to interpret his reality on willfully optimistic terms. Like the renewal of football season each fall—each team's and player's chance to rewrite over the previous year's (almost always) unhappy narrative conclusion—Peoples refuses to discount the possibility of his redemption. Though in his own once-forgotten narrative of adultery he plays the role of Roger Chillingworth, rather than Hester Prynne, Peoples "sticks to his guns" until the very end.[86] Only when he drives to Baltimore and sees in person that Nikki has made a new life for herself does he acquiesce to the finality of their separation, to "the ending of the movie, the one that was my old life."[87] Befitting his belief in silver linings, of course, Peoples's ultimate acceptance of one life narrative's ending allows him to pursue another: the concluding romantic partnership with Tiffany that provides the possibility for him "to endure nobly."[88]

Similar to Peoples's quest for Hollywood's happy ending, Exley's dream of fame informs his literary associations throughout the novel. Peppering *A Fan's Notes* with references to high-brow literary works, the author-narrator attempts to fulfill his need to have his "name whispered in reverential tones" by associating the events of his life narrative with the plots of works by Vladimir Nabokov, Saul Bellow, Ernest Hemingway, and J. D. Salinger.[89] A particularly young girlfriend is thus described as "Hudson's Rima, Spenser's Una, Humbert Humbert's Dolly," while Exley wishes he "had been a square-jawed, tight-lipped, virile Frederick Henry who loved, lost, and walked back to his hotel in the rain. But I didn't love in that way; and when I lost, I went quite off my head."[90] Rather than put himself in these novels, as Peoples does, Exley maps these novels—and their authors—onto his own life. In "throwing mental bouquets to those who had mastered the art" of writing, Exley marks reference points of literary prestige with which he wants to be associated.[91]

Finally it is Exley's own fannish connection to Nathaniel Hawthorne that helps him find a model for productivity at peace with his sense of identity. Returning to *The Scarlet Letter* because he has gotten a job as a high school English teacher, Exley admits that his "previous readings of Hawthorne had been hostile and sneering," likely because "his obdurate and unrelieved probing of the evil in men, particularly his so shackling the characters of his somber world with scarcely bearable yokes of guilt, had aroused in me an understandable distress."[92] In the wake of Gifford's crushing injury and Exley's own bloody and bigoted resignation to personal failure, however, he finds Hawthorne's depiction of enduring human turpitude reassuring:

> Having prostrated myself before the Freudians and found no relief . . . it seemed to me [that] not only are there certain things from which, this side of heaven, men should not be absolved . . . but employing all the psychological ploys available there are acts from which men never completely absolve themselves.[93]

Here, contra Lasch, Exley rejects the "psychiatric clichés, [that serve] him as a means of deflecting criticism and disclaiming responsibility for his actions."[94] Instead he recognizes that many of his actions have been reprehensible and should not be forgiven by others or, more crucially, by himself. His "deviations," in other words, are to be preserved in order that they *not* be revisited.[95] In contrast with Pat Peoples, then, the "guns" that Hester sticks to in *The Scarlet Letter* are for Exley unredeeming. Ultimate rehabilitation, of the saccharine kind that Hollywood and Peoples covet, is impossible.

The acceptance that his flaws are permanent but not redeeming for being such does not affect the mode of Exley's subsequent interaction with Hawthorne, however. "Reading [Hawthorne] in the light of this belief" that "sin and remorse are . . . a necessary parcel" in him, Exley thus "soon developed a crush on Hawthorne. I forced unanalogous parallels between his life and mine."[96] Rather unsurprisingly, then, Exley most cherishes the semi-autobiographical "Custom House" preface to *The Scarlet Letter*. In Hawthorne's description of authorial "languor" incurred "while working surrounded by men whose existence was bounded by the succulence of past and anticipated meals," Exley cannot help but see resonances of the ways in which "teaching children granted immunity from failure" and thus inculcated in him "a similarly impotent languor."[97] To find his own Scarlet "A" in storage, Exley retreats "when the summer holiday finally came" to his mother's attic, to write "these pages, [which] had begun to form themselves in my mind."[98] Physically incapable of being an athlete like Frank Gifford, Exley finds in Hawthorne a fan object whose actions he can quite literally mirror. Thus uninhibited, his efforts meet with success and *A Fan's Notes* is born. In effect, like Peoples, Exley's fan pursuits ultimately secure his identity, but not in the way he anticipated or intended. Fittingly so, because the foremost lesson of literary appreciation may be that life's silver linings are never foreseen or unambiguous. Like all truly complex narratives, human experience cannot be reduced to intended meanings or defined outcomes.

"I Never Tell Anybody the Way It Really Happened": Fandom and the Form of the Novel

Unable to tolerate "the bare facts [that] would prove inimical to my own version," Exley's "fictional memoir" represents the only narrative reality he can bear to reproduce.[99] "I never tell anybody the way it really happened," Exley asserts at one point, "any more than in a hundred places in these pages I have told what 'really' happened."[100] At least in part,

A Fan's Notes' generic indeterminacy reflects the fact that Exley's aesthetic choices about self-representation are inescapably influenced by the blurred uncertainty of his lived experience. The form of *A Fan's Notes* is, like its subject, inherently multiple. But the representative flexibility of the "fictional memoir" as a form also allows Exley to better demonstrate the capacity of sports and literary fans alike to inhabit varying positions of desire and analysis. Just as the sports fan naturally subsumes the "objective" statistical markers of an athlete's performance within an inherently subjective sense of that athlete's significance, the reader of literature similarly assigns personal importance to characters with varying consideration for the narrative "reality" conveyed by the words on the page. Exley's multiple modes of engagement with football approximate Rita Felski's notion of textual "enchantment" in *Uses of Literature*, in which a reader is immersed and emotionally invested in a text, even as he or she inevitably maintains "a state of double-consciousness . . . a distinctive bifurcation of perception [that] underlies modern aesthetic experience, whether 'high' or 'low.'"[101] In the context of textual engagement, Felski argues, enchantment is "a richer and more multi-faceted [experience] than literary theory has allowed."[102] It is in this vein that *A Fan's Notes* gives us reason to broaden the terms of textuality to include the sporting event as an episode of serial narrative and the sports fan as its doubly conscious reader. As its title suggests, *A Fan's Notes* both draws out the readerly resonances of sports fandom and highlights the fannish motivations hidden in the way we read. In form and content, *A Fan's Notes* illustrates the flexibility of fans-as-readers to assume multiple interpretive modes in a wide array of cultural contexts.

In the prefatory matter to *The Silver Linings Playbook*, Matthew Quick makes no genre-blurring claims: we are to understand that the novel is a fiction. The fact that Pat Peoples's New Jersey upbringing, struggle with mental illness, and Eagles fandom approximate many of Quick's own experiences is not overtly stated as it is in in the preface to *A Fan's Notes*. Even so, the novel and its narrator are obviously invested in exploring the fuzzy intersections between narrative interpretation and lived experience. As mentioned earlier, when Peoples reads the works on his ex-wife's high school American literature syllabus, he immediately relates them to his life history—such as he knows it—and his expectations for his future. Given the massive gaps in his memory, Peoples naturally attempts to graft other narratives onto his own story, and, perhaps because he understands that many of the events lost to lacunae will be unpalatable to him, he seeks in those narratives messages he can parse as positive or empowering. When applied to his own life narrative, this active participation in determining textual meaning leads Peoples to assert a kind of bifurcated consciousness. Like Exley's notion that above his fantasies "there was always one I, aloof and ironical, watching the other me play out 'his' tawdry dream," Peoples describes a feeling that he is "watching the movie of my life as I live it."[103] This kind of bifurcation might be considered symptomatic of schizophrenia, but it is also more than a marker of mental illness.[104]

As it is for Exley, Peoples's sense of bifurcation is a natural manifestation of his own self-reflective authorship within the narrative landscape of *Silver Linings Playbook*. Since the novel is formatted as a diary, Peoples writes the life he is observing as the book we read. "Watching the movie" of Peoples's "life as he lives it" also roughly describes the reader of *The Silver Linings Playbook*.[105] The semi-autobiographical novel blends the diaristic and epistolary forms of its narration seamlessly with the mass-mediated stories of football action conducted on the field and in the stands. It is not Peoples's psychosis that blends these narratives in informing what it means to be him—it is the experience of being human. That the on-field football happenings that Quick-qua-Peoples describes are true to the historical record—as Exley's are of Gifford—only intensifies the effect: the readers of *The Silver Linings Playbook*, like Peoples himself, are to understand that "reality" is a matter of blurred perspective and that no genre can, on its own, be fully true to life. The search for stories with which to associate oneself—sporting, literary, or mass-mediated—can never fully satisfy.

These realizations bring us back to Christopher Lasch and the notion that fandom is inherently narcissistic. It is the search for a satisfying story that animates narcissism, Lasch asserts, the need to fill "a yawning void, an insatiable hunger, an emptiness waiting to be filled with the rich experiences reserved for the chosen few."[106] Following particular sports entities partially meets this need for Exley and Peoples, as does reading literature, and in a similarly fannish mode of experience. But the eponymous silver linings mapped out in Quick's playbook are consolations in a cloudy life narrative, not definitional means of redemption. Rather than indicative of their reduced "grip on reality,"[107] Exley's and Peoples's narrative appropriations—of sports and literature alike—should be read as coping mechanisms, anchoring them to the possibility that their damaged lives can find positive outcomes without denying the damage already done.[108] That Exley's and Peoples's accounts of fandom and mental illness blur the bounds of genre in their written expression is only fitting given this context. Were their narcissism totalizing and their mental illness incapacitating, there would be no confusion about reality and fiction or about written words and lived experience—they would disappear as Henry Waugh does in the *Universal Baseball Association*. Instead, by representing the blurring of narratives in multiple modes of self-identification, the two men demonstrate the uncertainty we all must feel in making sense of who we are and what we might become. In so doing, they further show that while sports fandom may look or even feel akin to madness, like our connection to literature such fandom allows us to build identities on the firm footing of established communal narratives without denying the interpretive flexibility borne of our own idiosyncrasies.

Thus, while the novel allows Don DeLillo and Robert Coover to position fans as witnesses to history and rearticulators of what is "real" within it, the autobiographical novels of Frederick Exley and Matthew Quick internalize this blurring of seemingly authentic experience such that literary narratives themselves become legible equivalents. Yet most "real" sports fans consider their attachments to be matters of nonfiction, though they probably shouldn't, and narratives describing sports fan identification on fictive terms are relatively few and far between. The autobiographical novel provides a generic bridge, however, to the predominant form in which sports fan experience *is* narrated in print, one with a perhaps undeserved reputation for reflecting reality: the memoir.

3

RACE IN THE BASKETBALL MEMOIR
Fan Identity and the Eros of "a Black Man's Game"

Of all literary genres, it is the autobiography that seems most richly and strikingly American, offering as it does three features that are endemic to the American national character: private confession as public narrative; the invention or reinvention of the self; and personal history as salvation dramaturgy.

GERALD EARLY, "A Reading of *The Greatest*"[1]

Thus far I have examined only fictions of sports fan experience. Not only that: I have analyzed texts whose rhetorical prerogatives *as fiction* enhance their authors' abilities to plumb the depths of the sports fan psyche and explore the limits of fan creativity and expression. But the predominant form for representing sports fan experience, at least prior to the advent of internet blogs, was the memoir.[2] Though literary critic Paul John Eakin has argued persuasively that fictional narratives are only superficially less "real" or "true" than autobiographical accounts, memoirs of sports fan experience are manifestly strengthened in their appeal by the author-narrator's apparent existence on the same plane of reality as the reader as well as the athletes they memorialize.[3] This makes sense: the narrative potency of athletic events is premised on the unscripted, "real" nature of the unfolding competition as well as the contemporaneous, communal reception of the crowd, and the fan memoir purports to be built on the same edifice of unpredictability and shared experience. But the potency of memoir's appeal to the real has made the genre increasingly popular on subjects far beyond sport. In *Memoir: A History*, Ben Yagoda asserts that the publication of memoirs in America "increased more than 400 percent between 2004 and 2008" and that the form has consequently "become the central form of the culture: not only the way stories are told, but the way arguments are put forth, products and properties marketed, ideas floated, acts justified, reputations constructed or salvaged."[4] Though, unlike Eakin, Yagoda positions autobiographical writing as primarily based on demonstrable facts, he also contradictorily admits that memoir is a genre "defined and determined by its subjectivity," thanks to its foundation in the famously unreliable faculty of memory.[5] The form's veneer of "documentary truth," while sating American readers' thirst for supposed objectivity, also necessarily subverts that desire.[6] Memoir is, in other words, an extended written representation of the subjective narrative ordering of purportedly objective experiences—a process fundamental to the way humans construct their identities.

And like identities themselves, which "despite our illusions of autonomy and self-determination . . . we do not invent . . . out of whole cloth," memoir is inherently relational.[7] Classically understood as a "reminiscence of others" via the lens of the authorial persona, memoir is frequently used to remember or recontextualize someone prominent in its author's life, like a family member or a mentor.[8] Though technically this narrative is not focused on but facilitated by the author's persona, the form inevitably involves the articulation of her own identity in the process. Complicating the narrative construction of the self as it attempts to encapsulate the other, memoir is thus perfectly suited to the reminiscences of the fan.

In this chapter, I will examine five memoirs that demonstrate both the many opportunities for self-reflection and the active identity construction that the form allows, and that do so at the intersection of sports fandom and race. Sports fan reception and interpretation, however much the stick-to-sports types may protest, is inescapably influenced by social and political frameworks that impact fans' day-to-day lives. No fan's perspective is color-blind, however much she may want it to be, just as surely as no fan's perspective is free from social influences pertaining to gender and sexuality. The authors of all five works are fans of basketball, and, with one exception, the United States' premier professional basketball league: the National Basketball Association. The NBA is recognized among the "Big Four" American professional sports leagues[9] as having the biggest racial disparity between its athletes and fans: the majority of the former are black and the majority of the latter are white.[10] This demographic paradigm holds true for three authors I examine—Scott Raab, David Shields, and Bill Simmons—each of whom is a white male fan acutely aware of racial difference in constructing his memoir. The other two authors whose basketball memoirs I explore, John Edgar Wideman and Spike Lee, are African American fans of the game whose own experiences as black men inescapably and indelibly affect the way they receive it. In all cases, memoir itself facilitates the depth with which these authors consider race and basketball. As it is for the concepts of race and sports themselves—the former a genetically insignificant difference in melanin that has real consequences because of the human cultural construct of racism, and the latter a series of otherwise insignificant bodily movements that are assigned extrinsic competitive value by humans—the perceived "realness" of memoir is naturalized such that the form bears a gravitas that its fabricated nature does not inherently justify. At its core, memoir is an "inherent and irresolvable conflict between the capabilities of memory and the demands of narrative."[11] In telling their story of basketball from the stands, then, Lee, Raab, Shields, Simmons, and Wideman both read and write—reveal *and* remake—their own identities via their observations of the actions of others. They watch themselves watching the mostly black men whose physical abilities power their attraction and attempt to forge a compelling narrative from it.

Examining Lee's *Best Seat in the House*, Raab's *The Whore of Akron*, Shields's *Black Planet*, Simmons's *The Book of Basketball*, and Wideman's *Hoop Roots: Playground Basketball, Love, and Race*, I demonstrate the ways in which memoir's formal instability reveals the unstable reality of race and sports both for these fans as individuals and as representatives of fandom more broadly construed. As Gerald Early remarks in *A Level Playing Field*,

> High-performance athletes are not merely social roles or a collection of habits and customs; they are mythologies. On a certain level, athletes are a special sort of socially constructed mirror that reflects a romanticized version of cultural honor and cultural virtue. Athletes can be heroic and celebrated for their heroism in their performance in the way no artist or worker in another line of work can, for the

athlete can symbolize the honor of a group or nation in dramatic, even melodramatic, terms. High-performance athletics is perhaps the most theatrical and emotional form of ritualized honor that we have left in the world.[12]

In other words, every fan's experience of a sporting event functions as a kind of memoiristic enterprise—the signification of another through the self—and one that easily subsumes athletes within familiar narratives of group, nation, and race. The ways in which these authors write their observations of African American athletes into their memoirs are natural extensions of their actions as sports fans and reflect their desire to be identified as such, but they also call attention to the narrative nature of sporting events. Recognized as characters in memoir, the broad range of things that "real" athletes can be made to signify is readily apparent. Consequently, interpretations of sporting outcomes, rather than being limited by scores and statistics, are freed from the bounds of empiricism and afforded a full range of narrative potency.

Considering race and basketball through the lens of fandom also addresses power lines that are often ignored in conventional sports discourse. The distinctions between fan and player are multiple, and discussions regarding the attraction of the former to the latter usually leave assumptions of hegemonic whiteness, maleness, and heterosexuality unexamined. In part, this is because such discourse is predicated on the purportedly objective measurement of athletic merit, which "is the very thing," as Gerald Early puts it, that "dehumanizes the athlete":

> Merit is so pure in high-performance athletics that only the best athletes survive, no matter who they are. Athletics is such a perfect thresher that everything social seems subordinate or irrelevant or a form of adversity that the athlete has to overcome. On the one hand, we pretend that only the making of the athlete matters, but of course this is not true in the end. What athletes are, both socially and individually, has a great deal to do with how we respond to them.[13]

As Early recognizes, the notion that fans form attachments to athletes solely on the basis of competitive merit is laughable, but the idea is perpetuated because it obscures messy social realities and ostensibly depoliticizes the terms of that attraction. Colorblind racism, omnipresent in contemporary American culture at large, has long been inherent in sports discourse, but it is a particularly pressing matter in the modern NBA.[14] In *After Artest*, his definitive account of the NBA's "systemic assault on blackness" in the wake of the infamous 2004 Palace Brawl, David Leonard details the means by which commissioner David Stern and the league office have "focused on deracializing the league, on facilitating colorblindness, which they have considered key to [their] success."[15] This emphasis on colorblindness, Leonard demonstrates, effectively aligns league policy with the paradigm of "New Racism," which ignores systemic inequalities impacting people of color, particularly African Americans, and blames "personal failures and deficiencies all while denying the importance of race."[16] Leonard argues that the NBA's attempt at deracialization is effectively disseminated by the sports media to the league's consumers, who replicate it in their own discourse.

In contrast with Leonard's blanket assertion, however, each of the memoirs I examine makes a point of recognizing the league's blackness as both broadly and personally significant. Though sports critics have long argued, a la David Barash, that the sports fan's "yearning to be someone else, or at least, a very small part of something else" reflects his "dark desire for deindividuation," such a negative view of fan communitas as brainwashing oversimplifies the matter.[17] As media fan studies scholar Matt Hills puts it, the factors that foster fan association "are neither rooted in an 'objective' interpretive community or an 'objective' set of texts . . . nor are they atomised collections of individuals whose 'subjective' passions and interests happen to overlap. Fan cultures are both found and created."[18] Fans follow favorite individual athletes, both with *and* without regard for the larger interpretive communities of which they are a part. Moreover, fans identify *particular aspects* of those athletes' on- and off-court abilities and personas that personally attract them. In "seeking a coherent identity narrative," as journalist Eric Simons terms it, sports fans—consciously or not—articulate themselves individually and by association with others.[19] Shaping such an identity narrative in the public forum of memoir, Lee, Raab, Shields, Simmons, and Wideman's assertions of racial awareness are meant to distinguish them even as they assert their place within the collective body of basketball fans.

I do not mean to suggest that these fans' considerations of race and racism are equivalent, however. Attuned to race though they may claim to be, white fans Raab, Shields, and Simmons nevertheless problematically characterize black athletes as they attempt to humanize themselves via memoir. Race not only influences the way in which these fans read basketball meta-narratives but also powers their desire to write, and write themselves into, those narratives. Their reasons for loving basketball may be diverse and egocentric, but their recognition of racial difference is motivated by an underlying erotic fascination with black athletes. Despite its purportedly level playing field, notes Michael Eric Dyson in *Reflecting Black*, "for much of its history, American sports activity has reflected white patriarchal privilege."[20] Part and parcel of that privilege, the commodification and sexualization of sweating black bodies drives popular consumption of the NBA. Raab, Shields, and Simmons do not transcend these consumptive frameworks any more than they ignore them. In constructing "selves" on which to build their memoirs, they bend the NBA's malleable on- and off-court narratives to render the athletes they admire racialized fan-objects—characters they can ventriloquize—that aid in their self-articulation.

Lee and Wideman, by contrast, acutely and personally recognize the problematic nature of the consumptive frameworks by which the meanings of black athletic performance are made to suit a white audience. Lee, the famed film director of *Do the Right Thing* and numerous other films detailing African American experience, writes his memoir from a dual fan perspective: that of a middle-class Brooklyn kid with a passion for New York sports teams, and that of Spike Lee, celebrity fan and courtside season ticket holder for the NBA's New York Knicks. This dual perspective allows him to represent both the process of making meaning from the exploits of superstar athletes as an anonymous fan *and* what it feels like to have one's celebrity image consumed by the public in a similar manner. While Lee's fan insights mostly presume that the NBA ultimately benefits black athletes and black fans alike, John Edgar Wideman's memoir is premised on the notion that playground hoop, not the professional game, is the truest, most impactful version of what basketball can be, especially for people of color. As literary critic Tracie Church Guzzio puts it, playground ball "functions as an expressive space that Wideman uses to play, to criticize, to celebrate, to analyze African American experience."[21] Wideman, like David Shields, is an academic and professional author of intellectual acclaim, and *Hoop Roots* recognizes in basketball performance and the act of writing alike assertions of personal agency. Spectatorship, by contrast, seems to Wideman to be passive and prone to perversions in accordance with the prefabricated consumerist narrative of leagues like the NBA. But he also recognizes—now that his body has aged to the point where he can no longer play the game—that there is value in watching and learning from the game as it is played by others: in writing the basketball self, in other words, in a memoiristic mode.

Ultimately, while Wideman and Lee each in their own way reject just the sort of white fan appropriation that Raab, Shields, and Simmons can't resist (whatever their racial self-consciousness), the African American authors also recognize the potency and value of the game for black agency and resistance: on the court, in the stands, and in writing. So long as one doesn't presume that the sport's traditional consumerist narratives need dominate—of hard-working white heroes, naturally gifted black champions that are marketable so long as they hew to a politics of respectability, and hometown fans who have earned some measure of ownership over athletes owing to their consumer dollars and local orientation—Lee and Wideman assert the game's narratives always also contain the possibility for a radical freedom of expression. In a racialized rhetorical landscape in which autobiographical narratives have served as "one of the most historically successful ways that African Americans have liberated themselves from racist portraits drawn by whites" throughout American history, basketball presents a fundamentally similar emancipatory potential for Lee and Wideman: it allows for the articulation of the self on terms not (or at least not always) dictated by white supremacy.[22]

This chapter is organized in four sections. The first examines Raab, Shields, and Simmons's fan origin stories and their attendant recognition of the indelible racialization of basketball as well as the consequences of that racialization for the white fan authors' identities. The second section explores Lee's and Wideman's narratives of basketball awakening, and the ways in which the African American authors write back against stereotypes of black experience and an American popular culture built on the assumption of whiteness as a cultural default. In the third and fourth sections, I examine the rhetorical means by which the fan authors depict and personate their particular hoop heroes. In particular, in the third section, I argue that the three white memoirists' desire to closely associate with the African American objects of their fascination leads them to practice a mode of writing I call "aspirational homosocial ventriloquism." In doing so, Raab, Shields, and Simmons imagine, appropriate, and in fact give voice to the personas of their beloved athletes such that they reveal and embrace a reductive erotics of racial difference. As for Lee and Wideman, in the fourth section I argue that each implicitly recognizes the white authors' ventriloquizing behavioral mode and its archetypal toxicity. Even so, the two African American authors cannot help but engage in a similar—albeit less essentialist—ventriloquizing narrative mode in their own work. Taken together, these memoirs demonstrate that basketball fandom need not essentialize people of color or replicate the master narratives that serve the professional game's white billionaire power brokers, but it *is* a matter of authorship incumbent on shared source material. However we encounter basketball and whatever we make of it, the game (and every sport) is a social construct: its interpretive potency lies in the intersection between the self and the other—the very place that memoirs are constructed.

Origin Stories: "His History, Too, Was Ours": Learning to Love Basketball and Recognizing Racial Difference

In *Black Planet*, David Shields credits his childhood speech impediment with stoking his passion for basketball. Growing up as a stutterer, Shields found in basketball a mode of expression that speaking could not provide. As he writes in another memoir, *Body Politic*, "my whole life was structured around the idea of doing one thing so well that people forgave me for, and I forgave myself for, my 'disfluency.'"[23] Though recognized as such in childhood, a connection between race and basketball is never more apparent to Shields than when he finds himself in "Seattle the Good," one of the whitest cities in the country and one whose "ruling ethos" is obsequious politeness to the point of "forlorn apology for the animal impulses."[24] But his new passion, the Supersonics, called the "NBA's most impudent team" by *Sports Illustrated*, are "not like this at all."[25] They realize for Shields sociologist Richard Majors's notion of the "cool pose," wherein black males' "unique, expressive and conspicuous styles of demeanor, speech, gesture, clothing, hairstyle, walk, stance, and handshake [are designed to] offset an imposed invisibility and provide a means to show the dominant culture (and the black male's peers) that the black male is strong and proud."[26] The racialized basis of the Sonics' appeal is clear to Shields, and is, in fact, the intended theme of *Black Planet*. After all, as Shields explains in his prefatory remarks, in the NBA "white fans and black players enact and quietly explode virtually every racial issue and tension in the culture at large. Race, the league's taboo topic, is the league's true subject."[27] As the word "explode" suggests, *Black Planet* is a book that denies the possibility of a tidy resolution. It is a work worthy of the Public Enemy homage that is its title, unflinchingly and often uncomfortably examining the racial discourses that simmer beneath the NBA's veneer of colorblindness.[28]

Still, *Black Planet* is not an antiracist study, nor a broad-ranging one. Shields's work is a memoir, after all, and the fandom he represents is as particular as any fan's. His favorite player, the fulcrum of his interest in race and basketball, in blurring verbal and physical expression, is Gary Payton. Payton was an All-Star, one of the best defenders in the league, and notorious for his trash-talking. The first two factors contribute to Shields's interest, of course, but the last drives it. Describing himself as "the bad link in the whole thang[,] the fucked-up crew" and "the Problem Child" in an *Esquire* profile titled "The Joy of Yap," Payton actualized this self-conception on the court, constantly attempting to aggravate his opponents with his words as he played fierce defense against them.[29] Of this attitude, Shields exults: "*Language* is what's most alive and dangerous—Gary Payton knows this; so, qua stutterer, qua writer, do I."[30] This linguistic potency translates such that "Gary's game is better than everyone else's because his language is better than everyone else's. My identification with him is total."[31] Carried away by the author's self-reflective obsession, race and language invigorate every page of *Black Planet*, with Payton the memoir's touchstone of both desire and interpretation.

Payton's words are for Shields "alive and dangerous," particularizing for the memoirist what he calls white fans' "imaginary identification with black skin," in which spectators "pretend we want [the athletes] to be controlled and 'classy,' but really what we want them to do is misbehave, so we can equate their talent with inadequacy, reaffirming their deep otherness, their mad difference."[32] This notion echoes sociologist David L. Andrews, who has further suggested that white fans hold "the virulent assumption that these *innately* physical males would be misbehaving were it not for the involvement of their natural physical attributes in the disciplinary mores and stringencies imposed by the dominant (sporting) culture."[33] Shields wants credit for recognizing that Payton himself is "not really bad, he's only pretend-bad—I know that—but he allows me to fantasize about being bad."[34] Thus, though he uses the first person plural "we" to position himself amid this paradigm of racialized fan feeling in which white fans thrill to black players' "bad" behavior, Shields also attempts to distinguish himself within it. He is cognizant that not only racial typing, but any framework of "othering," is inherently disempowering for the athletes, no matter how wealthy or culturally prominent they become, asking "what adoration does not, by its very zeal, transfigure the other person into an icon, an object, a thing?"[35]

Recognizing this objectifying impulse and attuned to Payton's verbal expression, Shields nevertheless is ensnared within the economy of bodily commodification and desire. He finds himself staring at the Sonics' cheer-leaders, "showing off their bodies, with dollar signs in their eyes; [like] the players, showing off their bodies, with dollar signs in their eyes—this level of explicitness about bodies and money is weirdly exciting to me.... To be a pure body like this, to be looked at this way, to be admired and reviled for being so young, so physical, so unabashedly a body."[36] The "erotic delectation" that Shields detects extends into his own bedroom.[37] He recounts making love to his wife, "imagin[ing] that I am as tall, thin, and muscular as Gary Payton," and, in another instance, describing their intercourse as "more like fucking: a rough physicality that I realize later is my attempt to imitate the athletes I spend so much time watching and thinking about."[38] Such behavior realizes Henry Louis Gates Jr.'s notion, cited by Shields, that the black body has been "highly, menacingly sexual-ized," yielding it an "ambiguous dual role in the Western Imagination."[39]

On a broader fan register, Shields recognizes this eroticism in listening to his fellow fans, remarking that "it would be impossible to overstate the degree to which sports-talk radio is overshadowed by the homosexual panic implicit in the fact that it consists almost entirely of a bunch of out-of-shape white men sitting around talking about black men's buff bodies."[40] It is as if, as one of Shields's graduate students puts it,[41]

> watching men we can identify touch each other in that kind of way, an emotional way, watching emotional black men touch each other like that, close up like that, with the cameras right there, and all this excitement about *scoring*, well, that's threatening and it gets labeled as bad. In American culture the most dangerous symbol, the most frightening symbol, for white people, is black men in love.[42]

Black men's love for each other is threatening, in an atmosphere of carefully negotiated homosociality buttressed by homophobia,[43] because a large part of a fan's excitement has to do with bodily association, with Shields's sense that the players "are our dream-selves and we want to become them."[44] So long as they remain "transcendental signifier[s,]" as Shields describes Michael Jordan, unattainable and superhuman, the fans' desirous feelings are easily considered heteronormative.[45] It is when these men are considered *merely as men* that racism and homophobia are recognizable to the fans and subject to their self-reflective panic. Acutely aware that prefigured cultural narratives influence but do not excuse his behavior, Shields wonders if "black people [are] conscious of how excruciatingly self-conscious white people have become in their every interaction with black people? Is this self-consciousness an improvement?"[46] Whether or not it is in fact an improvement, Shields's self-consciousness of racial difference is vital to his identity construction in *Black Planet*.

Though Scott Raab also uses basketball narratives to make sense of his identity, in *The Whore of Akron* he conceptualizes his fandom, and the role of race within it, quite differently from Shields. To begin with, Raab takes an oppositional affective tack. His is not primarily a book about fandom, but *anti*-fandom. The subject of Raab's dispassion is LeBron James, the eponymous "Whore of Akron" in the author's estimation. James, an Ohio native drafted first overall by Raab's beloved Cleveland Cavaliers in 2003, led the team to the NBA Finals in 2007, only to fall short in his next three seasons. Following the 2009–10 season, James, perhaps the most coveted free agent in NBA history, left the Cavs to sign with the Miami Heat, joining Dwyane Wade and Chris Bosh as a member of the so-called Big Three.[47] James announced this news via an ESPN special titled "The Decision," which aired nationally and featured James answering questions about his future in front of a community center full of kids in his hometown of Akron, just forty miles from Cleveland.

Raab, a native Clevelander, supports the Cavaliers because of his regional affiliation, of course. But he also cherishes a deeper connection to the NBA franchise's futile history. "Being a Jew and being a Cleveland fan are inextricably entwined to me," he asserts, remarking that a "standard of fearful gloom [is] endemic to both the average Cleveland fan and the average Jew."[48] Having witnessed in person Cleveland's last professional sports championship, the Browns' 1964 NFL title game victory over the Baltimore Colts,[49] Raab declares that the city's forty-seven-year championship drought,[50] the longest in the nation, has rendered "Cleveland fans [a] veritable nation of Job, whose love burns yet through all the heartache and scorn."[51] To transform Raab's identification with an ethos of suffering—civic, religious, sporting, and personal, via tales of his own broken childhood and subsequent drug abuse—came James:

> What made [him] matter so much . . . was that he understood all of this and more. His pride in being a son of this soil was our own pride; his history, too, was ours. He hungered, like all of us, for affirmation and respect. He could rewrite history and restore our pride and finally, after half a century, make *us* matter.[52]

Dubbed "The Chosen One" by *Sports Illustrated* as a high school junior, James seemed poised to live up to that nickname for Cleveland fans. As Raab's italicized use of "*us*" indicates, it was supposed that James could transcend the notion, made famous by Jerry Seinfeld, "that fanhood is a matter of rooting for laundry . . . , that loyalty . . . is not integral to the business of pro sports."[53] James would redeem Cleveland fans because he was one of them. But he left.

That departure cues Raab's animus, and motivates his anti-fan memoir. Media fan theorist Jonathan Gray explains this type of transformation and its manifestations:

Fans can become anti-fans . . . when an episode or part of a text is perceived as harming a text as a whole. . . . Behind dislike, after all, there are always expectations—of what a text should be like, of what is a waste of media time and space, of what morality or aesthetics texts should adopt, and of what we would like to see others watch or read.[54]

James's departure "harmed" the NBA text for Raab, fractured it, and with it a fundamental aspect of his identity: "those teams [that] remain a psychic rock, an anchor for my wobbling, fretful soul."[55] But as Gray posits, it is not merely the fact of "The Decision" that fuels Raab's anti-fandom, but the details of James's behavior, the way the media portrayed him, the aesthetics of disloyalty he exhibits, and the way Raab's fellow fans reacted to the star's actions. All are tinged by race and racial difference. As Raab existentially wails,

What then can I read upon the stone heart of LeBron? What can I learn from the odyssey of a black kid, sprung from the loins of a teen mama, fatherless save for the seed of himself, who was a rock star at the age of fifteen, with girls lining up to lay naked with him just so that years later they could boast to their boyfriends that they boffed King James?[56]

As these comments about James's "teen mama," his fatherlessness, and supposed profligate teenage sexuality suggest, Raab's desire is based in schadenfreude and jealousy—in joy at James's failures and shortcomings—and those shortcomings are imbued, whether Raab consciously intends them to be or not, by racial stereotypes.

Though Raab inhabits the fan perspective, like Shields and Simmons he is relatively well-known as a writer (in this case for *Esquire* magazine) and capitalizes on the access a press credential affords him even as he skeptically regards the members of the sporting press. Bearing a tattoo of the Cleveland Indians' famously racist mascot, "Chief Wahoo," on his forearm, Raab remarks just a few pages into his memoir that

in a league full of athletes whose bodies can honestly be described as beautiful—one of the aesthetic delights of an NBA locker room is watching from a distance as the pack of mainly fat, mainly white members of the press gathers and ungathers itself as each chiseled specimen emerges from the shower—LeBron James is a masterpiece. Hewn of sinew, apparently impervious as iron—muscled yet sleek, thick-shouldered yet loose of limb, James looks different from every other player in the league, especially in a damp towel.[57]

Here is the very fulcrum of racialized homosexual pleasure and panic for white male fans: the locker room. Here are the archetypes of black male masculinity, muscled athletes nearly (and often actually) full frontal in their nudity, begrudgingly sharing carefully crafted, cliché-filled opinions on games past and yet to come. Himself admittedly fat and white, Raab nevertheless separates himself from fellow journalists as they suggestively "gather . . . and ungather" themselves before "chiseled specimen[s.]"[58] The specter of black male sexuality looms large in the space, and Raab amplifies it, though he recognizes finally that "there's nothing especially forbidding about a guy in a towel, even LeBron. He's a kid who just took a shower, and the fact that he can do things that I can only dream of— the physical summit of my day is a decent bowel movement—doesn't change that."[59] The diminution of James's physical stature by reference to his immature age and the supposed humor of Raab's scatological self-reference may be intended to detract from the eroticism of the synec-dochal tableau the author presents, but the deflection is feeble. Raab understands that racialized desire powerfully informs basketball fandom at large, even if he doesn't want to admit it.

Characterizing his own fandom, Raab admits that he doesn't "know or care how or where to draw a line between fan and fanatic."[60] But the statement belies his awareness of, and desire to transgress, the line between conventional modes of spectatorial investment and rabid disregard for others that he exhibits in recounting another visit to the Cavaliers locker room just weeks before "The Decision":

[LeBron James] turns to finish getting dressed. I walk away, straight into the towel receptacle, a large wooden open-topped bin on wheels, waist high for normal folk. I stagger on the thick carpet, but manage to right myself without falling. And as I gather myself, I catch a sideways glimpse—here I'm going to flout what is unarguably sports journalism's most precious and closely guarded rule—just a snapshot, really, of the Chosen Junk. Eh—nothing special. Proportional, which is to say larger than my own cock last time I managed to find it.[61]

Again using self-deprecation ostensibly to minimize the impact of his words, Raab recognizes that athlete nudity, a locker room constant, is respectfully unreported on by those journalists granted access. Commenting on the size of a black man's penis, Raab plays into racist tropes concerning black male sexuality—in which "the black athlete (as the quintessence of blackness) assumes the preeminent position as *the* 'penis-symbol' and becomes a fantastic trope through which anxieties concerning the fragility of western (male) sexuality are played out."[62] But he also inverts the trope insofar as he minimizes the "Chosen Junk," calling it "nothing special."[63] This comment is surely intended to insult James personally, but it also counters the old racist notion that white men should fear "hypersexual" black men in accordance with the supposed enormity of their penises. Raab thus both embraces the implicit racist eroticism of his—and others'—fandom, and resists doing so in a way that would acquiesce to conventional modes of racist bigotry. James may seem superhuman on the basketball court but he is fallibly human off it, and neither sense of him, Raab's characterization suggests, can be uncomplicatedly ascribed to conventional stereotypes concerning his race.

Though he doesn't shy away from the racially charged implications of his rhetoric, Raab does consider that his views on James might not be shared by African Americans. After "The Decision," in preparation for James's return to Cleveland as a member of the Miami Heat, Raab heads to the historically African American section of town because, as he puts it,

I want to have a conversation with a black guy about my animus toward LeBron. Jesse Jackson and Maverick Carter and a few black voices in the media have weighed in on the role race played in the reaction to the Decision. Some claim it's a factor, some deny it—I'm not looking for antipathy or absolution: I just want to know what I don't know. I want to think about what I haven't thought of yet.[64]

To sate his curiosity, Raab converses with Jimi Izrael, a fellow nationally recognized writer and native Clevelander, in a black barbershop. As a barber shaves "QUITNESS" into Raab's hair, he describes his anti-fandom and asks for Izrael's take as a black man. Tellingly, Izrael represents "white Cleveland" as feeling "like they fed LeBron, clothed him, and never called him 'nigger' in so many words—so the least he could do is wear his body down for another few years carrying a team of glamour boys and flat-foots."[65] When Raab insists that James flaunted his local roots—"wore [them] like he meant it. Like he *wanted* to be here"—Izrael importantly identifies an epistemological distinction:

> Listen: Freedom means something different, maybe something more, to black people. White folks look at LeBron and see a traitor who turned his back on his city. Black folks, even hardcore fans, see a black man making choices that suit him and his family—without hesitation or regret. Just like white folks do.[66]

James's "Decision," Izrael recognizes, was merely that: a decision. Outside the context of sports, people change jobs and cities all the time. That such an action is excoriated in an NBA context, Izrael reminds Raab, is not completely unrelated to the demographics of its players. That a black man is expected to stay where the mostly white fans desire him to, no matter how much he will be compensated, recalls a history in which black men didn't have the right to move where they liked.[67] Raab does not comment on the substance of Izrael's argument, ending the section shortly thereafter. But the mere fact that Raab records it as such implies some degree of self-criticism at the racial undertones of his own feelings.

Making sense of his own life narrative through sports is for Bill Simmons, like Scott Raab, induced in part by his parents' divorce, with fandom functioning as a psychic salve in childhood. Young Bill would end up going to a lot of Celtics games on his father's lap, and the team became a focal point of bonding between them. Though the Celtics had already been wildly successful in the 1950s and 1960s, winning an unprecedented eleven championships thanks to the excellence of Bill Russell, Simmons retrospectively considers the 1973-74 season, his father's first as a season ticket holder, as "the perfect time" to buy into "Celtic Pride."[68] Boston was especially excited about these Celtics because of stars John Havlicek and "reigning MVP Dave Cowens, a fiery redhead who clicked with fans the way Russell never did."[69] In attempting to understand why, Simmons recognizes racial difference as an important factor:

> The Celtics were suddenly flourishing in a notoriously racist city. Was it happening because their best two players were white? Was it happening because of the burgeoning number of baby boomers like my father, the ones who fell in love with hoops because of the unselfishness of Auerbach's Celtics and Holzman's Knicks, who grew up watching Chamberlain and Russell battle like two gigantic dinosaurs on Sundays, who were enthralled by UCLA's win streak and Maravich's wizardry at LSU? Or was Cowens simply more likable and fan-friendly than the enigmatic Russell? The answer? All of the above.[70]

Typical of Simmons, the paragraph's explicit reference to others' racism coexists with his own racially troubling language that attributes two teams' unselfishness to their white coaches and metaphorizes two of the NBA's greatest post players, both black, as "dinosaurs." But on the surface, at least, Simmons asserts a racial sensitivity that was present even in his childhood fandom. He recalls his "racial identity crisis in the first grade," when he insisted on calling himself "Jabaal Abdul-Simmons" because "my favorite sport was black" and "it pissed me off that I was white."[71] The anecdote, exhibiting childish naiveté that is meant to be humorous, nonetheless reflects Simmons's desire to discuss racial tensions between the NBA's mostly black players and mostly white fan base in an atmosphere in which "everyone's sphincters tighten whenever a white guy discusses race and sports."[72] As his anal reference makes clear, however, Simmons's desire to discuss race and sports is frequently lodged in the crude homophobic rhetoric of white male privilege such that his purported awareness can look more like ignorance or bigotry. In many ways, he fits neatly within the paradigm of New Racism cited by Leonard, relying, as Ben Carrington puts it, "upon a static definition of racism that is so limited and narrow that only overt forms of white supremacy that lead to intentional acts of genocide, violence, or public persecution get to 'count' as racism."[73]

Simmons, ever the commenter on his own authorial process, records toward the end of *The Book of Basketball* that "one of my first choices for a title was *The Book of Basketball: A White Man's Thoughts on a Black Man's Game.* My publishing company talked me out of it. Can't play the race card in the title."[74] Obviously regretting that decision, Simmons's discussions of race in the work are prominent and frequently sexually charged. To deflect from the controversial nature of such discussions, Simmons asserts that biracial pop science impresario Malcolm Gladwell "loves talking about race. And I do too. . . . But when you're white, the degree of difficulty skyrockets. You can't screw up."[75] Amounting to little more than a "some of my best friends are black" defense, Simmons feels no compunction about playing to stereotypes. He delights in remarking that African American Celtics guard Dennis Johnson was "hung like a tripod" and creates what he calls the "All-NBA Dick Team," upon which, "you're never going to believe this, but there were no white guys."[76] Simmons, in a manner even more straightforward than Raab, recalls Franz Fanon's formulation, as paraphrased by Carrington, by which "the black man is effectively reduced to the phallus" in the white imagination.[77] He further "others" black men by rendering their skin tones alien—remarking that Sudanese NBA star Manute Bol had "skin so dark that it made him seem purple"—and by comparing them to beautiful and expensive objects— asserting that proximity to NBA All-Star David Robinson, known for his impressive physique, was "like standing a few feet away from a prize thoroughbred or a brand-new Ferrari Testarossa. . . . He was strikingly handsome and even the most devout heterosexual males would have admitted it. Really, he was just a specimen."[78] That Simmons does all of this with an air of defensiveness is revealing. In articulating his sports fan persona, Simmons is not content to ponder (and linger in productive uncertainty about) his own racist and racialized behaviors like Shields and Raab. Instead, even as he ascribes racism to others, he reacts to recognition of his own racially problematic rhetoric with a tone of whiny sarcasm and "post-racial" justifications of white male privilege that cater to his desire to be seen as an ideal homosocial compatriot to others—to be, as the saying goes, "just one of the (white) guys."

In *Darwin's Athletes: How Sport Has Damaged Black America and Preserved the Myth of Race*, a book that lambasts the culture of sports, and basketball in particular, as detrimental to African American life—John Hoberman calls the NBA a "theater of pseudo-reconciliation [which] serves to mitigate the pathos of American segregation . . . by creating one-sided relationships between white fans and the black athletes they admire from afar."[79] Simmons exemplifies Hoberman's characterization quite effectively. Raab and Shields are less exemplary, if only because they are under fewer illusions about the American reality of de facto segregation and the basketball arena's incapacity to reconcile it. Even so, they are unable or unwilling to extricate themselves from the racial frame via anti-racist action—they are rubber-neckers, not Good Samaritans. But Hoberman, too, misunderstands the value of the NBA's drama since he consider the white audience's dominant media frame as the only one that ultimately matters. As Spike Lee and John Edgar Wideman demonstrate, such deference ignores the expressive value of the game for black players and fans.

"A Stake in the Game": The Power of Hoops Beyond White Audiences

Growing up in Brooklyn, New York as a member of the "first black family in the neighborhood," Spike Lee describes a childhood so oriented to spectator sports that "it would be *impossible* to overstate the impact of sports on my life."[80] And while Lee details his attachment to baseball and football icons like Jackie Robinson and Joe Namath, it is only "the Game [of basketball that] danced in everybody's blood in New York."[81] What's more, according to Lee, the city has reciprocated, as basketball became a cultural force thanks to

> brothers from the city, like [Lew] Alcindor and Tiny [Archibald,] who imprinted The Game with a distinct style and a life of its own, who made it Broadway as an entertainment spectacle, whose athletic artistry and creativity lifted pro hoop from the distant outposts of its origins and ethnic urban subculture base into the world-wide consciousness today. . . . [In] the city, we know that when the Game is played both creatively and well, it can become an art form.[82]

New York's cultural symbiosis with basketball is for Lee both marked by the blackness of "brothers from the city" *and* aesthetically valuable as "an art form" beyond any measure of its "Broadway" popularity.[83] Given his New York–centric notion of basketball's significance, it is no surprise that his more particularized passion for the game centers around the New York Knicks, their NBA championship teams of 1970 and 1972, and the star of those teams: Walt "Clyde" Frazier.

Frazier was for Lee a "hero and idol" on account of "the method of [his] game. . . . I wanted to emulate his cool professionalism and styles. I admired everything about him. He made me see that producing while making it look easy was the epitome of skill."[84] Recalling Richard Majors's notion of the cool pose and the terms of David Shields's attraction to Gary Payton, Lee's connection to Frazier is premised on personal expressive flair, but only insofar as that self-styling accentuates his on-court effectiveness—style without substance does not interest him.[85] Lee's attraction to Frazier's style is inextricable from his blackness, to be sure, but that attraction is not of the fetishizing type that counterpoises the blackness of the team against a white public (as it is for Shields in *Black Planet*). Not only is New York a hub of American diversity—as Lee's own childhood experience attests—but the Knicks of this era, particularly the 1970 championship team, have been popularly celebrated via tropes of the "melting pot," an interpretation that Lee does not resist. "All the fans had a stake in the game," he writes,

> a personal stake, and many ethnicities were represented, and classes too. [Bill] Bradley was followed by the elites, some of whose ilk had given him a hard time at Princeton. He'd brought in a whole new crowd—and an opinionated one, at that. Immigrant classes spawned [Dave] DeBusschere, [Mike] Riordan, [Red] Holzman. Then you had the brothers, ranging from deep southern rural to Midwestern to Chicago slick to Gary, Indiana, hard. . . . [T]here was no formal affirmative action then or, if there was, it was not the kind that favored black people. You earned your way into the Knicks rotation. No matter who they were or where they were from, it was like the politics of the city and the nation were revealed in their backgrounds, their games, and by those who followed them. This is a reason they are remembered so fondly.[86]

Lee's own fond memories involve attending games in Madison Square Garden's then-cheap upper deck "blue seats," including Game 7 of the 1970 NBA Finals, a game famous for the performance of the team's injured star, Willis Reed, and one that Lee calls "an original composition of basketball. It *was* like music!"[87] Yet, as the melodic simile suggests, Lee had music on the brain: he almost missed the game because his father, a jazz musician, had an important performance that night which all the members of the Lee family were expected to attend. While young Spike loved and respected his father, he was "serious and . . . insulated in my devotion to the Knickerbockers. . . . I opted to go to the game. I felt I had no choice."[88] The repercussions of missing the concert did not turn out to be severe, but Lee recognizes the choice as a definitive one: it cemented his fan identity in the eyes of the family. Subsequently describing the game to his brother, Lee recalls "a half-smile playing across his face. As I think back on it, he didn't care so much as he knew how much I did."[89] The degree to which young Spike's identity is premised on his sports fandom is already so pronounced that his family members have come to embrace its expression.

Just as it is for Spike Lee, John Edgar Wideman's attachment to basketball is deeply familial, and *Hoop Roots* describes not only his emotions in watching his children play basketball, but also his own childhood memories of his grandmother's house in Pittsburgh's Homewood neighborhood, and the pick-up basketball court just down the road where he honed his game.[90] Wideman, who went on to star as an All-Ivy forward at the University of Pennsylvania, reveres the game for its embodied performance, and his memoir is elegiac insofar as his aging body no longer allows him to play the game. "Whatever you make of this book, I need it," Wideman writes, "need it the way I've needed the playground game."[91] Pick-up ball is the paragon of hoops performance for Wideman, and he particularly values "how relentlessly, scrupulously [the playground game] encloses and defines moments."[92] This contrasts starkly with "writing autobiography, looking back, trying to recall and represent yourself at some point in the past, [in which] you are playing many games simultaneously. There are many selves, many sets of rules jostling for position. None offers the clarifying, cleansing unity of playing hoop."[93] Ultimately Wideman relates the frustrating multiplicity of writerly consciousness to that of the fan, urging his reader to "pity the poor writer. He or she's a benchwarmer, a kind of made-up spectator who may or not be spectating the game in front of his face, or other games, other places, other times, or a mixture of the actual, of memory, wishes, dreams of game, a fictitious fan."[94] In Wideman's work, naturally, there is no particular affection for the NBA game that fosters the love of hoops extolled by the other memoirists examined in this chapter. Even so, in part because of his physical infirmity and in part because of sports spectatorship's obvious resonances with his authorial identity, Wideman is forced to grapple with fandom as a mode of experience and identity formation. Ultimately, he arrives at some degree of appreciation for the fan's art of narrative.

Both of these aspects of Wideman's memoir—playing basketball and coming to grips with the benefits (and detriments) of merely watching it—are fundamentally imbued with an understanding of basketball as connected to African American experience. Like many young black boys, Wideman saw basketball as a way out of poverty. Unlike most of them, he successfully leveraged his basketball ability, in conjunction with his immense intellect, to escape that poverty. But the specific details of Wideman's success are far less important to him in *Hoop Roots* than explaining the broader necessity of the dream itself:

> Growing up, I needed basketball because my family was poor and colored, hemmed in by material circumstances none of us knew how to control, and if I wanted more, a larger, different portion than other poor colored folks in Homewood, I had to single myself out. . . . The idea of race and the practice of racism in our country work against African-American kids forming and sustaining belief in themselves. . . . You need the plausibility, the possibility of imagining a different life for yourself, other than the meager portion doled out by the imperatives of race and racism, the negative prospects impressed continuously upon a black kid's consciousness, stifling, stunting the self-awareness of far too many.[95]

One of the kids unable to overcome the "meager portion" that Homewood doled out was Wideman's sibling, Robby, who, unlike his Rhodes Scholar–winning older brother, never left the neighborhood. After being present at a robbery gone wrong in which the white victim was fatally shot by another man, Robby was convicted of murder in 1976 and is still, as of this writing, serving a life sentence without the possibility of parole.[96]

As if to compound Wideman's pain and sorrow, just ten years later, his sixteen-year-old son, Jacob, was convicted of murdering a fellow summer camper while on a trip to Arizona.[97] Needless to say, John Edgar Wideman personally understands the grimmest possibilities awaiting young black men who lose their way, and thus feels compelled to describe the power of basketball to resist the "negative prospects impressed continuously upon a black kid's consciousness" on stark terms.[98]

Wideman also acutely understands, and unwittingly responds to, David Shields's observation about white people's self-consciousness in their interactions with African Americans.[99] Remembering a childhood experience watching a group of white men play pick-up hoops, Wideman recalls being called courtside by one of the players:

> Here, kid. C'mon. Try one. I wish I could describe the man who called me over because remembering him might demonstrate how conscious we made ourselves of white people as individuals, aware of their particular features, character, the threat or advantage a specific person posed. In a way, the last great campaign for civil rights, commencing in the southern states in the early fifties, during the same period this scene on Finance Street occurs, was a demand, a concerted political movement to secure, among other things, the same attentive, circumspect recognition of us as individuals that I was compelled, at my peril, to afford this white guy who handed or passed me a ball.[100]

In effect, Wideman tells Shields that yes, black people are aware of his self-consciousness. And yes, it is an improvement—after all, being perpetually self-conscious of white people's hegemonic power was *and is* necessary for the survival of black people. "One of the worst trials for Americans of visible African descent (and maybe for invisible crossovers too)," Wideman writes, "is the perpetual fear of not measuring up to standards established by so-called white people who imagine themselves the standard issue and also presume themselves to be the issuers of standards."[101] Translated onto the court, while Wideman agrees with Shields (and Hoberman, to some degree) that the NBA and other highly mediated basketball contexts serve as a platform for corporations to "cash . . . in on the paradox of white fascination with blackness" in a problematic manner, he would seem to welcome Shields's protestations of excruciating racial self-consciousness insofar as it leads to the recognition of black athletes as individuals.[102] And yet, in considering the consumption of Michael Jordan—Shields's "transcendental signifier"[103]—Wideman positions "this modern, media-driven, vicarious, virtual possession of a black body" as a mode of self-aggrandizing power "better than buying a slave, with all the attendant burdens of ownership" and one, alternatively, that allows white men who crave transgression, like Shields, to "represent 'bad' without worrying about paying dues bad black boys pay—poverty, jail, apartheid, early graves."[104]

Compelled by anti-racism to a kind of anti-fandom of the NBA, Wideman's memoir nevertheless shares much in common with the other works examined in this chapter, especially Raab's and Shields's texts, which are also self-consciously concerned with the means by which white people consume the performances of black bodies. But *Hoop Roots* is also formally distinct from the other four texts, exploring narrative modes and commenting on authorial process in ways that demonstrate not only Wideman's own awe-inspiring artistic talents, but also the broader creative possibilities of sports spectatorship as a mode of consciousness. *Hoop Roots* is less a memoir of basketball through the authorial self—as *Best Seat in the House*, *Black Planet*, *The Whore of Akron*, and, to a lesser extent, *The Book of Basketball* are—than it is a memoir of authorship through the basketball self. "The game's a way of perceiving the world," Wideman writes, and it is the game's possibilities for perceptivity itself, rather than merely the world it reveals, that drives his interest in it.[105]

"I Ain't Your Fuckin' Plaything": Aspirational Homosocial Ventriloquism

Shields, Raab, and Simmons identify the particular subjects of their obsession and recognize, with varying degrees of self-criticism, that race permeates the way their fandoms are constructed, but for all three, another mode of fan interaction remains unsatisfied. What is missing, what they crave, is social contact. Unlike the average fan, all three memoirists have writerly credentials enough that they have been able to physically enter the locker room and speak in person to the athletes with whom they associate as fans (or anti-fans). They have become, to differing degrees, professional

"Big Name Fans," with all the fraught hierarchies such a title implies.[106] And yet, despite their access and renown, Raab's, Shields's, and Simmons's interactions with the athletes that fascinate them—as represented in the extreme by Raab's voyeuristic, taboo-breaking description of his glance at LeBron James's "Chosen Junk"—are often nasty, brutish, and short. The athletes, well aware of their position in American celebrity culture, generally speak only to the required limits of game-related questions they are required to answer, and then only in the vagaries of the notoriously hollow idioms that constitute "jock speak." For the purposes of journalists writing game recaps, this level of interaction is sufficient. But for many committed fans, and male fans like Raab, Shields, and Simmons in particular, it is far from adequate. The athletes' true voices, heard only when the locker room doors are closed to outsiders, is what these fans crave. Not only would unfettered conversation yield deeper insight into the athletes as such, it would bring them into a state of homosocial intimacy desired by many fans.

Simmons exhibits this desire in recounting the closeness of the players on the Boston Celtics' 1969 championship team:

> Right after [Bill] Russell's Celtics won . . . a crew of friends, employees, owners and media members poured into Boston's locker room expecting the typical routine of champagne spraying and jubilant hugs. Russell asked every outsider to leave the locker room for a few minutes. The players wanted to savor the moment with each other, he explained, adding to nobody in particular, "We are each other's friends." The room cleared and they spent that precious piece of time celebrating with one another. Lord knows what was said or what that moment meant for them. As [NBA great] Isiah [Thomas] told Dan Patrick, we wouldn't understand. And we wouldn't.[107]

Fulfilling Simmons's paradigmatic notion that the key to NBA success is "The Secret," a measure of camaraderie among good players that makes them a great team, Russell's example is notable because it emphasizes exclusivity. That "we," the fans, wouldn't understand the intimate locker room discourse among the closely bonded players on a championship team is not merely the product of said fans' inability to play basketball at the highest level. It is always also, because it is unattainable, the source of the fans' deepest homosocial desire: to not merely know the athletes, but be their friends (and, in some cases, lovers). Lacking this access to the players, many fans—Shields, Raab, and Simmons included—imagine what it would be like to have that intimacy. In doing so, they operate much like media fans who write "Real Person Slash" (or "RPS"), a genre of ethical concern for many in the fanfiction writing community, which writes real people into imagined (usually non-heteronormative) sexual relationships. Though Raab, Shields, and Simmons do not prerogatively narratively embody the athletes (as do the practitioners of RPS), they do take the liberty of voicing the athletes, putting them in imagined conversation with their own narratorial personas, in a practice I call "aspirational homosocial ventriloquism." This ventriloquism is sometimes conducted with careful attention to the racial valences of the authors' larger works, but it must always privilege the fan's perspective. By disregarding the fact that their biases necessarily skew these imagined conversations in their favor, Shields, Raab, and Simmons fail or decline to recognize that their fantasy dialogues can be just as objectifying as the racism latent in their sexualized consumption of the black male physique. They demonstrate that they think of black culture, as Todd Boyd puts it, "as if it's always being performed for a white audience . . . forcing the culture to accommodate whatever perceptions might already be in place as opposed to allowing it to exist on its own terms and give off its own representation."[108]

For Shields, Gary Payton's language is available on the court via snippets of the player's oral expression and body language. Interpreting the latter, Shields often imagines Payton's accompanying words. When "a fan offers him a high-five . . . Payton quite pointedly refuses; . . . *I ain't your fuckin' plaything*, I feel Gary telling the fan, *I ain't your buddy, you don't know me, don't go thinkin' you can slap my palm*."[109] Voicing the All-Star in italics, Shields imagines a hostility toward the (implicitly white) fan that plays to the stereotype of angry and dangerous black masculinity but that also recognizes the player's potential resentment toward fans who would believe they share in (or even control, as indicated by "plaything") his accomplishments. Gary Payton's verbal expression is available to Shields at greatest depth through *The Gary Payton Show*, a Seattle radio program on the local sports station, in which fans can call in and speak to the man himself. Shields never calls, but he records the dialogue between other fans and Payton, with an eye to the subtextual. Though Payton is mostly guarded in his responses, Shields freely expands on the point guard's words. At times, this ventriloquism speaks to the homosocial intimacy and exclusivity coveted by Simmons. When a caller asks about an angry on-court exchange between Payton and an opposing player, "Payton says, 'He said something he wasn't supposed to.' *It's our camaraderie.*"[110] Though Payton's vague response ostensibly censors a potentially FCC-unfriendly comment, Shields reads his imprecision as a measure of homosociality: the circle of "camaraderie" is closed to fans, even when the discourse involves opposing players.[111]

But the players' interactions are also notably racialized by Shields. When a radio host suggests, in a follow-up to the fan's question, that one of Payton's white teammates, Detlef Schrempf, was responsible for restraining him and preventing his conflict with the opposing player from escalating, Shields records that

> Payton strenuously resists this scenario: "I know when to back off and not get the other tech so I won't get kicked out of the game. That's all Det was trying to tell me." *I'm not just a body; I possess consciousness; I don't need blond, blue-eyed Schrempf to imprint upon me the consequences of my actions.*[112]

Here is Shields's racial self-reflection transposed onto Payton's voice and onto the court. The player's response is strategic: getting two technical fouls would result in Payton's expulsion from the game, something that would benefit neither him nor his team. But Shields detects in Payton's voice anger born of systemic injustice. That the German American "Det" would need to impart to Payton this obvious bit of strategy is to imply, for Shields, that the linguistically gifted point guard is little more than a megaphone-laden body. In asserting a racialized subtext to the point guard's words, however, Shields also sees fit to presume that his concerns are Payton's—that he can determine the areas in which racism impacts the All-Star's life. He assumes as much, if not more, about Payton than the radio host did in making his initial suggestion.

Does Shields's glib use of aspirational homosocial ventriloquism reflect his own white privilege? Or does the authorial device effectively call attention to his fellow spectator's colorblind assumption that white players can better control their emotions? He intends the latter, but the answer is surely both. In a guest column for the *Seattle Times*, Payton writes of fans' tendency to equate on-court behavior with personality: "People see us on the court and automatically judge us by our demeanor on the court.....[They] don't understand that we might be tough on the court, but off the court we're a lot nicer than what they think."[113] Payton's assertion that on-court performance does not define him as a person leads Shields to ventriloquize again: *"It's all just theater: we're not the lunatic niggers you want to think we are."*[114] Voicing Payton, Shields feels he can use the n-word with impunity; the intimacy he desires would assume blackness such that he can reflect the shame of American racism back on other white fans. This response intensifies Payton's words and makes their racial connotations explicit, but it also answers Shields's earlier claim about fan desires for athlete misbehavior. It not only relies on Shields to racialize Payton's assertions of performative agency but also allows him to overzealously employ what, coming from him, is a racist epithet. He realizes for himself something akin to film director Quentin Tarantino's motivation in making *Pulp Fiction*, which, Shields asserts, "just comes down to Tarantino's getting to play the only white character in the history of the movies who is cool enough to say 'nigger' to a black man and use it—mean it—as black vernacular."[115] Shields, speaking for Payton, likewise attempts to use the n-word as black vernacular, and that he doesn't, or won't, recognize that this is just as problematic for him as it is for Tarantino, speaks to the off-key nature of his ventriloquism.

Because *The Whore of Akron* is a tale of anti-fandom, one would think that its author would have little desire to interact with the object of his scorn. Yet Raab, a recovering addict, uses the veil of Valium to put himself in imagined discourse with LeBron James. Raab's aspirational homosocial ventriloquism is also built on online interaction, however, as mediated by the social media platform Twitter. Doped up at 2 a.m., hoping the drug will help him sleep, Raab logs on to his computer and notices a tweet from "@King James," James's twitter handle, that reads: "*I love my chef B so much (pause)! He made the meanest/best peach cobbler I've ever had in life. Wow!!*," with a picture of the dessert attached.[116] Mocking James for "scarfing cobbler and tweeting about it like he's ten years old" in the early morning of a game day,[117] Raab nevertheless lusts after the cobbler's "huge rough-cut hunks, gold-crusted and gleaming" and asks "Can I hate the sinner and love the sin? I do," before tweeting in reply "Note to self: Cobbler hard to hate."[118] Chortling amid the "slow rush of narcotic joy" and hurtling into the realm of fiction, Raab's internet interaction is hallucinogenically transferred to the nearby couch, where "LeBron is sitting . . . and he has a dish of cobbler for me."[119]

As Raab digs in to the hallucinated cobbler, the specter of James scolds him for "killing [himself] with a fork and spoon."[120] Recognizing Raab's self-consciousness at his own obesity, this remark begins a five-page dialogue, presented with James's imagined words in italics, that allows Raab to ventriloquize his anti-hero's responses to the author's fannish indiscretions. Chief among these, of course, is a confrontation about Raab's reportage on James's locker-room nudity:

> *"Why did you write about my cock? What's wrong with you?"*
> I don't know, kid. I thought you were staying in Cleveland when I saw your dick. You fucked up—you quit. You lied. You left.
> *"What does any of that have to do with my cock?"*
> Nothing. Not a thing. It just seemed funny, almost falling over the towel thing, looking over, boom.[121]

Raab's lame justifications in response to the imagined James's surprisingly legitimate inquiries—surprising because they ultimately emanate, as they must, from Raab himself—amount to little more than petty revenge and sophomoric humor. However intoxicated he may present himself to be, Raab performatively recognizes that he transgressed journalistic ethics and the locker room's code of privacy. But he does not do so explicitly or in his own voice. Instead, the ventriloquized voice of James as interlocutor allows Raab to overtly maintain his bloviating hatred while implicitly recognizing the problematic basis of his actions.

Beyond the sexual, this spectral dialogue also probes the broader base of Raab's anti-fandom:

> *"How dare you judge me?"*
> You spit on millions of people.

"I don't answer to them. I do what's right for LeBron."

Is that what you tell a West Akron kid who cried when you left the Cavs?

"I spit on nobody. I played my ass off for seven years. Those kids never once heard of me with drugs or guns or any of that stuff. Not once. Those were the best years that team ever had, and you judge me for leaving like it's the worst crime ever committed."

I can't think of a parallel betrayal in the history of American sports.[122]

The imagined James quite reasonably points out that his supposed "betrayal" should rank far lower on the scale of possible athlete indiscretions than those involving drug use (whether performance enhancing or merely narcotic) and violent crime.[123] And Raab's response, while condemning in tone, is hollow in substance. What's more, the potential crimes mentioned by the spectral James relate directly to Raab's confessed history of drug use and associated gun ownership. By the time the imagined discourse concludes, it is abundantly clear that the ventriloquized James is meant to evince a mea culpa from Raab, not himself:

"What's the worst thing you ever did?"

Summer of 1994. I got the woman I love pregnant. She was afraid to have the kid. I wanted the kid—I was forty-two years old, I'd destroyed everything in my life, including my marriage. I *still* wanted that kid. All she wanted in return was the promise that I'd sober up. Just the promise.

"What happened?"

She had the abortion. I drove her to the hospital myself. Drove her there, drove her home, went back to my place, got fucked up, got out my shotgun, and put it in my mouth.

"What happened?"

I couldn't do that, either.

"You crying?"

It's the cobbler, LeBron. It's the meanest/best cobbler I've ever had.[124]

Hearkening back to the lusted-after cobbler that sparked the entire imagined exchange, Raab recognizes, in this moment of confession, that his vitriol at James is rooted in self-hatred—the flaws he sees in the basketball star are not analogous to his own, but they evince them. That Raab's racist expressions of anger toward James—highlighting his mother's supposed sexual profligacy, insinuating the criminality of his "posse," and, of course, measuring his penis—are all noticeably absent or weakly defended in this dialogic framework is telling. Airing his own troubled past, Raab recognizes that his vitriol, like James's cobbler, tastes best when meanest, but is no less trivial for its objectification. In a book that refers to its fan object as a "whore" in its title, this moment demonstrates the nuance and self-reflection possible in fan feeling. While it doesn't excuse Raab's troubling and often racist rhetoric, it does demonstrate the memoir's capacity, no less than the autobiographical fictions explored in the last chapter, to represent the sports fan's consciousness on terms that blur the line between reality and fiction, and the valuable critical and creative insights that blurriness enables.

Where Shields's and Raab's uses of aspirational homosocial ventriloquism manage to recognize white male fans' desired intimacy with black players and provide complex, if still problematic, imagined landscapes for their interaction, Simmons's use of the authorial device is flatly objectifying. The athlete ventriloquized is not Larry Bird, Simmons's favorite player, who is white, but Michael Jordan, a figure of such legendary skill, star power, and corporate power that sociologist David L. Andrews refers to him as "a Reaganite racial replicant: a black version of a white cultural model who, by his very simulated existence, ensures the submergence and subversion of racial Otherness."[125] Contrary to Andrews's notion, Simmons presents Jordan in a distinctly racial way. Simmons prefaces his interaction by declaring that "I'm telling this story in the present tense because, as far as I'm concerned, it still feels like it happened three hours ago. Come back with me to [the] 2006 [NBA] All-Star Weekend in Houston. I am drinking Bloody Marys on a Saturday afternoon with my buddy Sully and his Boston crew."[126] Firmly ensconced in his own homosocial milieu, Simmons is thrilled when former All-Star (and noted friend of Jordan's) Charles Oakley occupies the table next to his, escorted by "three lady friends," and is soon followed by Jordan himself. Though Simmons and his friends are at a restaurant, not a basketball arena, the presence of superstar athletes enhances the homosocial potency of their outing, for, as Michael Eric Dyson rightfully asserts, "the culture of athletics has provided an acceptable and widely accessible means of white male bonding."[127] Simmons and his friends have no compunction about eavesdropping on the subsequent conversation, ordering food and drinks in order to stay at the table as long as Jordan and crew do. They hope to absorb what Dyson has characterized as the "black cultural nuances of cool, hip, and chic" for which "the black athletic body is deified, reified, and rearticulated within the narrow meanings of capital and commodity."[128]

Though Simmons and company can hear much of Jordan's conversation, little of it is reported directly. Instead, Jordan and his dialogue are characterized such that their relevance to the eavesdropping crew is prioritized. Describing the procession of people who "stream over to say hello, pay tribute to Jordan, kiss his ring," Simmons makes him out to be "the real-life Michael Corleone" a power broker who, when asked by his agent how late he stayed up the previous night, "say[s] 'Seven-thirty,' as we nod admiringly."[129] Like Michael Corleone, Al Pacino's infamous character in *The Godfather* trilogy and a pop-culture touchstone for Simmons and his ilk, Jordan is both revered and criminalized, respected and feared. His response to David Falk, his agent, is informational until amplified by Simmons and friends—staying out all night is a measure of masculinist mischief for these men, a sign that Jordan has no obligation to polite, and thus implicitly feminized, society. Simmons effectively incarnates Michael Kimmel's characterization of "the Self-Made Man," who "turned to leisure activities, such as sports, to give his manhood the boost he needed and strove to develop some all-male preserves where he could . . . be alone with other men."[130] Jordan's response to Falk both demonstrates that display and intensifies the homosocial intimacy of Simmons's eavesdropping sporting enclave.

Such a feared boss figure must wield the threat of violence to gain such awe and reverence, and Oakley—Mafioso enforcer Luca Brasi to Jordan's Corleone, according to Simmons—fills that role. Simmons recounts how

occasionally Oakley stands up and saunters around just to stretch his legs and look cool while I make comments like, "I wish you could rent Oak for parties." At one point, Oak thinks about ordering food, stands up, looks over at all of us eating, notices our friend Rich's cheeseburger . . . and I swear, we're all waiting for Oak to say the words, "Oak wants your cheeseburger, and he wants it now." But he doesn't. He ends up ordering one himself. Too bad.[131]

At best, Simmons is oblivious to stereotypes and assumes black male "cool" to a laughable degree. At worst, the notion that he could "rent Oak," as if the former NBA All-Star were just performing himself as a commodity, and that Oakley would speak in the third person while holding up "Rich" for his cheeseburger, is astonishingly racist. To make matters even more troubling, Simmons uses a footnote to assert that he gave his son the middle name "Oakley" because, as he rhetorically asks: "Will you grow up to be a pussy with a middle name like Oakley? No way."[132] Here is Shields's notion of the white fan's implicit desire to see black players misbehave, inextricably intertwined with an idea of masculine toughness that Simmons hopes to pass on to his son.[133] Simultaneously made to serve Simmons's desire to flaunt his homosocial toughness via misogyny and characterized according to racist stereotype by the process, Oakley is little more than a puppet in a show, a threatening figure to fit the fan author's preferred narrative of masculinity.

In this milieu, Jordan himself, with Oakley supposedly at his beck and call, "isn't Corporate MJ, the one you and I know. This is Urban MJ, the one that comes out for the Black Super Bowl, the one that made an entire league cower for most of the nineties. It finally makes sense."[134] Using the dog whistle term "urban" to signal a threatening blackness not normally associated with the Jordan represented to white America in Nike and Gatorade commercials, and "the Black Super Bowl" to racialize the NBA All-Star game (and by contrast the Super Bowl itself), Simmons thrills at his supposed exposure to unfiltered blackness. He imagines that he has witnessed what David L. Andrews calls the "dreaded metamorphosis from 'Michael Jordan the person to Michael Jordan the black guy,'" a narrative trope that emerged in the wake of media coverage of Michael Jordan's gambling proclivities and the (unrelated but nonetheless popularly associated) murder of his father in 1993.[135] But what "makes sense" about "urban" Jordan to Simmons is a reflection of Simmons. Jordan, ventrilo-quized and essentialized, is made to be what Simmons, as a fan, desires to be. That is, until his "wife shows up."[136] "Uh-oh," writes Simmons:

Everyone makes room for her. She sits down right next to him. Poor MJ looks like somebody who took a no-hitter into the ninth, then gave up a triple off the left-field wall. The trash-talking stops. He slumps in his seat like a little kid. The cigar goes out. No more hangin' with the boys. Time to be a husband again. Watching the whole thing unfold, I lean over to Sully and say, "Look at that, he's just like us." And he is. Just your average guy getting derailed by his wife. For once in my life, I don't want to be like Mike.[137]

Misogyny at its most unfiltered, the passage is also the moment of the most potent homosocial commonality. Though to Simmons they may represent black "others" that are powerful, threatening, and cool, Jordan and his friends have their homosocial intimacy disrupted by the shrewish figure of a wife. The other women present, mentioned earlier in accompaniment of Oakley, are regarded as mere commodities—welcomed on the edges of the inner circle—but Juanita Jordan demands respect, and the crude social customs of male buddyism must be suspended. This is misogyny's common ground, from Simmons's perspective, reducing Jordan to the level of the fan—of such distaste for feminism that he no longer "want[s] to be like Mike" because the player is rendered normal, "just like us."[138]

Simmons's ventriloquism differs from Shields's and Raab's insofar as it is not an imagined dialogue and Jordan is not his favorite player, though the "Jumpman" is certainly revered by him, as he is by millions of others. Despite—or perhaps, one could argue, because of—the fact that Simmons does not imagine Jordan's words, as Shields does for Payton and Raab for James, his aspirational homosocial ventriloquism is the most misogynist, most racist, and least self-reflective of the three. Aware of other fans' racism as Simmons may claim to be, he does not or cannot recognize the ways in which race structures and influences the NBA narrative as he imbues it with personal resonance. He may have once called himself "Jabaal Abdul-Simmons," but that blackface naming did not provide him with any depth of understanding about African Americans or himself. Simmons understands blackness through the lens of popular narratives that basketball and other entertainment provide him. As Jeffrey Lane puts it,

Too often the understanding that whites have of blacks is profoundly skewed by the simple fact that . . . whites interact with blacks only indirectly, through the consumption of a very limited number of representations. Listening to black music, watching black athletes on television, and seeing black criminals on the news function in lieu of direct communication. Since each of these forums is a space removed from everyday life—being famous or a criminal is to exist in the extreme—a transfiguration occurs in which blacks become characters, icons, symbols, or caricatures—that is, something other than human beings.[139]

This is what Shields—and even Raab, for all his bile—can see: that the objects of their fan desires are rendered just that, objects. That to the fan these athletes must be little more than "characters, icons, symbols, or caricatures" is a self-reflective authorial burden for Shields and Raab.[140] But reducing human beings to fictional characters is also the price of articulating the self as a memoirist. Simmons's insensitivity is personally motivated, no doubt, but it is also grounded in the kind of wide-ranging objectivist, "post-racial," pseudo-biographical ambitions that his broad title, *The Book of Basketball*, betrays. Simmons behaves, in other words, as if the ventriloquizing narrative of Jordan that he creates is not a constructed story (with obvious racial overtones) but a recap of "real" events. Like the multitudes of sports fans who thrilled to Jordan's physical exploits without recognizing their behavior as readerly (and autobiographical), Simmons disavows or pretends not to recognize the stakes and responsibilities of his role as a storyteller.

Veering into overt fiction writing, Raab, Shields, and (though he may not recognize it) Simmons use aspirational homosocial ventriloquism to more directly associate themselves with desired athletes. But they also do so for another reason: it implicitly demonstrates their authorial talents as it facilitates their fan identity. That these fictional imaginings should be considered distinct from the rest of their memoirs' "nonfictional" narrative may seem strange to literary scholars, like Eakin, who accept that autobiographical accounts are "always a kind of fiction."[141] But, because sporting events (other than professional wrestling) are usually publicly perceived to be "real" (and implicitly nonnarrative), the premise that their outcome is never predetermined is vital to the competitive stakes and the fans' excitement. If their ending is known, or known to be predetermined, their action loses dramatic potency for fans in medias res. For Shields, "a sports event takes place inside a very brief temporal frame; the moment the frame is broken, the artificiality of the event—its utter inconsequentiality—overwhelms it."[142] Commenting on the decision by Seattle's ABC affiliate to delay the broadcast of Monday Night Football, he argues that "the fact that the game is not unfolding in real time makes a mockery of everybody's fandom."[143] Contributing to what Philip Auslander calls the "diminution of previous distinctions between the live and the mediatized," television furthers the cultural "blending of real and fabricated situations."[144] But for Shields, and many sports fans, an emphasis on "liveness" lends a sense that that the game is a "real" event and not a story or show—and thus makes their fandom "real" by association with "the trappings of sacred 'authentic' competition," as Sam Ford puts it.[145] That the games are statistically recorded and quantified only adds to the scientific feel of the event as a happening, not a narrative. But like human confidence in the accuracy of our own memories, this denial of the narrative construction of the sporting event is a convenient, and sometimes necessary, distortion.

The truth is, of course, that each fan interprets a sporting event differently. Beneath the umbrella of the event's "winner" and "loser," between the numbers in a box score, beyond the public metanarrative provided by the media, each fan inescapably builds a narrative from his own perspective. Like "the manner in which the reader experiences [a literary] text," as literary critic Wolfgang Iser puts it in "The Reading Process," the sports fan's interpretation "will reflect his own disposition. . . . Thus we have the apparently paradoxical situation in which the reader is forced to reveal aspects of himself in order to experience a reality which is different from his own."[146] Or as Scott Raab reflects, amid his vitriol at LeBron James, "What another sees in you will reveal that person. What you see in another reveals your self. We are—each of us and all of us—mirrors."[147] This is perhaps Raab's deepest insight in the memoir, for though millions of people in the Cleveland area share some distaste for James, *The Whore of Akron* is finally a narrative of Raab via James, not the inverse, as it would be under the classical rhetorical terms of the genre.

"Black Bodies Still Occupy the Auction Block": Reconsidering One's Own Blackness Through Another

While Raab, Shields, and Simmons thrill to their imagined intimacy with black athletes that fascinate them on terms predicated on racial difference, Lee and Wideman necessarily feel a distinct associative desire. Both men recognize, to varying degrees, white fans' impulse to objectify black athletes and seek to resist it. Lee's Knicks, once celebrated for exemplifying the American fantasy of the "melting pot," by the late '70s had been derisively dubbed the "Niggerbockers" as part of a broader perception on the part of the white public that the NBA was "too black."[148] This led Lee to embrace strident black athletes and coaches like Georgetown's John Thompson and "any black person the mainstream media vilifies.... I start to ask myself, 'Why do they hate this guy so much?' He must be doing something good here. He must be telling them to kiss [his] black behind, also."[149] But as Lee rose to fame for films like *She's Gotta Have It* and *Do the Right Thing* in the late 1980s, he also became close with superstar athletes as a matter of course. In fact, thanks to his famed guest appearance as Mookie (the protagonist of *She's Gotta Have It*, portrayed by Lee) in a series of commercials for Nike's Air Jordan shoe line, Lee has become popularly associated with—and indeed relishes his connection to—Michael Jordan himself.

Lee opens *Best Seat in the House* by recounting a conversation with Jordan, conducted in the Bulls superstar's Range Rover as they drive back from recording a commercial in 1996. In this moment, there is nothing aspirational about Lee's homosocial intimacy with Jordan. Yet "riding shotgun with the greatest ball player in modern sports history, probing his mind" still provides a thrill, despite Lee's own celebrity and the rather mundane nature of the conversation he relates.[150] But Lee is not oblivious to the critique of Jordan's commercial success, levied by Wideman and many others, to which he can be said to be an accessory. Asserting that "the ads for Air Jordans that we shot were not aimed primarily at inner-city kids [but rather] tapping into the authentic black basketball cultural motif more than trying to get an exclusively or predominately black clientele," Lee bristles at "negative publicity for Nike, Mike, and me. Community activists said Michael Jordan and

Spike Lee were the opiate of the masses."[151] Lee's bond with Jordan is strengthened, then, by a perception that both have been unfairly rendered pariahs for supposed complicity with the crass capitalism of the sports-industrial complex. And the source of this victimization is notably racialized for Lee: "sometimes African-Americans are too quick to look for a savior, somebody to lead us out of the wilderness. . . . No athlete or entertainer is going to stop young brothers from killing each other, no matter what."[152] Putting limits on the degree to which any role model can be said to impact social change, Lee presumes to speak for Jordan in defense of them both—against African American cultural leaders who consider both men complicit. Lee's ventriloquism of Jordan thus doesn't cross racial lines, but it is fundamentally similar to Raab's, Shields's, and Simmons's attempts to voice a hoops icon insofar as it combines the creative and autobiographical possibilities of the memoir to address race and his own personal insecurity about it. In this way Lee, no less than the three white memoirists, uses his passion for basketball and authorial privilege to reveal, and reckon with, his fears and desires regarding the commodification of black bodies.

But Lee must also reckon with public perception of his own black body in an NBA context as well. He spends much of the book discussing his exploits as one of the NBA's most prominent celebrity fans, paying particular attention to his famous turn as a verbal sparring partner to Indiana Pacers' star Reggie Miller during the 1994 NBA Eastern Conference Finals. Never ashamed to "get on" opposing players from his courtside seat, Lee's verbal antagonism sparked particular furor in the Pacers' three-point specialist in Game 5 at Madison Square Garden.[153] With the Knicks up twelve at the start of the fourth quarter, Miller caught fire from beyond the arc, at several points "turn[ing] and look[ing] directly in [Lee's] face as the ball split the net."[154] Before long, Lee recollects, "it was like Reggie was playing me as well as the Knicks."[155] The national television broadcasters from NBC noticed, and the famous (and infamous) play-by-play announcer Marv Albert admonished Lee, "saying on the air that I was not part of the game and that I 'should realize that.'"[156] Yet, Lee insists, "Reggie made me part of [the game,] then left me lying there" as Miller and the Pacers triumphed, 93–86, and headed back to Indiana with a chance to win the series at home.[157] Lee understands that he has become a prominent part of the public narrative surrounding his favorite team, recognizes that many fans will inevitably misrepresent his role, and still embraces the opportunity. Though he was "getting killed over the airwaves and in the papers" and "had gone from being known as the Knicks biggest fan to a being a well-meaning lunatic," Lee bought a courtside seat to Game 6 in Indianapolis, watched the Knicks triumph, and left in a hurry as Indiana fans threatened his life.[158] The fans' anger at Lee was clearly marked by racial hostility—though Miller and most of the Pacers players were also African American—and while he doesn't explicitly call it as much in *Best Seat in the House*, Lee has subsequently said: "I've never been to a [Ku Klux] Klan rally, but [in Indianapolis's] Market Square Arena, if they could have strung me up that night, they would have been happy."[159] The Knicks went on to win Game 7 in New York, after which Lee attests to feeling as if "I'd played forty-eight minutes myself. I was toast, physically and emotionally."[160]

Familiar with what it means to be flattened to the utmost stereotype by basketball fans, Lee still clearly relishes his privilege as a celebrity "Big Name Fan" who can enter the locker room, talk to the players, and consider himself part of the game.[161] But he also understands that his intimacy with the players is related to the hypercommodification of the game. "It's . . . a much different [Madison Square] Garden crowd" than the one of his childhood, Lee reflects: "The whole financial landscape has changed. The average working stiffs who bleed orange and blue are not really able to afford season tickets."[162] While *The Best Seat in the House* provides Lee immersion among his fellow fans, he comes to understand that the narrative landscape of the modern NBA is built on a racial divide buttressed by the unequal allocation of global capital, in which "basketball shows what we as [black] people can do if the environment allows us to put our stamp of definition and creativity on it" and yet, thanks to a managing structure of franchise ownership dominated by extremely wealthy white men, "we [African Americans also] make up the cattle—that's what the players are—to be bought, sold, traded at will."[163] While Lee stops short of calling the players "Forty Million Dollar Slaves," as African American *New York Times* sports columnist William C. Rhoden did in titling his history of the black athlete, it's clear that Lee is troubled by the way in which the NBA's (largely black) millionaire athletes are manipulated by its (almost exclusively white) billionaire team owners.[164] Lee sees, in other words, *why* aspirational homosocial ventriloquism exists—he craves, and is lucky enough to enjoy, interpersonal intimacy with NBA players that fans like Shields, Raab, and Simmons can only imagine—yet he also perceives why such an impulse can further deepen interracial misunderstanding and inequality.

Disaffected by the NBA game, Wideman nevertheless has basketball heroes whose exploits and interactions he relates. Chief among these is Ed Fleming, a Homewood pick-up hoops legend, whom Wideman runs into at the funeral for his own nephew, Omar.[165] Though he "almost didn't recognize the broad-shouldered man in a dark suit," Wideman is soon describing his old acquaintance as if the two were on the court, remarking on the "gliding, effortless go and flow in his movements . . . alert for whatever might be required next, fighting through a pick, planting an elbow in somebody's chest, tensing himself for a collision with a two-hundred-fifty-pound body hurtling toward him full speed."[166] This focus on physicality endures: the substance of their "little chat" is largely omitted from the text, though some history of Fleming's college and professional playing career is provided.[167] Instead, Wideman figures Ed Fleming largely as a representation of the black body. He calls

> Ed Fleming's body type and color a stigma, a danger to the bearer for five hundred years in racist America. Convict body, field hand body, too unadulterated African, too raw, too black, too powerful and quick and assertive for most whites and some colored folks to feel comfortable around until Michael Jordan arrived and legitimated Ed Fleming's complexion and physique, mainstreaming them, blunting the threatening edge, commodifying the Jordan look, as if the physical, sexual potency of a dark, streamlined muscular body could be purchased, as if anybody, everybody—Swede, Korean, Peruvian, Croat, New Englander—could be like Mike.[168]

For Wideman, Jordan forever altered, but did not destroy, the means by which "though chattel slavery is a thing of the past, black bodies still occupy the auction block."[169] Jordan's transcendent abilities made the "convict body, field hand body" marketable, and allowed marketers to realize the degree to which "the black body's power to stir desire and sell things transcended any individual black pitch-person."[170] Thus, per Tracie Church Guzzio, "paradoxically, for Wideman, basketball operates both as a celebration of African American culture and as a sign that white America still equates African Americans primarily with athletic ability."[171] Ed Fleming, as a kind of Jordan precursor, ineluctably carries in his person the commercial potential of "the black body as a field of dreams where whites can play out erotic fantasies."[172]

With few of his own words represented on the page, Ed Fleming becomes for Wideman a figure of symbolic preeminence in his bodily mediated consideration of race in professional basketball. His physical presence is ventriloquized (qua Jordan) to serve Wideman's rhetorical purposes on the subject. But Ed Fleming is also more than a lesson in the objectification of black bodies. He further elucidates for Wideman the power of naming within the narrative landscape of the playground game. "You take care of yourself now, John," Fleming remarks as the two men part ways: "don't be a stranger."[173] This seemingly quotidian salutation gives Wideman pause:

> *John.* I don't believe I'd ever heard Ed Fleming say my first name. A baptism of sorts, in Warden's [funeral home] of all places. He'd always called me Wideman on the court. . . . A single name's enough on the Homewood court, and if it's your surname, *Wideman,* it's said with a little intentional chill of depersonalization, the way a referee calls you by your uniform number, foul on *Ten,* in high school or college games. . . . You can go years, a lifetime, playing alongside guys and know them only by their court handles.[174]

This nomenclature matters in the playground game, not because anyone is actually keeping stats (as in the officiated game), but because it brings into being the player that is Wideman, rather than the person that is John.[175] It is as if they are distinct characters. Wideman—or John, rather—is deeply affected by this recontextualization of his sense of self in relationship to Ed Fleming. It forces him to reconsider his own means of identifying his interlocutor:

> To some of his peers he was *Ed* or *Fleming.* Always *Ed Fleming* in my mind. Both names necessary, three inseparable syllables, more

incantation or open-sesame mantra than a name. A mini-sound bite like those heroic epithets identifying characters—Ox-eyed Hera, Swift-heeled Achilles.... That's just not any old Ed or Fleming. He's *the* Ed Fleming. Implacable. Irresistible.... When I call him *Ed*, the single, naked sound coming out of my mouth almost as surprising for me to hear as hearing *John* pass through Ed Flemings lips.[176]

This is not aspirational homosocial ventriloquism, exactly, but Wideman's depiction of this legendary playground figure is marked both by his desire to be closer to Ed Fleming and by his self-reflective attention to how he represents him. Wideman's awkward response to meeting "Swift-heeled Achilles" in extra-diegetic repose in Ithaca, rather than in the mad action of *The Odyssey* itself, sheds light on the comforting nature of the impulse to objectify or flatten players into characters, even within the far-more-intimate confines of the playground game. But it also reminds Wideman of the immersive nature of the game as an "unfolding narrative, told and retold," one in which "a counterreality is dramatized. Playing hoop, African-American men act out a symbolic version of who they are, who they want to be."[177] As Guzzio puts it, "Wideman inscribes basketball as a possible form of resistant expression that addresses and refutes stereotypes of black masculinity and reveals the spurious nature of even the notion of such a cultural construction as 'black masculinity.'"[178]

Thus, while participation in the playground game may have ultimately rendered Ed Fleming *the* Ed Fleming—Homewood's Swift-heeled Achilles—it also allowed Ed himself the personal agency to forge that symbolic version of himself. "Playing ball," Wideman writes, "you submit for a time to certain narrow arbitrary rules, certain circumscribed choices. But once in, there's no script, no narrative line you must follow."[179] Only "the unpredictability of language ... sometimes approximates a [playground] hoop game's freedom" for Wideman, in which the "we are doing this together and it's just us out here but the game has been here before" and the "players ... are also the truest fans. The medium the message."[180] Where the NBA game is a product, shallow and disposable, "playground basketball and writing ... result in the most basic sort of self-knowledge.... They're about the seeking, the inquiry, process not destination."[181] Wideman's major problem with the NBA game—with spectatorship itself—is his belief that fans necessarily prioritize ends over means, satisfaction over reflection: they do not produce, only consume. But toward the end of *Hoop Roots*, as he cantankerously comments to a female companion about the flaws in a playground game which he is now helpless to join, Wideman begins to recognize he is

> acting like an old man the action has passed by . . . fussing at the game. Am I mad simply because playground hoop has changed. Different now from what it was before, when it was my game. . . . What is this man's playing telling me about his life. My life. What might he be saying that I don't want to hear. What truth about him. About myself. The game. Our tangled lives in these daunting, unhinged, uneasy, challenging days and times. I try to see what's going on with fresh eyes. . . . So for the little time left I shut up and watch and listen. Remember.[182]

In this moment Wideman realizes, albeit reluctantly, that he *can* produce something through hoop without playing it, that, as this book has argued, fandom is as much about writing the self as it is reading the game. Reflection on the task of fan writing is all it takes to produce something beyond mere mindless consumption. For Wideman and every fan, on the sideline as on the court, "hoop isn't me. But I'm the game."[183]

"A Completely Imaginary Love Affair in Which the Beloved Is Forever Larger Than Life": Vanity, Identity, and Narrative Control

Wideman's realization that his connection to basketball is forged in writerly agency beyond the limits of his body—that he can be the game even when he can no longer play it—is well-earned in the richly textured narrative expanse of *Hoop Roots*. Not everyone can realize the possibilities of authorial agency in sports fandom so richly, of course. In "From National Hero to Liquid Star: Identity and Discourse in Transnational Sports Consumption," Cornell Sandvoss argues that the combination of "affection and identification" that characterizes sports fan attachment can be considered

> a form of narcissism, in which the fan's fascination with the fan object lies in its misrecognition as an extension of self, maintained through

processes of self-reflection in which sports stars and teams function as a mirror to the fan. On a rhetorical level, this is reflected through the use of "we" . . . in speaking about their favorite team; on a narrative level, it is reflected through their characterizing and describing the object of their fandom in terms and qualities that reflect both the fan's self-image, values, and beliefs and their wider social positioning.[184]

Sounding much like Christopher Lasch in *The Culture of Narcissism* some thirty-three years prior, and less like the rather more sanguine fan studies scholar of his own earlier monograph, *Fans: The Mirror of Consumption*, Sandvoss here posits that the athlete as fan object functions as a vessel for the fan's articulation of self in a manner that does not reflect intentional interpretive action or authorship, but only narcissism and misrecognition. Importantly, however, Sandvoss suggests here that as the fan's sense of self changes, the athlete's qualities of attraction do as well: even without self-conscious authorship of her fan narrative, the fan maps qualities she fancies in herself onto the athlete as fan object (rather than the reverse) and thus alters the object in their mind's eye. At the point at which the fan can no longer do this—when the athlete's cultural position changes drastically such the fan ceases to find a way to recognize herself in the athlete—the connection is severed and a new one formed. Pessimistic though his narcissism-based framing may be, Sandvoss's formulation aptly characterizes many of the narrative qualities of fandom in the present tense. Still, Sandvoss fails to account for the degree to which the fan's past fandoms are likewise altered to fit her active articulation of self. While Scott Raab recalls cheering for James when he starred for the Cavs, he maintains throughout that he did so on uneasy terms—as if he could anticipate betrayal.[185] Likewise, Lee professes, at the moment of the injured Willis Reed's emergence from the tunnel before Game 7 of the 1970 NBA Finals, that "Knicks fans knew we were going to win. We had waited. Now we were positive."[186] In doing so, Raab and Lee unwittingly connect Sandvoss's notion of narcissistic projection to Paul John Eakin's claim, in *Fictions in Autobiography,* that "autobiographical truth is not a fixed but an evolving content, [and] the materials of life history are freely shaped by memory and imagination to serve the needs of present consciousness."[187] The terms of sports fandom, like those of memoir, are always influenced by active self-definition. Recognition of change is possible, of course, but an unbiased account of the fan one *was* is no more possible than any accurate recollection of a past version of the self.

This constant reorganization and rearticulation of self-narrative is possible, in part, because of the notorious unreliability of memory. A further consequence of this self-defining process, especially in a sports context, is a tendency toward teleology in reconstructing the past. Association with players allows fans to correlate their personal successes—or failures, in Raab's case—with publicly recognized figures whose glories resonate on a plane of shared emotion. It is in this vein that Shields reports his "empathy for the church-goers. They go to church for the same reason fans go to the games: adulthood didn't turn out to have quite as much glory as we thought it would; for an hour or two, we're in touch with transcendental things."[188] Projecting their senses of self onto a wave of communally signified emotion defined artificially by the rules and score, the fans deterministically translate the athletes' performance into their carefully constructed narrative. Viewed in retrospect, the event's winner and loser seems no less predestined that any memoirist's self-assured notion that who she is the person she was destined to become. Significant happenings are accentuated or minimized by media and fans to account for the narrative determinacy mandated by the outcome. And yet, as Wideman puts it, "A story interesting to one person may bore another. Writing describes ball games the reader can never be sure anybody has ever played. The only access to them is through the writer's creation. You can't go there or know there, just accept someone's words they exist."[189]

Simmons, for one, embraces the fact that "basketball is an objective sport *and* a subjective sport, dammit. That's what makes it so much fun to follow."[190] He revels in the imaginary imperative such recognition provides him. "The single best thing about sports is the unknown," he asserts, "it's more fun to think about what *could* happen than what already happened."[191] The predetermined narrative must be denied in live competition, but such narrative construction for an imagined future constitutes, for Simmons at least, the single greatest pleasure of sports fandom. Gerald Early somewhat cynically agrees: "In athletics, everyone is always assuming that the past is prologue. Sports fans thrive on and live for the mad, endless speculations about the future, fixated on prophecy, on who will win or lose; but everyone is also buried in the empirical tomb of past performance, the quantitative graveyard of the Ghosts of Athletic Greatness Gone By."[192] This makes a kind of reciprocal sense; if rooting for a team, or player, or result lends some narrative coherence to fans' personal lives, then narratively mapping their futures allows the fans effectively to outsource their identity construction to an outside entity—to fantastically project personal outcomes and emotions in a lower-stakes narrative environment. One could argue, as Mark Freeman does in *Rewriting the Self*, that our lives' inherent uncertainty drives external passions. Freeman finds it "curious and noteworthy that so many . . . insubstantial and unreasonable things have such a remarkable hold over us. Indeed, isn't it the case that the things we care about most—ourselves, others, music, art, nature—are precisely the things for which there is the least reason to do so?"[193] Many a detractor of spectator sport has made the same query, as does Shields: "Why do I care so much? That's what I would like to know. It's a safe love, this love, this semi-self-love, this fandom; it's a frenzy in a vacuum, a completely imaginary love affair in which the beloved is forever larger than life."[194] The answer lies in the last three words. Because the beloved sports narratives are "larger than life," they transcend the fan's own life narrative even as they enhance it.

But if fandom is a "frenzy in a vacuum, a completely imaginary love affair," as Shields puts it, why chronicle it publicly?[195] If one takes memoir to be a self-justifying construct—if you can write one about your life, then you must have had a life worth living—can we say the same for fandom? Does it follow that if sports are meaningful to you, your fandom has meaning? The more sanguine memoir theorists, such as G. Thomas Couser, firmly believe that "in writing one's life one may bring a new self into being. If this is true, then in reading life narrative, we witness self-invention."[196] Those more critical of the memoir's formal claims to truth in representation, like Paul John Eakin, are not quite so buoyant, but nevertheless recognize that "we inhabit systems of social intercourse in which the ability to articulate an identity narrative . . . confirms the possession of a working identity."[197] Either way, sports lend material to claims of selfhood in that they aid in that articulation. Whether the love affair is imaginary or not, it defines fans against the void of non-identity, as Frederick Exley so adamantly asserted in *A Fan's Notes*. Humans may rely on "illusions of autonomy and self-determination," as Eakin puts it, but "we do not invent our identities out of whole cloth. Instead, we draw on the resources of the cultures we inhabit to shape them, resources that specify what it means to be a man, a woman, a worker, a person in the settings where we live our lives."[198] One such specifying resource is the sports fan milieu. Anonymizing as the roar of the crowd may seem, it perpetually assists in the articulation of selfhood on an individual level.

Reading Lee's, Raab's, Shields's, Simmons's, and Wideman's memoirs serves the same purpose. As the authors articulate their identities as fans and writers throughout their narratives, their readers cannot help but "ask questions about ourselves . . . by observing others as they struggle to find answers."[199] But what do fans really learn about race and the NBA by reading *Best Seat in the House, The Whore of Akron, Black Planet, The Book of Basketball,* and *Hoop Roots*? Not all basketball fans prioritize a racial frame when viewing the game. One hopes, however, that the authors' awareness that race inescapably imbues their fandom allows their readers to recognize, as David Leonard puts it, that "notwithstanding the efforts of the NBA to obscure or mediate racial difference—to deny or minimize the existence of racism both inside and outside its arenas—race and dominant white racial frames continue to impact the NBA's organization and reception."[200] In the process of writing their memoirs, Lee, Raab, Shields, Simmons, and Wideman demonstrate the inescapable influence of socially constructed racial meta-narratives even in self-constitutive efforts that would attempt to resist them. They likewise undermine the veneer of objective reality and demonstrate the fundamental narrative flexibility of sports.

4

IT'S BEEN A PROBLEM WITH ME AND WOMEN
Failed Masculinities in Depictions of Sports Fans on Film

> Women may be doing sports almost as much as men are, but they
> don't like to talk about it very much. Maybe the stronger women get,
> the more men love *to talk about* football.
>
> MICHAEL KIMMEL, *Manhood in America*[1]

In the novel and the memoir, the flexibility of the written word elucidates
fans' ability plumb the depths of the self and imagine possibilities for
sports narrative. But such abilities are almost never represented on mainstream media platforms like newspapers or television networks. Meanwhile, media fans are increasingly depicted in popular media, like CBS's
hit sitcom *The Big Bang Theory*, and are "no longer considered 'weird'" in
quite the same way.[2] As Lucy Bennett and Paul Booth assert in *Seeing Fans*,
"the popularity of fandom has exploded ... [even as it] sits in an uneasy
position in the media industries. Both courted and held at arms' length,
fans are still seen as deviant and pathological, even as their enthusiasm
is channeled into more 'authorized' avenues."[3] Media producers have
realized, in other words, that fandom is pervasive and that recognizing
media fans' presence—instead of ignoring them, as they largely had in
media ecologies prior to the turn of the century—is profitable, even when
such recognition comes with a side of stereotypes. Sports fans, however,
haven't received quite the same attention. Sports are hugely profitable,
of course, and media companies—no less than any other story-telling
enterprise—have endeavored to capture these rich narratives on screen.
Yet in doing so, when they depict fans at all, media companies, and Hollywood movie studios in particular, tend to present them as ciphers for

the audience, that is, as faceless consumers with little to add to the story. When individualized, filmic sports fans are usually secondary characters, often women (think Annie Savoy in *Bull Durham*) or children (à la the kids in Disney's *Angels in the Outfield*), whose actions are clearly subordinated to the masculine agency of the men on the field. As Aaron Baker puts it in *Contesting Identities: Sports in American Film*: "when it comes to sports films, the overriding example of hegemonic representation is their repeated endorsement of the viability and usefulness of self-reliance—and therefore the irrelevance of a social identity based on one's membership in a group."[4] Thus the crowd's roar merely accentuates the beleaguered athlete's great triumph at film's end, signaling his reacceptance into the mainstream and cueing the moviegoers' goosebumps—the individuated athletes and/or omniscient narrator contrasting with the mass of the adoring audience. Per Baker, for Hollywood sports films, "athletic excellence matters most, thereby reducing the status of the spectator to that of consumer rather than producer of value."[5]

Apart from hegemonic incentives to deemphasize audience members' interpretive agency, the main obstacle to depicting the behaviors of fans as I have described them in this book—that is, as self-reflective readers and rewriters of sports narratives—is the interior nature of those activities. Reading and writing are almost impossible to depict compellingly onscreen, the life of the mind being, if not antivisual, then at least so inward-focused as to be unrecognizable to others. While Don DeLillo, Fred Exley, and John Edgar Wideman can compelling represent interiority on the page, the narrative consequences of such scenes are largely philosophical or imaginary, with little material effect on athletes, or even other fans. Providing a backdrop for the heroic exploits of athletes or presented as a kind of shorthand for the mania brought on by the pressures of modern life, then, Hollywood's sports fans are usually faceless, feckless, or pathological.

Even so, there are films that focus primarily on sports fans, of course. In this chapter, I examine four of them: *The Fan*, *Fever Pitch*, *Big Fan*, and the film version of *Silver Linings Playbook*. All four movies ostensibly serve as cautionary tales about the social consequences of sports obsession, and though they arrive at vastly different conclusions regarding those consequences, each film specifically relates fandom to the protagonist's defective manifestation of masculinity. That these fans' failure is a matter of gender is in one sense attributable to the fact that, as Aaron Baker puts it, "to some degree every sports film is about gender, whatever it has to say about other aspects of social identity."[6] But it is also more than that: these fans are emasculated not merely because they are fans, but because they are self-reflective, narrative-oriented fans. By carefully considering the meanings of sport on their own terms, rather than those of conventional consumerism and the Hollywood sports drama, these fans have misappropriated sport as normative cultural touchstone. That these heterosexual white male protagonists are rendered "losers" by their sports fandom provides evidence that, as Mel Stanfill puts it, "the equation of fandom to failed masculinity, heterosexuality, and whiteness persists."[7]

This chapter is organized thematically according to Aaron Baker's similarly formulated "essential traits for the normative idea of masculinity in many sports films," by which these fans manifest their failure: "middle-class self-definition," "heterosexuality," and "whiteness."[8] These fans are losers, the films imply, because their obsessions prevent them from conforming to social norms in these areas, resulting in isolation and delusion. They are thus associated not with the violent, frenzied pathology of the sporting masses, but with the negative stereotypes of social ostracization most often associated with dedicated media fans of the science fiction and fantasy genres. This is particularly notable because, as Henry Jenkins and many others in fan studies have noted, these stigmatized media fan groups were some of the first to enthusiastically embrace fan agency and authorship as a cultural phenomenon capable, if not inherently, of stimulating creative and critical discourse. This is not to say that the fans of *The Fan*, *Fever Pitch*, *Big Fan*, and *Silver Linings Playbook* write fanfiction or attend fan conventions—far from it. But they do engage in textual interpretation and meaning-making that belies their supposed inadequacy. They are, in other words, writers of sport—not merely passive recipients. And, as it is for Jenkins's "textual poachers," this idiosyncratic reception and attendant authorship is marked as feminine. As Stanfill affirms, "fan failure at gender is a key component of the dissociation of fandom from normativity," and, not coincidentally, to a concomitant "failure of whiteness."[9] Since the white heterosexual male remains Hollywood's assumed subject position for cinema consumers, then, the self-reflective and thus feminized male sports fan is naturally pathologized, even in films in which he is the protagonist.

"Do You Work for a Living?": Fandom as Economically Emasculating

The immense impact of mass production and the attendant crisis in masculinity it provoked in the twentieth century is evident in the history of the cinema just as surely as it is in athletics: John Wayne's western action hero and Theodore Roosevelt's muscular Christian athlete are variations on the same overcompensatory theme. And when these two hypermasculinities overlap in films of sports heroism, there can be little doubt who the producers of capital are, the NCAA's illusions of amateurism be damned: the athletes. Even as sports films render their own viewers the passive consumers that their plots ignore or, in the case of *The Fan*, *Fever Pitch*, *Big Fan*, and *The Silver Linings Playbook*, mostly denigrate, they inescapably link "patriarchy to issues of capitalist control."[10] These films simultaneously imply that sports fans are insufficiently manly because they are economically impotent, and that they are economically impotent because their fandom unmans them.

Director Tony Scott's *The Fan* is a prime example of this conundrum. It was not a popular or well-regarded film, despite its all-star cast. Based on Peter Abraham's 1995 novel of the same name, *The Fan* aims at being a thriller, starring Robert DeNiro as crazed baseball fan Gil Renard and Wesley Snipes as the object of his obsession, San Francisco Giants slugger Bobby Rayburn (a Barry Bonds–like figure). That the film fell far short of its aspirations at the box office—netting just $18 million despite a budget of $55 million—reflects its failings as an overwrought melodrama. But no less significant, it seems to me, is that the film allows its viewers little sympathy for its fan protagonist.[11] Nor, presumably, can that audience relate to the terrorized millionaire athlete or the cadre of professional athletes, agents, and media members that make up the other major characters in the film. In effect, *The Fan* alienates the very eponymous sports fans it would seem to need to attract. If the conventional athlete-focused sports film presents Richard Dyer's "conservatism of utopian entertainment" by presenting the individualist bootstraps ethos of the (white, male, heterosexual) status quo as triumphant, then *The Fan* presents a dystopia in which DeNiro's deranged fan represents the ultimate consequences of the failure to adhere to that capitalist moral standard.[12]

From the outset, Renard's mania is predicated on his failed masculinity, evidenced by his nostalgia for his boyhood. The opening scene of the film focuses on fragments of grainy, black-and-white images of boys playing baseball. Bobbleheads, miniature baseball helmets, newspaper clippings, and other old-timey ephemera are displayed in tight shots, signaling Renard's attachment to an idealized (and notably white) version of baseball's "golden" past. As these stills are shown, the viewer hears Renard recite a poem, ostensibly written by him, in which the fan extolls "the grace from the field [that] arouses the crowd, / reflects on the days when I was quite proud."[13] Reflecting on his boyhood playing career and the joys of Opening Day—for its "high that I crazily lust"—Renard hints at his current difficulties: "I really am quite close, just a break away / from straightening things out, and being okay. / I can help my team to regain its glory / with just a little twist to the same old story."[14] Foreshadowing with "a little twist" Renard's expertise with and violent propensity toward knives, the opening scene ends by zooming in on the eyes of a boy, as if the viewer is entering Renard's developmentally arrested psyche, a landscape of deformed or aberrant masculinity.

The connection between "unsuccessful heterosexuality and liminal adulthood" is a longstanding one in the depiction of fans,[15] as Henry Jenkins famously pointed out in highlighting William Shatner's infamous "Get a Life" Saturday Night Live sketch in *Textual Poachers*.[16] In a sports-specific context, Marjorie Kibby similarly asserts that nostalgia, whiteness, and masculinity are inextricably interconnected in depictions of sports on film:

> If contemporary sport had been tainted by greed, scandal, feminism, and social liberalism, then the sport of a misremembered boyhood safeguarded hegemonic masculinity in providing an arena where individual success, male-male bonds, the reaffirmation of the father, and the rejection of the feminine, could be comfortably accommodated.[17]

Sports films encourage white males to ignore social change via nostalgia, Kibby argues, by suggesting that they can succeed in the present by hewing to values corresponding to a fictionalized version of the past. Via Renard, *The Fan* affirms the impulse but rejects the consequences. Renard is a failed (and then fired) salesman at the knife company his father founded, a divorced father of a son who doesn't share his love for or skill at playing baseball, and a deluded former youth player who thinks he can still compete with the "greedy" athletes he purports to admire. Renard's nostalgic obsession does not power his rise and redemption via the bootstrapping myth of success via overwhelming effort, but rather distracts him from self-betterment on those terms. Unlike athlete-centric "Reaganite" sports films like *Hoosiers* and *Rudy*, which, as David Leonard puts it, "respond to a crisis in white masculinity [by] offering a world in which white males dominate sports," *The Fan* is a cautionary tale of the failed white man, not a celebration of the triumph of the successful one.[18] Renard cannot succeed because he does not produce capital: rather than focused only on his own bootstraps, his narcissistic obsession is mediated via baseball, a "space and discourse presumably dominated by black 'others.'"[19] Renard's economic failure is thus always also a failure of whiteness, a racial—and racist—reality of neoliberal capitalism that drives the macabre horror plot that is the film's second half, and a topic I will return to in the third section of this chapter.

Where *The Fan* offers a fear-mongering portrait of fan investment by taking the fan's attempts at compensating for his economic emasculation to violent extremes, director Robert D. Siegel's *Big Fan* complicates and mitigates the earlier film's horrific conclusions. Though it stars a comedian, Patton Oswalt, as the eponymous "big fan" of the New York Giants football team, the film is a drama, premised on a violent interaction between a fan and his favorite player. Like DeNiro's Gil Renard, Oswalt's Paul Aufiero is portrayed as a feminized, unproductive loser—he works as a parking garage attendant and lives at home with his aging mother—whose deep attachment to his favorite team infantilizes him and implies mental instability. And like Renard, Aufiero alters the narrative of that team by personally interacting with its African American star, in this case a linebacker named Quantrell Bishop. But Aufiero renounces his failure to adhere to patriarchal capitalist moral standards in a fundamentally different manner than Renard. Rather than egomaniacally lashing out in order to demonstrate his power over his sports hero, Aufiero embraces the alternative moral economy sports fandom provides him. If, as Leo

Braudy famously postulated in *The Frenzy of Renown*, "fandom mediates the disparity between the aspirations fostered by culture and the relatively small increments of personal status possible in a mass society," then Aufiero embraces that mediation rather than allow himself to be frustrated by fandom's inability to enlarge those small increments in any material way.[20] Valuing his own textual production and the affective rewards football fandom provide him over the normative values of his family, Aufiero understands and self-consciously rejects the hegemonic economic standards that would characterize his existence as aberrant.

Aufiero is introduced as he listens to sports radio and prepares to call in. From his attendant booth at the parking garage, he scribbles down a monologue that he intends to deliver to the "Sports Dawg" about his beloved Giants. With premeditated authorial intent, then, Aufiero prepares to engage the cacophonous media forum that David Nylund calls "an attractive venue for embattled white men seeking recreational repose and a nostalgic return to a prefeminist ideal."[21] Meanwhile, a driver, perturbed at having to pay for a brief stay in the garage, derisively tells Aufiero to "have fun in your box."[22] While the driver ostensibly refers to the parking attendant structure in which Aufiero labors, the dismissal serves as a kind of epigraph for the film and for any exploration of self-reflective fandom. Is "fun in your box," in this case the "box" of sports fandom as a defining personal enterprise, enough to satisfy a person in lieu of the traditional markers of family and career success?

According to the 2005 romantic comedy *Fever Pitch*, the answer is at first yes, and then no. Loosely based on Nick Hornby's 1992 soccer fan memoir of the same title, the American film stars Jimmy Fallon as Red Sox baseball super-fan Ben Wrightman and Drew Barrymore as his love interest, Lindsey Meeks. Directed by the Farrelly Brothers, proprietors of "dumb white guy comedies . . . about young men who fail to live up to patriarchal ideals," *Fever Pitch* inverts the traditional presentation of masculinity with regard to neoliberal social norms for the production of capital.[23] Ben, a fatherless New Jersey transplant who attended his first Red Sox game at the age of seven with his uncle Carl, is a math teacher who spends his summers at Fenway Park—in effect sacrificing his earnings potential to be a more dedicated fan. Lindsey is a corporate executive with high-powered female friends, all of whom fetishize white-collar labor, its attendant earnings, and a culture of luxury—signaled by the film through scenes featuring spinning classes, elaborate costume parties, and rounds of golf. Discussing her work for MarquisJet—a luxury private jet service—with a group of middle schoolers brought to her workplace on a field trip by Ben, Lindsey describes her office as a "church of numbers, and every day is Sunday."[24] Indicating the film's sanctioning of capital as a moral measure, this focus on numbers also fosters the relationship between Ben and Lindsey, as the mathematical nature of baseball becomes common ground.

Still, in talking over her relationship with Ben with her girlfriends, Lindsey reflexively questions if she can be compatible with someone who is not driven by capitalist measures of success, and wonders: "why does everything in my life have to be a trophy? Who am I trying to impress?"[25] Commenting on Ben's "good vibe," Lindsey's friends affirm her tendency to "date yourself" in the form of such trophies, or "poodles," but they do not question the neoliberal criteria for doing so.[26] "Where's he been?" one friend asks, remarking "Why's he still on the market? . . . How has he not been tranquilized and tagged?"[27] Invoking free-market ideology and wildlife management in describing her romantic interest, Lindsey's female compatriots both assert for her a natural degree of dominance in choosing a mate and imply that Ben must be defective—not "man" enough to have found a partner already. Crucially, Ben's insufficient masculinity is directly tied by one friend to his economic inadequacy: the problem with teachers, she asserts, is "they have a small . . . income."[28] The pregnant pause amplifies the double entendre, linking economic limitations to sexual inadequacy.

Ben is at first untroubled by the role reversal between Lindsey and himself when it comes to the traditional gendering of economic production. He is able to provide for her in other ways: caring for her when she is sick, bringing humor and levity to her overly serious daily life, and incorporating her into the close-knit group of season-ticket-holding fans he calls his "Red Sox family." But when the demands of his fandom compete with Lindsey for attention, and he initially chooses fandom over her, she breaks up with him and begins to date a man she met at work. To win her back, Ben decides to sell his season-tickets—an heirloom passed on to him by his uncle Carl—for $125,000, signaling both his abandonment of the "childish pursuits" of fan practice and his embrace of capitalist gain as a measure of satisfaction.[29] That Lindsey rejects Ben's action just before the film's sappy conclusion—which features the couple celebrating on the field after the Red Sox won the 2004 World Series—does not change the fact that the film authorizes economic prowess as a prime mover of social understandings of masculine virility. Ben is ultimately only happy in his box because Lindsey jumps over the outfield wall to join him in it.

Like *Fever Pitch*, David O. Russell's *Silver Linings Playbook* ends by emphasizing fandom's positive possibilities. Though the basic contours of the plot remain the same as in Matthew Quick's 2009 novel, the filmic adaptation ultimately redeems its fan protagonist in a melodramatic manner one might expect from a big-budget Hollywood movie. Starring Bradley Cooper, Jennifer Lawrence, and Robert DeNiro, the film reaped the rewards of that expectation, earning more than $100 million at the box office and winning an Academy Award for Best Actress thanks to Lawrence's portrayal of Tiffany. But the film version of *Silver Linings Playbook* lacks many of the narrative elements and formal features that power the novel's more nuanced portrait of fandom and mental illness.

Narrator and protagonist Pat Peoples, renamed Pat Solatano in the film, is shown fully ensconced in Eagles fandom and, to a lesser extent, reading the books on Nikki's syllabus with an eye to self-improvement. But the very process of representing these actions externally—via third-person camera portrayal instead of first-person diary entry—reduces the complexity with which Solatano self-consciously assigns value to those activities. In other words, the way in which he incorporates these narratives into his sense of self, and the degree to which they can address his psychological trauma, are limited by the generic conventions of the dramatic film in a way that they were not in Quick's pages. Further bound to a melodramatic conclusion, Russell's movie, like a conventional recap of a sporting event or an accounting of corporate profits, seems only to care about the final score—that the home teams, in this case the Philadelphia Eagles and Pat Solatano, come away with the win.

At the crux of this impulse to turn Quick's conciliatory silver linings into the triumphant sunshine of a Hollywood ending—and the driver of capital both on screen and with regard to the film's reception—is the character of Pat Solatano Sr., played by Robert DeNiro. Sixteen years removed from his turn as Gil Renard in *The Fan*, DeNiro's portrayal of the elder Eagles fan exemplifies the film's impulse to mitigate the negative outcomes associated with pathological fandom's relationship to masculinity, in part by connecting economic prosperity to positive paternal behavior. In Quick's novel, Pat Peoples Sr. is marked as a man whose mania in life, as in sports, is no less pronounced than his recently institutionalized son. Violent intimidation determines his power in the household. Banned for life from his beloved Philadelphia Eagles' football stadium because he "lost it, attacked [a] Dallas fan, and beat him within an inch of his life. [Pat Peoples Sr. was] arrested, convicted of aggravated assault, and incarcerated for three months."[30] Peoples Jr. recognizes that his father's unsavory outbursts "make him sound crazy," and at one point in the novel, the elder Peoples is so enraged he destroys his television.[31] The notion that sports can function as a masculine bonding space in which "individual success, male-male bonds, the reaffirmation of the father and the rejection of the feminine, [can] be comfortably accommodated" is evident in Quick's novel only via transmission of trauma.[32] The film version's father figure, Pat Solatano Sr., by contrast, is driven by mania of a seemingly much more justifiable sort. While his supposed capacity for violence in the form of the stadium ban is briefly mentioned in the film (Pat Jr. calls him "the explosion guy"), the fandom Solatano Sr. manifests on screen is characterized by compulsive disorder of the type that trades in hyperorganization and routinization rather than violent outbursts.[33] Obsessed with lucky handkerchiefs, the particular way in which the television remotes are held during the game, and the order of the envelopes in which he collects bets for his book-making business (an illegal practice that Pat Peoples Sr. does not partake in), Pat Solatano Sr. comes across as quirky, not intimidating.

The transformation of Pat Peoples Sr. into the more palatable Pat Solatano Sr. does not lessen the realism of the fan father figure as a character—resisting the assumption that sports fan behavior is necessarily violent and uncritical is one of the core purposes of this book, after all. Rather, DeNiro's friendlier patriarch diminishes the potency of the context in which the narrative's protagonist, Pat Jr., reflects on his own fan behaviors.

Rather than a reminder of the violent tendencies and mental illness he is trying to overcome, Pat Solatano Sr. is a marker of positive possibility for his son. Yes, the elder Solatano runs an illegal operation as a bookmaker, but he claims to do so only in order to garner enough capital to start a legitimate business: a family restaurant. To heighten the stakes, in the events that provide the film's climax, Solatano Sr. also wagers all of his available funds on a prop bet involving an Eagles game and the results of Solatano Jr.'s dance competition with Tiffany (something Peoples Sr. does not do in the novel). But this potentially ruinous behavior is not only rewarded with capital when both are successful in their exploits, but in intimacy with his troubled son—in whom he puts his faith and confidence and with whom he endows the strength of character to recognize his love for Tiffany and to move on from Nikki at film's end. Solatano Sr. is, in other words, a bridge to Pat Jr.'s individual happy ending. Yet this happy ending is fully accessible to both men, Stanfill rightly posits in the abstract, "because their phenotypic whiteness carries a cultural expectation of an innate capacity for self-control."[34] The Solatanos' redemption from pathological fan stereotype is grounded in an assumption that the sports fan *can* leverage the homosocial bonds fostered by fandom to right the ship and triumph, provided the fan in question is white, male, and heterosexual, of course.

"Happy Is Family! Children!": Fandom as Heterosexual Failure

Pat Solatano Sr.'s economic reward for investing in his son's success in the film version of *Silver Linings Playbook* isn't the only measure by which his masculinity is presented as an ideal toward which his son must strive: the elder fan's patriarchal benevolence is also represented in his relationship to his wife, Dolores. Rather than abusive and strained, as the Peoples's marriage is depicted in Quick's novel, the Solatanos' relationship is nurturing and supportive. They present a model of heterosexual coupling to which the younger Solatano, recently institutionalized because of his violent outburst toward his wife's lover—and thus implicitly a double failure, both for beating the man with whom his wife committed adultery and for being the kind of man who is cheated on in the first place—can aspire. The younger Solatano's egregious failure to hew to the mode of heteronormative coupling provided by his parents marks his masculinity as aberrant. But since Solatano's father is an even bigger Eagles fan than he is, the relation of this aberrance to Solatano's fandom is not immediately or obviously apparent.

In *The Fan*, by contrast, Gil Renard's fandom seems to be primarily stigmatized as a rather stereotypical outgrowth of toxic masculinity: he misogynistically refers to Jewel, a female sports radio host, as a "bitch"; completely disregards his ex-wife on parenting matters; excoriates his son Richie for being hesitant about little league tryouts; and screams profanities at players and fans while at the Giants game.[35] Renard thus fully reifies Kibby's notion (via Michael Messner) that nostalgia preserves sport as "the most significant arena in which males could prove their power over, and separation from, the feminine."[36] Abandoning Richie at the ballpark in order to meet with an important client (who, in turn, skips out on him), Renard returns to find his son missing. He then forcibly enters his hysterical ex-wife's house to find the boy distraught, returned home by a concerned fan. Over the screams of his ex-wife and her new partner—both locked out of the room—Renard and his son share a short-lived father-son moment of tenderness. But it is the last sympathetic scene the film affords its title character. After losing his job the following day, something breaks in Renard and the film heads toward its macabre terror plot.

In a film that is hardly shy about its phallic imagery—Renard offers a tiny knife called the "Little Pecker" to at least three characters in the film, as if announcing his metaphorical impotence—the scene immediately following Renard's firing makes director Tony Scott's message of failed masculinity explicit. As Renard lies despondent on his bed, listening to sports radio, the host interviews a "doctor" who intones: "In a Freudian sense . . . the catcher is the father, and the son is the pitcher . . . the bat speaks for itself, and of course the ball is the ejaculate."[37] Comic though this cartoonish representation of baseball on Freudian terms may seem, the film doesn't play it for laughs. After a restraining order is filed against Renard and he is kicked out of his son's baseball practice, a similar scene depicts him throwing knives at the wall as the explicit Nine Inch Nails song "Closer" plays, with lead singer Trent Reznor wailing about wanting to sexually violate his listener. Renard's misplaced obsession with professional baseball—the simulacra of the phallus—having unmanned him, the crazed fan resorts to violence to restore his masculine agency.

Asked in a radio interview why he is slumping, Bobby Rayburn blames it on having lost his lucky uniform number (11) when he signed with the Giants. The slugger indicates that he needs "all the help [he] can get" in talking some sense into Juan Primo, the Giants' other star outfielder and the player who wears lucky number "once" ("eleven" in Spanish). Hearing this, the desperate Renard takes matters into his own knife-wielding hands. Confronting Primo in the steam room of the team hotel, Renard stabs him to death. Murdering the naked player as the song "Closer" again blares in the background, with its lyrical focus on fucking as a mode of domination, Renard's fan obsession is queered. Linking fans' desires to "get intimate with all that profundity," as David Foster Wallace put it, to Renard's desire to fuck and kill first Juan Primo and subsequently Bobby Rayburn, *The Fan* homophobically stigmatizes his failed masculinity by associating fan behavior with a malignant and violent manifestation of homosexual desire.[38]

Renard's masculine sexual inadequacy and implicit queerness is also a failure of heteronormative family relations, via his own son, and Tony Scott's dystopian film soon maps this patriarchal relationship onto *The Fan*'s campaign of terror toward Rayburn. After a period of mourning for Juan Primo, Rayburn begins to excel, and the team rises. When asked the reason for his success by Jewel, the sports radio host, the star says: "I wish I knew." Renard, listening at home, exclaims "That's it!" and decides that he must make Rayburn grateful for his murderous assist.[39] Stalking Rayburn to his beachfront home, Renard watches with binoculars as the slugger's son, Shawn, begins to flounder while swimming in the surf. Rushing to intervene, Renard saves Shawn from drowning. Rayburn, thanking Renard profusely, invites him into the house. When Rayburn asks if he likes baseball, Renard says: "I'm not obsessed with it or anything. Are you a player? Barry Bonds?"[40] Relieved that his son's rescuer is "not one of those die-hard baseball guys," Rayburn asserts that "those guys are losers." Incredulous, Renard asks: "Aren't the fans what it's all about?" Rayburn answers, tellingly:

The fans are like women. When you're hitting, they love you. When you're not, they'd just as soon spit on you as look at you . . . they don't understand that you're the same person whether you're hitting or you're not. You know? The only person you should play for is yourself.[41]

Simultaneously impugning women as fickle *and* emasculating Renard by association with this misogynistic stereotype, Rayburn's wholly self-centered ethos of athletic excellence also ostensibly endorses the boot-straps model of capitalist uplift. Read another way, however, we might understand "play[ing] for yourself" as more accurately Renard's modus operandi than even the millionaire athlete, insofar as it indulges Renard's masturbatory dream notion that he could still compete as a ballplayer, rather than Rayburn's lived economic reality. Renard's fandom represents a failure of heterosexuality then, not merely via misogyny, queer desire, or patriarchal insufficiency then, but because it is fundamentally onanistic. Fandom is therein marked as a an infantile immersion "in the realm of desire," as Ross Pudaloff puts it, much as the rapture of nineteenth-century novel readers were linked to masturbation by overzealous moralists.[42]

The stigma of self-gratification also marks *Big Fan*'s portrayal of fan behavior as fostering aberrant sexuality. Having departed his "box" in the parking garage and returned to his room in his mother's house—decorated with a life-size poster of idolized football star Quantrell Bishop—Paul Aufiero, aka "Paul from Staten Island," calls the "Sports Dawg" and delivers his previously written rant against "Philadelphia Phil," an Eagles fan who often calls the New York station to taunt Giants fans. Talking over the plaintive objections of his mother in the next room, Aufiero finishes his monologue and hangs up the phone, only to immediately call his friend and fellow listener, Sal, who informs him that he was "on fire."[43] Satisfied, Aufiero climbs into bed, gets out a bottle of lotion and pulls up the covers to masturbate. Directly connecting sexual satisfaction to praise of his fan identity, *Big Fan* positions both as lonely enterprises. Aufiero's masturbation in response to his friend's praise also exemplifies, as Stanfill puts it, the pathologizing notion that "the homosociality of fandom forever threatens to collapse into homosexuality."[44]

The ostensible shame of fannish self-gratification is reinforced later in the film, when Aufiero's mother, excoriating him for being single, yells, "I know exactly who you date! Your hand!"[45] Unlike the athletes whose muscular exploits convey manly success, Aufiero's obsessive fandom manifests masculine sexual failure. While many athlete-centric sports films similarly "emphasize[s] male homosocial relationships" via the locker room, "establish[ing] male-only social groupings and prioritize[ing] male/male friendships over cross gender relationships," Sal and Aufiero's bond isn't one of respite, or sanctuary, from a modern world that delimits masculine behavior.[46] Rather it has become a primary mode of existence and identification: there are no women-as-objectified markers of heter-onormative success waiting for them outside the locker room. All the two fans have is each other, and the Giants.

The film's figuration of fans' homosocial intimacy as in conflict with heteronormative maleness is only exacerbated when Aufiero and Sal seize an opportunity to interact with Quantrell Bishop in person. Seeing the All-Pro linebacker and his friends filling up at a Staten Island gas station, the fans follow their hero's car to a Manhattan strip club. Entering the club despite their complaints about its stiff cover charge and expensive drinks—an indicator of the fans' economic inadequacy—the two sit at the periphery of the player's circle, rebuffing lap dances in order to gawk at the athlete. Ignored, the fans decide to buy Bishop a drink. When Bishop turns down the offering, Aufiero and Sal approach the football star in pursuit of personal affirmation. At first received warmly, the interaction turns sour when Aufiero and Sal indicate that they followed the football star's vehicle from Staten Island. Crossing a perceived boundary of polite behavior by stalking Bishop, the revelation of this information leads to a physical confrontation. The brief fight concludes with Bishop punching Aufiero and knocking him unconscious.

Aufiero awakens three days later in the hospital, his left eye completely blackened. When he learns that it is Monday—the day after the Giants' game—he immediately asks Sal, at his bedside, "How did we do?"[47] A solemn shaking of the head is Sal's only reply. Bishop has been suspended from the team pending a criminal investigation, for which Aufiero's testimony is required, as the police detective puts is, to "nail the son of a bitch."[48] Visibly troubled by this phrasing, Aufiero claims that his memory is foggy and tells the investigator that he will get back to him at a later date. But his problem is existential, not one of mental clarity. As his first-person plural phrasing regarding the Giants' fortunes indicates, Aufiero, like many fans, feels a deeply personal connection with his chosen NFL team. To damage the team's fortunes by impacting the availability of any player, let alone one of its stars and his favorite athlete, seems to him a betrayal of his own self-interest.

Aufiero's subsequent decision not to cooperate with the police investigation—maintaining that that he himself was drunk and partly to blame—isn't the end of his difficulty regarding the assault, however. Aufiero's brother Jeff, a personal injury lawyer, first urges him to charge Bishop in civil court and then, when rebuffed, files the lawsuit on Aufiero's behalf, claiming that his brother is "not mentally competent to make decisions for [himself.]"[49] The pathologizing notion that obsessive fandom is a form of mental illness is thus literally realized in the film. When Aufiero learns of the lawsuit and furiously protests that he is mentally sound, Jeff responds: "You're a 36-year-old man who lives at home with his mother, who depends on her for food, for laundry, and countless basic fucking life necessities, alright? On paper you're basically a fucking vegetable!"[50] Explicitly articulating the ways in which Aufiero has failed to live up to the normative expectations of American masculinity, Jeff's use of the word "vegetable" to convey both mental passivity and physical dependence effectively characterizes his brother's fandom as a drain on personal *and* familial possibilities, a net negative that affects far more than one person. This figuration of Aufiero's economic failure also plays in to the means by which, per Aaron Baker, "commercial sports have consistently been portrayed as disproving the idea of a socially constructed identity. Sports movies at least in part follow this representational tendency."[51] Whether or not Aufiero is a success, his brother, neoliberal popular rhetoric, and the world of sports asserts, is a mere matter of his own effort, and has nothing to do with his circumstances.

As for Aufiero's mother; she is more concerned with normalizing her son's behavior than her lost resources. After she interrupts one of his calls to "The Sports Dawg"—in which he characterizes the violent interaction with Bishop as "an unfortunate misunderstanding"[52]—the two argue about the nature of happiness:

Aufiero: Why are you doing this to me?

His Mother: I'm not doing nothing to you, you do it all to yourself!

A: I'm sick of you treating me like a baby!

M: You are a baby, with your calls and your little playmate Sal, why don't you grow up and get a life!

A: I have a life!

M: No you don't!

A: I'm happy with my life!

M: No you're not!

A: I think I would know!

M: Happy is family, children.

A: Says you!

M: Says everybody! There's basic stuff, every person needs! You're brother has them, your sister has them!

A: I don't want what they've got! I don't want it! I don't want it! I don't want it![53]

This exchange is the film's crucible, the moment in which *Big Fan* most clearly recognizes and implicitly sanctions an alternate value system for fans. Asserting his autonomy and indicating his own careful consideration of the patriarchal standard his family, and indeed society at large, expects, Aufiero uses the refrain of "I don't want it!" to punctuate his rejection of the notion that "basic stuff" is in fact "basic," or even necessary for personal fulfillment. Intractable though it may seem, Aufiero values the success of the Giants as his own, cherishes the creative outlet contributing to sports radio provides him (it's his authorial contribution, in this case), and finds in his homosocial relationship with Sal satisfaction, not disappointment. As in its presentation of economic viability, *Big Fan* presents a more complicated picture of the outcomes of fandom, even when such behavior manifests as failed masculinity.

As in *The Fan* and *Big Fan*, *Fever Pitch* intimates that the fan's investment inevitably infantilizes him. The winking romcom cliché that is Ben's surname in the film, "Wrightman," is troubled by more than jokes about the size of his income. Befitting the "dumb white guy comed[y's]" generic impulse to "undermine and satirize masculine prowess," the Farrelly

Brothers' representation of fan loserdom "ask[s] audiences to laugh at their nerdish characters' failed masculinity, a process that still upholds those same ideals as natural and desirable."[54] Though Ben is a teacher, he is not a respected adult authority figure to his students, but more of a peer, depicted laughing and joking with them. In a scene played for laughs, Ben is shown seeking relationship advice from an unseen interlocutor who turns out to be Ryan, a kid on the baseball team he coaches. To Ben's incredulous assertion that Lindsey "expects me to miss a Yankees game," Ryan measuredly responds: "you love the Sox. But have they ever loved you back?"[55] But it doesn't matter to Ben if his love is unrequited. Turning down an opportunity to meet Lindsey's family early in the film, Ben instead travels to Florida for spring training with the Red Sox. As Lindsey watches in horror from her parents' couch in Baltimore, Ben is interviewed on ESPN. Steve Levy—an actual ESPN anchor and one of several sports personalities with cameos in the film—picks Ben out of a crowd of boisterous fans and asks: "Where do the Sox rank in terms of importance in your life?" To which Ben responds: "I say Red Sox, sex, and breathing!" Subsequently asked what he does for a living, Ben exclaims: "I'm a teacher. I mold young minds!"[56] The implication is obvious—fandom has reduced Ben to a fool, a teacher with less maturity than the young minds he purports to mold. As Lindsey's dad puts it from the couch, ostensibly unaware of the identity of the crazed fan in question because he has yet to meet Ben: "Can you believe this asshole?"[57]

As the metonymic representation of Ben as an "asshole" indicates, Ben's fandom hinders his heterosexuality by stunting his sexual maturity, rendering him a child or a hormonal teen. When Lindsey invites Ben to go to Paris and he declines, citing some important upcoming games for the Red Sox, she breaks down and reveals that she is "late" and may be pregnant (it is later revealed to be a false alarm). Lindsey had planned "to go to Paris and . . . tell you there . . . but no, you don't see us tangled up in the sheets with the Eiffel Tower in the window, you see the Mariners are coming and Pedro is pitching Friday night." Ben responds, characteristically, "Saturday. Schilling is on Friday," before admitting, "I should have reacted differently."[58] Beyond matters of inappropriate affect, Ben's arrested development is also manifested materially. When preparing to meet Lindsey's parents at last, Ben emerges from his Red Sox–festooned room in a Hawaiian shirt and a jock strap. They share a laugh and Lindsey remarks, only half-jokingly: "This is not a man's closet! . . . You have one pair of dress shoes! You're like a man-boy! Half man, half boy. You should see the way my sister's husband dresses. He had a professional come in and do his closet. It's like: suit, suit, suit, suit."[59] Setting aside the class assumptions about having "a professional . . . do" one's closet, the message is clear: Ben is an overgrown child. And he owns up to it: "Sometimes I like to be 11 years old," he tells Lindsey, "I like to be a part of something that's bigger than me. . . . It's good for your soul to invest in something you that you can't control."[60]

The only thing Ben can control is his degree of dedication to that investment, and Lindsey asks him to compromise his zeal. Late in the film, after a memorable night out, Ben realizes he has missed one of the most remarkable comebacks in Red Sox history. Upset and blaming Lindsey, he proclaims his bona fides as a fan of "23 years! Do you still care about anything you cared about 23 years ago? How about 10? How about 5? Name a single thing that you've cared about for 23 years." This measure of dedication signals to Lindsey Ben's failed masculinity, as she retorts: "23 years ago I was 7, and if I still wanted to marry Scott Baio I would think that my life went terribly wrong. I just thought tonight was so different, and you broke my heart, Ben."[61] Measured against Lindsey's girlhood desire for then-teen heartthrob Scott Baio, Ben's Red Sox fandom is overtly marked as childish. Read another way, however, given the film's—and indeed the larger romcom genre's—concern with heterosexual marriage as the desired "happy ending," Lindsey's desire to "marry Scott Baio" is still a desire to marry, even if Ben isn't a teen heartthrob. The core problem with Ben's fandom itself isn't his childish passion itself, per se, it is his unwillingness to adapt or redirect those childhood desires in order to settle for anything less than Scott Baio, as Lindsey has. As Lindsey puts it: "All those things that you feel for that team, I feel them, too. For you."[62] She is willing to adapt the desires of her fantasies to meet her reality, and Ben, at least until he demonstrates his willingness to sell his season tickets at film's end, is not.

But Ben's failed masculinity is also presented as something other than arrested development—it is also framed as queer when he attempts to explain his fandom to Lindsey early in the film, through the implied construct of the closet. The two initially meet in the winter, and when Ben reveals that he will be going to spring training, instead of meeting Lindsey's family, he feels the need to come out, in a manner of speaking. "Okay, I've been avoiding this," he remarks worriedly, "There's something you don't know about me . . . I am a Red Sox fan. I'm like a big, big Red Sox fan . . . it's a passion. I mean, it's a very big part of my life. And it's been a problem with me and women."[63] Having confessed to his fandom on terms that mark it as affecting his performance of heterosexuality, Ben is pleased to find that, at least in this early moment in the film, Lindsey is understanding of his obsession. Moments later, as if to reify his commitment to heteronormativity, Ben gets down on one knee, extends to her a small jewelry box, and opens it to reveal . . . tickets. "Lindsey, will you go to opening day with me?" he asks. She says "yes," enthusiastically, as the music swells, but by the end of the film Lindsey is turning down an actual marriage proposal from Ben. "This isn't you," she tells him, "this is the other guy. . . . It's October. [The Red Sox are] one game from elimination. You're becoming winter guy again. I already know I like winter guy, it's summer guy that broke my heart."[64] Lindsey has come to realize that Ben's apprehension at "outing" himself as a Red Sox fan—and figuring that fandom as a potential threat to their heterosexual coupling—was well-warranted. And it is this rejection of "winter guy" that finally motivates Ben to agree to sell his tickets.[65]

Silver Linings Playbook's Pat Solatano is also stuck in teenager mode, both mentally and in material terms, jobless and living with his parents upon his release from the mental health facility. Presented, at least in the film version, with his parents' idyllic heteronormative example and obsessed with his own failed relationship with his ex-wife, Nikki, Pat's immaturity connects his failed masculinity to his fandom via his interactions with Tiffany. Unable to present the audience with the diary entries and written correspondence that power the book, the film relies on an incredible awkwardness in their affective relationship to one another. Both insist they are still wed to their former partners, though neither is legally married and Tiffany's husband is deceased. Pat bluntly dismisses Tiffany's sexual addiction as aberrant without titillation, after she asserts: "I hate the fact that you wore a football jersey to dinner because I hate football, but you can fuck me if you turn the lights off, okay?"[66] That neither initially recognizes nor sanctions their potential romantic coupling—as all the married people around them do—speaks both to their individual battles with mental illness and to Pat's inability to figure his fandom as something other than a redemptive narrative ineluctably tied to an eventual reconciliation with Nikki.

Since the *Silver Linings* film's narrative goals are more akin to *Fever Pitch*'s romcom imperatives than the more ambiguous takeaways of Matthew Quick's *Silver Linings* novel, Pat Solatano eventually manages to properly contextualize his Eagles fandom—as a social endeavor rather than a narrative of existential importance. Thus he ultimately chooses participation in his dance competition with Tiffany over watching the Eagles and rejects an offer of reconciliation with Nikki. The film concludes with a heteronormative patriarchal tableau in which Pat and Tiffany, like Pat's parents, along with his brother and sister-in-law, gather to watch the Eagles game. Properly contextualized, the film ultimately suggests that fandom can strengthen masculine heterosexual ideals, rather than detract from them. But there is something else that *Silver Linings*' redemptive nuclear family tableau obscures or at least represents as completely unremarkable: the film's people of color. Pat's repaired masculinity only thrives in a family environment that is notably, and intentionally, white.

"Some Big Black Moulinyan Jackoff Asshole That Gave You Brain Damage": Fandom as a Failure of White Supremacy

Though the four films treat race on overtly varying terms, all present fandom as based in whiteness and buttressed by structural racism. Of the four, Tony Scott's *The Fan* is the least subtle, explicitly positioning fan pathology as manifesting anti-black racism. Having rescued Bobby Rayburn's son, Shawn, and been told by the African American slugger that "fans are like women" in that they are fickle and disloyal, Gil Renard seeks to return to his idealized childhood glory. With DeNiro's gleeful glint in his eye, Renard asks to pitch to Rayburn, to prove that he has "a couple innings left." As they play on the beach, Rayburn asserts that Primo's death had nothing to do with his recent successes, except insofar as it reminded him that baseball is "just a game," that "we're not curing cancer." Enraged, Renard drops the pretense of civility. Demanding Rayburn admit that he's "happy that [Primo is] dead," and that he provide "a simple 'thank you' . . . for the man who lays down the sacrifice," he throws the ball at the All-Star's head.[67] It is the first violent act that pivots the film toward its conclusion of racial terror. Having saved Rayburn's son from the surf, symbolically reifying his patriarchy, Renard attempts to leverage the power of white supremacy over the black athlete.

Frightened and upset, Rayburn calls it a night and returns inside. Minutes later, after brushing his teeth, Rayburn goes to check on Shawn. The boy has disappeared, taken—along with Rayburn's Hummer—by Renard. Once he kidnaps Shawn, Renard's nostalgic attempt to reestablish his "mis-remembered boyhood," also becomes more explicitly racialized.[68] By equating the purported selfishness of the modern player with an African American star, the "links between whiteness and love of the game," as David J. Leonard puts it, have been signaled for much of the film.[69] But when Renard threatens to kill Shawn unless Rayburn hits a home run and "tell[s] the 50 million viewers that this home run is dedicated to Gil: a true fan,"[70] he uses the terror of family separation—one of the insidious practices of human bondage—to signal white supremacy.[71] Having also quite literally cut the brown skin of Rayburn's Latino teammate, Juan Primo—and left a piece of Primo's shoulder (branded with coveted number 11) in Rayburn's freezer—Renard's stated desire to restore respect for fans is also obviously also an attempt to use violence to assert the dominance of white men.

The Fan thus represents the danger of fandom not merely as a delusion that emasculates and disempowers, but also as one that produces explicit violence and racism. Intended or not, Tony Scott's film implies that the implicit injustices of the status quo—of systemic racism, misogyny, and structural violence hidden in plain sight, all in service of global capital—is the rightful alternative. Only what Ben Carrington calls the "static definition of racism" gets to "'count' as racism" in *The Fan*, and is marked as pathological in Renard.[72] After Shawn is kidnapped, a flurry of action sequences ensue—including Renard's murder and on-field impersonation of a Major League umpire—after which the eponymous fan is shot to death on the pitcher's mound. Bobby Rayburn survives, despite being stabbed by Renard, and his son is rescued. How can the survival of the African American millionaire athlete represent a return to the white, patriarchal, neoliberal order? Easily, if one accepts that, as David L. Andrews has argued of Michael Jordan, black superstars "pander to the racial insecurities and paranoia of the white majority primarily because of their ability to shed their black identities in promotional contexts," their "racially neutered image displac[ing] racial codes onto other black bodies."[73] Renard is marked as pathological, at least in part, because his racism is of the old, visibly violent type, rather than the less overt structures of white authority maintained under the auspices of "new racism." And Rayburn is implicitly a "good" black man because his primary mode of labor, athletic competition, is visibly meritocratic.

What's more, Rayburn is easily read as a correction for the famously pathologized absent black father figure detailed in the infamous Moynihan Report and often reproduced in popular culture. *The Fan* doesn't end when Renard is shot to death by police at Candlestick Park, but when Shawn and Bobby Rayburn are reunited in a different stadium: the little league park where, a yellowing newspaper clipping reveals, a home run by Renard won the youth-league city championship. Below a picture of the triumphant boy *Fan*, a subhead reads: "local son hoisted up by team after home run." After Rayburn and his son embrace and proclaim their love for one another, Trent D'arby's song "Letting Go," written for the film, plays over the credits. Obsession over another's exploits is never healthy, the song intones, only surrender to the normal rhythms of life: at the core of which are familial intimacies like the embrace of a father and son. Renard's fan-based failure in heteronormative family relations is corrected by Rayburn's example of nurturing fatherhood.

While *The Fan* grimly writes the fan's violence against athletes of color into the narrative, *Big Fan*'s violence is perpetrated against the fan. But Aufiero's masculine failure and his decision not to get legal revenge against his favorite athlete is also marked as a failure of whiteness.[74] Absent his own father, and traumatized by his family's lack of respect for his life choices, *Big Fan*'s Paul Aufiero is forced to reckon with his feelings for Quantrell Bishop as he recovers from the injuries the star linebacker inflicted upon him. Morose, Aufiero daydreams about his favorite player. A vivid sequence shows the African American star linebacker against a black backdrop, evocatively lit in his blue and gray uniform on a lush grass field. The eroticism of this moment is obvious, visually representing Ben Carrington's assertion that the "black athlete is . . . positioned as a site for voyeuristic admiration . . . controlled by a complex process of objectification and sexualization that once again renders the threat of negritude controllable to the white patriarchy."[75] Cutting to a scene in which Aufiero gazes at the poster of Bishop in his bedroom, the dream sequence connects the favored athlete's mute black body to a place of intimacy for the white fan. This transition thus emphasizes the problematic nature of Aufiero's narrative control over the athlete via preferred representation, rather than the attributes and complications that Quantrell Bishop, the real person, poses for him. It represents fans' connection to preferred narratives in sports, as well as the real-life context that leads so many to resist conceptualizing sport on narrative terms.

But Bishop's blackness is more than a matter of sexualized narrative fantasy for Aufiero; it also figures prominently into his family's denigration of his fan identity. Irate that a lawsuit has been filed against Bishop on his behalf and without his consent—on account of him amounting, as his brother Jeff puts it, to little more than a "vegetable"—Aufiero vociferously asserts his agency. Questioning that agency as a matter of fan practice, Jeff also racializes Paul's fan pursuits, retorting: "I know you're a fan of this guy, but you've got stop looking at him as some kind of fucking hero, and start looking at him some big black moulinyan jackoff asshole that gave you brain damage!"[76] Derived from the Italian word for eggplant, "moulinyan" is widely recognized as a racial slur used by Italian Americans to refer to people of color. Though Aufiero doesn't comment on his brother's use of the derogatory term—he responds only by asserting that his "brain is fine!"—its inclusion is particularly significant, signaling racial intolerance on several registers. First, and most basically, the term's history marks it as part of the process by which Italian Americans, like Irish Americans, Jewish Americans, and other descendants of immigrant groups not initially recognized as "white" by earlier incarnations of Anglo American cultural arbiters, separated and elevated themselves as an ethnic group by denigrating and asserting their superiority to African Americans. For Aufiero to consider a black man his hero is, his brother implies, to disregard or undo the work Italian Americans have done to mark themselves as "white" and reap the benefits of white supremacist social norms and structures. On another register, the slur's eggplant etymology connects it, as a phallically shaped vegetable, to both the stereotype of black men that marks them as hyper-sexual physical specimens—connoted here also by the prefix "big black" and the sexual suffixes "jackoff" and "asshole"—and to the notion that Paul himself, by virtue of his loss of consciousness upon being assaulted and lack of interest in patriarchal social norms of masculine agency, is himself a "vegetable." Paul's fan passion, Jeff's racist remark implies, marked him as a victim before any assault took place. By looking upon a black man as a hero, instead of a "moulinyan jackoff asshole," Aufiero failed in his duty to uphold the structure of racial dominance in which black men are disposable and white men are the heroes.

Enraged as Aufiero is at his brother's usurpation of his agency in the matter of the lawsuit, it is ultimately his fan rival, "Philadelphia Phil," who sends him over the edge: from anger into action. Aufiero cringes as "Philadelphia Phil" taunts him over the airwaves of his favorite sports radio station, revealing to "The Sports Dawg" audience that regular caller "Paul from Staten Island" is in fact the person Quantrell Bishop allegedly assaulted at the club. Phil then invites Aufiero to "switch over" to Eagles fandom and join him at a Philadelphia bar in advance of the Eagles' big matchup with the Giants: an invitation that shifts the film toward a denoue-ment designed to thwart the viewer's expectations.[77]

Taking his mother's car without permission, Aufiero drives to a sport-ing goods store, where he purchases a Philadelphia Eagles jersey along with silver and green face paint. Changing into the gear at a rest stop, a handgun bulges from Aufiero's pocket as he resumes driving down the highway toward Philadelphia. Seeking out Phil in a crowded bar, Aufiero recognizes his radio nemesis's voice and introduces himself as "Mark." He nods along as Phil shouts that he wants the Eagles "to mass fucking murder these motherfuckers" and refers to a blue-clad spectator shown on TV as "a giant fag! Not a Giant fan, but a Giant fag!"[78] Joining in as the Eagles fans shout further homophobic slogans like "Giants suck cock!" a pained expression crosses Aufiero's face. Finally, the game over and the Giants defeated, Phil gets up to use the restroom, exclaiming that he needs to call New York sports radio because he has a "big bag of salt that needs wounds for rubbing into."[79] Aufiero follows, pushing his way into the same stall as Phil, pointing a gun at him, and beginning this exchange:

Aufiero: "Be quiet. Quiet, okay? You didn't have to be mean."
Phil: "What are you talking about, mean?"
A: "Everybody's always so mean. . . . It wears me out."
P: "You got the wrong guy."
A: "No, I got the right guy."[80]

At that, Aufiero opens fire, hitting Philadelphia Phil multiple times in the chest. Horrified, Phil reaches up with his hands to feel the wounds, revealing a red-stained right hand. Seemingly surprised to still be conscious, Phil then lifts up his left hand to reveal . . . blue paint. Aufiero, still pointing what we have learned is a very realistic-looking paintball gun in Phil's direction, solemnly utters: "Eagles suck." Since the New York Giants' colors are blue and red, this azure revelation conveys—rather than murderous mania—Aufiero's undying loyalty to his chosen squad. Which isn't to say that this assault isn't a criminal act, merely that the film isn't interested in equating fan mania with blood lust. Since we have no notion of Aufiero's internal reasoning, like we do for Exley and Raab, the viewer can only extrapolate the narrative reasoning behind it.

While it is likely not an explicit homage to Tony Scott's vision of psychotic fan carnage at the conclusion of *The Fan*, this penultimate sequence in Robert D. Siegel's *Big Fan* certainly resonates with it. Though Aufiero's rage in extremis is directed toward a fellow fan and not the athlete with whom he previously found violent conflict, the notion that the perceived disrespect of others toward a super-fan—who otherwise enjoys the privileges that white males enjoy in American society—would drive him to lash out with deadly force is utterly believable given popular conceptions of fan pathology and the United States' extensive history of gun violence. Despite the film's rather morose tone, plot, and pacing, however, *Big Fan* subverts its viewers' expectations when the blue paint on Philadelphia Phil's chest and hands is revealed. Aufiero hasn't used deadly force, he merely conveyed its possibility to Phil. If fandom is not considered "real" enough to satisfy Aufiero's family's expectations for what dictates his life choices, neither then is the physical force with which his rage is manifested.

As if to double down on this subversive denouement, the film finishes with dark humor; after Aufiero flees the scene of his (unexpectedly non-deadly) crime and is tackled by police, the film cuts to a final scene that consists of Sal visiting Aufiero at a penitentiary. Both men are initially somber as they talk on phones from across a partition, Aufiero commenting that his mother has been to visit as well, but is "not really taking this too well."[81] Suddenly Sal's eyes light up, and he excitedly presses a crumpled scrap of newspaper up to the glass barrier. "It's out?" Aufiero asks incredulously.[82] "It" is the Giants' schedule for the upcoming football season, and the two proceed to prognosticate great success for their chosen squad. Proclaiming the slate "cake," Aufiero pauses on a game scheduled for November 20 against the New England Patriots: "I get out that week!," he exclaims, "Patsies are toast, there's no way we're losing with us in the parking lot!" Sal calls this prediction "totally realistic" before Aufiero utters the film's final line: "It's gonna be a great year."[83]

Big Fan's ending thus embraces the endless renewal of possibilities that the seasonal rhythm of sports promises, both for the team and the fan. Far from the macabre imagery and forewarning against obsession that closes *The Fan*, the ending of *Big Fan* is odd and humorous. It cannot be said to be entirely celebratory; the viewer is meant to both take seriously Aufiero's crime and laugh at the prospect that he and Sal are exultant over the release of a football schedule while he is still incarcerated. Still, transposed onto Aufiero's circumstances, their mood suggests in closing that perhaps fandom *can* and *does* fulfill people despite life situations that others might consider less than ideal. It argues, in effect, that fan attachment might not be much more delusional than the social bonds one builds through marriage or employment. Yet critical readers will rightly dampen this hopeful possibility somewhat by pointing out the privilege that Aufiero and Sal automatically enjoy as white men. In a nation that has criminalized blackness such that African American men are incarcerated at a grossly disproportionate rate and one in which white defendants regularly receive much more lenient sentences than their black counterparts convicted of the same crimes, the oddness and humorousness of Aufiero and Sal's interaction is indelibly supported by their whiteness. The further fact that the football-playing bodies they fetishize are largely black only adds to the racialized tableau: in the football locker room or the penitentiary, Aufiero does not belong, the film implies. He may be a loser by virtue of being a fan, but at least he is not black.

Tellingly, the two films inclined to more positive conclusions as to obsessive sports fandom's possible outcomes are the two that pay the least attention to race, at least overtly. *Fever Pitch*, for its part, is an almost entirely whitewashed film—there are no people of color in any of the major speaking roles. In one early scene, in which Ben's friends compete for a chance to go to a game with him, two African American friends appear in the background, watching nonplussed as Ben's three white friends dance awkwardly for Yankees tickets. They have no lines of dialogue. Because actual footage of the Red Sox's historic 2004 season is spliced between shots of Ben and Lindsey in the stands, baseball players of color appear in the film, of course, but none have speaking roles. All of Lindsey's female friends are ostensibly white, as are all of their partners. Almost all the students and teachers at Ben's school are white as well. And, most significantly given the fan context of the film, all of the members of Ben's "summer family" are white.[84] Though the group of Red Sox season ticket holders is diverse in other ways, including fans young and old, male and female, and even a pair of women that the film strongly hints are lesbians, none of the dozen or so members of this intimate fan group appear to be anything other than white. In *Fever Pitch*, as in the majority of American films, "when it goes unmentioned, whiteness is positioned as a default category, the center or the assumed norm on which everything else is based," as Harry Benshoff and Sean Griffin put it in *America on Film*.[85] The conspicuous lack of diversity among Ben's "summer family" is meant to be utterly unremarkable in just this way—the fact that all of the people wealthy (or in Ben's case lucky) enough to sit in such a prime location are white is not meant to be examined or second-guessed. In authorizing and signaling her own incorporation into Ben's Red Sox fandom, Lindsey does not complicate this tableau of whiteness as the default—nor did she *ever* threaten it, despite her difficulties accepting Ben's dedication to the Sox as a defining aspect of his masculinity. Given Boston's fraught history of race and racism—basketball legend Bill Russell called the city "a fleamarket of racism" in his autobiography—*Fever Pitch*'s conspicuous whiteness and lack of consideration of race and racism is notable, if somewhat predictable, given the "color-blind" rhetoric prevalent in much sports fan discourse.[86] But Ben's redemption is also connected to his whiteness, Stanfill rightly argues, since popular conceptions of "whiteness depend . . . on self control" and thus "fans who are white men are . . . represented as fully able to 'achieve' normative white, heterosexual, masculine self-control, as their deviance comes from correctably bad decisions."[87] Ben can overcome the deviance of his Red Sox super-fandom and reassert control such that he "gets the girl" in the end, the film suggests, in part because such control was always inherent in his white masculinity.

Silver Linings Playbook, for its part, includes two prominent characters of color: Danny, Solatano's friend from the mental rehabilitation institution, and Cliff, his therapist. In addition, Solatano's favorite Eagles player, DeSean Jackson, whose jersey he receives as a gift from his brother, is African American (as is his equivalent in the novel version, Hank Baskett). Yet each of these characters, while significant, is ultimately rendered peripheral to the tableau of familial whiteness that concludes the film. Danny, who arrives at the Solatano residence on the lam from the mental institution, is rendered a kind of pet by Pat Sr., who comes to believe that Pat Jr.'s friend brings the Eagles a measure of luck when he sits in the right place, holding the television remotes in a particular way. Returned into the institution, Danny reemerges later in the film as comic relief, picking up on the romantic tension between Tiffany and Solatano at a dance practice and dancing suggestively with Tiffany before telling both to "black . . . up" their routine.[88] Portrayed in this way, Danny—played by well-known comedic actor Chris Tucker—effectively fills a variety of stereotypes of black men: as runaway slaves, as house negroes, and as inherently physical and hypersexual beings. In conjunction with Tucker's hyperactive affect and laugh lines, the cumulative effect is to render Danny no less peripheral than DeSean Jackson, Solatano's favorite player. Both are stock types, beloved but only for their usefulness in allowing Solatano to articulate his fandom and reclaim his identity.

Unlike Danny, whose similar battles with mental illness mark him as someone Pat can position himself as superior to, Cliff, by virtue of being a court-appointed therapist, is necessarily an authority figure for the recuperating protagonist. The South Asian American mental health professional exercises his power over Solatano before their first meeting, playing the song that triggers his violent outbursts.[89] This puts the two at odds, but their relationship soon warms when Cliff reveals that he is an Eagles fan and feels that Solatano's favorite player, DeSean Jackson, "is the man."[90] Sanctioning Eagles fan identity as a path to a positive mental health outcome, Cliff also urges Pat to move on from Nikki and to pursue a relationship with Tiffany. Nudging Pat toward the patriarchal fan tableau that is the film's conclusion, Cliff also complicates this outcome midway through the film when he arrives to a tailgate Solatano is attending, along with his fellow members of the "Asian Invasion" Eagles fan club. The group of Asian fans, whose camaraderie with Pat Peoples and his white friends fuels the book protagonist's notion that "all it really takes for different people to get along is a common rooting interest and a few beers," augur in the film those same warm feelings but also inadvertently trigger Solatano's violent impulses.[91] While the fight in the stadium parking lot also appears in the novel, there it is triggered by the rivalry between Eagles and Giants fans. In the film, instead of an interteam fan squabble, it is an intrateam conflict based on racism. When white Eagles fans start accosting and attacking members of the Asian Invasion, Solatano can't stop himself from flying into a fit of rage in defense of his therapist and his friends. The conflagration of Solatano's mental illness in the form of violence is thus mitigated by his defense of someone wronged by racism. Even still, like the manifestation of Danny as Solatano's "black friend," this incident, along with Cliff's attendant sanctioning of Solatano's rehabilitation through his new romantic partnership with Tiffany, ultimately serve as window dressing. Solatano's fractured masculinity is only truly rehabilitated by his adaptation of his fandom to the notably white, heterosexual, patriarchal space of the family presented at the film's end. Cliff, like Danny, may help him along the way, but neither serves as meaningful parts of the final apparatus of Solatano's rehabilitated identity.

Though some of them are able to redeem themselves, the fan protagonists of *The Fan*, *Big Fan*, *Fever Pitch*, and *Silver Linings Playbook* are invariably emasculated on account of their obsession. In their economic shortcomings, heterosexual inadequacy, and failure to hew to the dictates of hegemonic white supremacy, each fan fails to some degree to manifest their masculinity according to the prevailing dictates of American popular culture. Even so, in spite of themselves, these films also inescapably render these fans' self-reflection and textual productivity. And though they are incapable of capturing the introspective agency that powers that production, these films do not—or cannot—destroy that agency even if they feminize and pathologize it.

Gil Renard, psychotic though he is, authors the poem that opens the film. Paul Aufiero carefully composes his comments before calling in to "the Sports Dawg." Pat Solatano Jr. writes letters that he believes are delivered to his ex-wife. Ben Wrightman, the only fan protagonist whose textual production is not represented in some way, nevertheless articulates the power of sport to help him make meaning of his existence, albeit through the power of numbers rather than words:

> Ben: You know what's really great about baseball? You can't fake it. Anything else in life you don't have to be great in. Business, music, art: you can get lucky. You can fool everyone for a while. It's like not baseball. You can either hit a curve ball or you can't. That's the way that it works. You can have a lucky day, sure, but you can't have a lucky career. It's a little like math. It's orderly. Win or lose, it's fair. It all adds up. It's not as confusing or ambiguous as, uh . . .
> Lindsay: Life?
> Ben: Yeah! It's safe.[92]

The safety Ben finds in baseball is surely meant to associate his pleasure with arrested development, but his articulation of the game's ability to help him order his existence when faced with existential uncertainty nevertheless reveals his intentional valuation of his fan identity.

Even so, these filmic portraits of self-reflective fans unequivocally lack the depth of complexity and creativity that marks their counterparts in the textual representations that I have examined thus far. Given the inherent difficulty in depicting interiority and the prerogative financial imperatives of the Hollywood film industry, this is not surprising. The very fact that these films focus on fans at all, however, is of the utmost significance to my claims about fan possibility in this book. For, in building filmic narratives around fan protagonists, rather than the athletes or teams with which they associate, these films recognize the relatability of sports fandom itself as a significant mode of being. This recognition is part and parcel of the larger trend depicting fans in popular media, as noted by Bennett and Booth in *Seeing Fans*, as well as the fact that, as Stanfill puts it, "sports fandom is commonly understood as integral to normative American masculinity."[93] The decision to pathologize these fan protagonists, then, can be considered part of what Matt Hills calls "the newly ascendant figure of the 'superfan,'" created in popular media "in order to reinstate fan-cultural distinction and difference in the face of so many shades of fandom."[94] Whether they rely on tropes about maniacal murderers (Gil Renard), loveable losers (Paul Aufiero), "dumb white guy[s]" (Ben Wrightman), or comeback kids (Pat Solatano Jr.), these films cannot help but crack the door of possibility to the valuation of fan expression *beyond* the stereotypes they trade on. Their fan protagonists may be relatively unsophisticated readers and writers of the corpus of sport, but they are readers and writers nonetheless. Pathologize fans though they might, these films are premised on the notion that the lives of the sports-obsessed are worth knowing and caring about, not merely to those intellectually inclined to care about the inner lives of others, but to the widest possible range of consumers.

Since sports fans fizzle in Hollywood films largely because of generic limitations and the creation of the "super-fan" as a bankable trope, we might think about alternative possibilities on technological terms. Just as the textual forms of history, memoir, and the novel each inflect fan narratives in distinct and powerful ways, so too do the technological capabilities and limitations of film. Perhaps the capacity to compellingly "articulate, and animate the experience" of "we spectators" requires a more personal, accessible, and adaptable expressive platform than that of big-budget film.[95] That platform, twenty-first-century fan practice suggests, is online: fans' ability to create metanarratives out of sport's visual feast—and, crucially, distribute them—has been utterly transformed in the internet era.

5

REIMAGINED COMMUNITIES
Web-Mediated Fandom and New Narrative Possibilities for Sport

I think any "community" is sort of bullshit, but it'd be hard to think of FD as anything else. Or at least a sort of communal hub. Or at least a sort of rec centre with NBA League Pass on the bigscreen, except everyone watches games with the sound down because they're funnier than most of the announcers and talk about players in terms that bring them to life better than points-in-the-paint graphics and corporate-sponsored replays. Someone I know once described FD as "a bunch of semiotics majors who went to Brown." I wasn't really sure what that was supposed to mean, and when I asked Shoals he said, "You can be a semiotics major?" I don't know. But, in some way, aren't we all?

PASHA MALLA, quoted in Shoals, "The Day Never Ended"

Figuring fans' consumption of popular texts on narrative terms, as I do in this book and media studies scholars have done for decades, means emphasizing fans' individual interpretive agency. This approach seems especially appropriate in the contemporary media landscape, given the overwhelming array of niche media products that characterizes the "long tail" of consumption in the internet era (Anderson cited in Hundley and Billings 2010, 1). Yet sports are often thought to be one of the last concentrated mass cultural touchstones. Because sports' unscripted competitive construct incentivizes live viewing, media theorists and advertisers consider them differently: as defined by a mass audience that consumes them contemporaneously. While movies and television shows are increasingly consumed on demand via streaming services, sporting events—especially "MegaSport" events like the Super Bowl—still command millions of simultaneous viewers and attendant sums of advertising capital (Hundley and Billings 2010, 2). One unfortunate consequence of this notion of sports as the last bastion of true mass media is the perpetuation of an anachronistic consideration of its fans as passive dupes. Yet, as I have demonstrated in this book, such a portrait of sports fans oversimplifies and mischaracterizes. This is even more evident online, in which fan-authored blogs and social media threads have demonstrated the myriad ways fans analyze, personalize, and re-narrativize the stories that unfold on the fields, television screens, and computers in front of them. As they rewrite them online, these fans treat sports narratives as a rich metatextual corpus, and they create their own literature of sports experience within it. Fan critiques of sports spectatorship and its narrative ramifications for personal identity long predated the web. But the internet era powered a definitive shift in the form and pervasiveness of those critiques, and has amplified their potential to effect change in the sports industrial complex.[1]

In tracing that definitive shift, the fan-authored American sports blog is often credited to Bill Simmons, for the platform's popularization if not necessarily its innovation. Simmons emerged from relative obscurity as a contributor to the late-'90s proto-blogosphere to write for ESPN.com beginning in 2001. Eschewing press row and the locker room for first-person accounts of TV broadcasts, littered with pop culture references and jokes, Simmons quickly gained a massive online following. Two best-selling books—including the aforementioned *Book of Basketball*—a documentary series, and the creation of his own web empire later, Simmons became one of ESPN's most valuable personalities before a feud with management led to his departure from the Disney-owned sports broadcasting behemoth in 2015. I have previously credited Simmons's rise to media star from the performative authorial perspective of a fan "exactly like you or me" (Gladwell 2009, xii) to his ability to "retroactively rescript the master narrative [of sports, and invest] it with further potency via authorial self-reflexivity and autobiographical detail" (Cohan 2013, 131). In doing so, I asserted for the "sports fan author," the capacity to "demonstrate not only the narrative possibilities of sports but also the narrative possibilities of the self" (132). In this chapter, I will examine that assertion beyond Simmons to consider the significance of fan blog innovators that Simmons foreran if not inspired.

In particular, I will analyze three blogs that demonstrate digitally influenced innovation in their expression of an alternate understanding of sports narratives: FreeDarko.com, FireJoeMorgan.com, and Power Forward. I have chosen these blogs for their relative prominence as well as the creative and critical innovations that led to their recognition and (in many cases) their authors' professionalization as writers and journalists. On the one hand, these fan bloggers, like the print authors I have written about in this book, are distinct from "ordinary" fans insofar as that recognition has made them "Big Name Fans" with a reputation and certain privileges (Pearson 2010, 93). On the other hand, when these blogs began, the authors (almost all of whom used pseudonyms) were little different from any fan posting on Facebook or Google's "Blogspot" platform—they rose to prominence based on the strength of their writing and innovative thinking. In this chapter, I consider the work undertaken on these three blogs with an eye to three frameworks through which their authors reorient what it means to be a sports fan: modes of fan attachment, narrative reconceptualization, and identity politics. I will demonstrate that the accessibility and communicative flexibility of the blogosphere enhances and further develops fans' capacities to rearticulate the ways in which athletes and games are presented, interpreted, and assigned personal meaning. Reaching an audience of fellow fan-readers far beyond their living rooms or the corporate communicative contexts of major sports media entities like ESPN.com, these sports fan-authors use the public forum of the internet to develop new narratives and build imagined communities of an alternative scope.

Modes of Fan Attachment

In *Sports Fans: The Psychology and Social Impact of Spectators*, Daniel Wann, Merrill Melnick, Gordon Russell, and Dale Pease name eight primary motives that influence the socialization of the "highly identified" sports fan: group affiliation, family, aesthetic, self-esteem, economic, eustress, escape, and entertainment (2001, 4, 31). Wann et al. use psychological and sociological data sets to determine the "origin of team identification" (5). In taking such a macro approach, the scholars can be said to have outlined the parameters of much, maybe even most, fan experience. But they also failed to capture the fact that, as Garry Crawford puts it, "being a fan is not just a label or category; it is also an identity and a performance" (2004, 20). Narratives fuel that sense of self and its performance, and sports provide such narratives in abundant and multifaceted ways that allow fans to reach far beyond Wann et al.'s rather monolithic notion of "team identification" (2001, 5). Though the team construct naturally enforces the kind of divisions thought vital to the formation of imagined communities (Abercrombie and Longhurst 1998, 116), it also imposes implicit spatial and temporal constraints that electronically mediated fandoms easily subvert, allowing for the formation of alternate modes of affiliation.

One prominent example of the capacities of fans to work beyond the conventional boundaries of sports' imagined communities was manifested on the NBA blog FreeDarko.com. Active from 2005 until 2011, FreeDarko was born from the message board of a fantasy basketball league. Calling themselves "the Masters of the Klondike" to evoke a spirit of exploration, FreeDarko's group of friends and internet acquaintances posted under pseudonyms like "Dr. Lawyer IndianChief," "Silverbird5000," and "Bethlehem Shoals." The site's eponymous imperative—to free Detroit Pistons draft flop Darko Milicic from the confines of the team's bench—was rarely ever its focus. Instead, the site concerned itself with basketball appreciation predicated on critical frameworks that transcended the conventional boundaries of sports' imagined communities. To wit: the "collective," as they called themselves, coined the term "Liberated Fandom" to refer to a new paradigm of investment in the NBA, "the capacity to watch basketball with an eye toward individual narratives that is not bound to allegiance to a particular team" (Recluse Esq. 2007, "Dropping (Three) Jewels"). For Bethlehem Shoals this meant having "no belief whatsoever in the endless maze of sport upon which ESPN is premised," to watch basketball for reasons having "nothing to do with the importance of what's on or one's moral obligation to check it out. . . . If you have love of the Association there's at least one game per night that will illuminate you. Maybe this is the ultimate articulation of FreeDarko Liberated Fandom—we *chase* product, rather than waiting till we can brag about ours to others" ("Against the Endless Maze," "Save your Claws," emphasis in original). In effect,

Shoals and the other FreeDarko blog writers forswore inherited favorite teams and "zip code messiahs" (emynd 2006, "Off the Head")—the prime source of "group affiliation," to put it in Wann et al.'s terms (2001, 31). They had, it seemed, cast aside interpersonal socialization as a primary motive of fandom.

But how and why did this practice manifest itself in the blog era of the internet? Two reasons: one having to do with communication technology and the other having to do with the narrative-based experience that technology engenders. For the first, the internet architecture of the blog itself allowed for fan communitas on precisely the terms that would, in a larger fan context, seem to reject socialization. Which is to say that while the then-Seattle-based Shoals couldn't turn to a Supersonics fan in the stadium stands or sports bar and likely find someone sympathetic to his appreciation for the Phoenix Suns or Gilbert Arenas on aesthetic terms, he could do precisely that on the internet. For those like FreeDarko contributor "Gordon Gartrelle" who find "mainstream sports discourse [to be] as uncritical, stale, retrograde, and conformist as mainstream political discourse" (quoted in Shoals 2011, "The Day Never Ended"), FreeDarko was a revelation, and the blogosphere provided the necessary connecting piece for that segment of sports fans, be they merely a "niche" audience or representative of something more. Dan Shanoff argued that they are the latter in eulogizing the site in 2011, asserting that "FreeDarko's essential tenet of 'liberated fandom' dovetails with the essential foundation for our current media era. . . . FD acolytes [are] given intellectual permission to pursue cheering for funky players with no position or stuck on the wrong team or otherwise bending the orthodoxies of the NBA" (quoted in Shoals 2011, "The Day Never Ended").

In effect, FreeDarko's aesthetic mission amounted to more than a new paradigm for fan interpretation and expression: it was example par excellence of the expanded capacity for critical thinking that digital interactivity allows. Realizing N. Katherine Hayles's notion in *How We Think: Digital Media and Contemporary Technogenesis* that digital media is "an important resource for contemporary self-fashioning, for using plasticity both to subvert and redirect the dominant order" (2012, 83), the authors of FreeDarko incorporated hyperlinks, images (often obscure, or seeming non sequiturs), YouTube videos, criticism from non-sports related sources, and unconventional statistical analysis enabled by the data access and processing power that computers provide. The cumulative effect, as much as anything else, of Liberated Fandom was to free FreeDarko's authors, "collective" though they may have called themselves, to individually reflect on the intellectual possibilities of basketball beyond any socially prescribed interpretive boundary. As Will Leitch put it, "FreeDarko . . . made me realize the power of caring this much, of thinking this hard, and investing this much . . . and how the Web could harness and unleash that power" (quoted in Shoals 2011, "The Day Never Ended").

From a literary-critical perspective, one might suppose that FreeDarko engaged in a hermeneutics of suspicion—positioning themselves at a critical distance from the NBA text. Rejecting conventional fandom as an uncritical mode of responsiveness overdetermined by competitive outcomes and a "from-the-gut hermeneutics of greatness," the Free-Darko collective espoused the "active role we take in fandom" (Shoals 2006, "Strength Begat Mind," "The Ever-Renewing Cauldron"). But to characterize FreeDarko authors as utterly suspicious readers is to miss the enchantment and recognition, to borrow Rita Felski's terms, that they found in the NBA metatext (*Uses of Literature* 74). Shoals affirmed the notion that modern consumers "find an identity based in culture, which in America is an open market of freelance commodities and personal collage" (2006, "You Can Grade Me Shorter"). FreeDarko–an NBA identity formation may have rejected interest in the NBA based on the standard metrics of competition, but aesthetic rapture and personal association were fundamental to their ethos. As contributor "emynd" put it in the context of Allen Iverson:

> The game done changed and the winnings and losings are only as important as the winners and losers that play the . . . game. I suppose finding some sort of grand-scale enjoyment in each and every one of AI's performances regardless if they result in a win is akin to liking the music that an artist makes whether or not he wins a Grammy for it. (2006, "The Heart of a Perpetual Loser")

The conventional public metric of success is mostly irrelevant to the liberated fan, but she still sees herself in the text, or invests in it emotionally. As Felski notes in *Uses of Literature*,

The experience of being immersed in a work of art involved a mental balancing act . . . even as we know we are bewitched, possessed, emotionally overwhelmed, we know ourselves to be immersed in an imaginary spectacle: we experience art in a state of double consciousness. (2008, 74)

Though Felski considers art to encompass a wide range of imaginative texts, her immediate context does not consider sports performance. Even still, her characterization aptly describes the mindset of the FreeDarko-an liberated fan. Though the site's authors mostly forswore the conventional fan practice of identity construction via team affiliation, they nevertheless realized that, as Nick Abercrombie and Brian Longhurst put it in their influential study of *Audiences*, "analytical performance is intrinsically linked to emotional attachment" (1998, 177).

The relationship between emotion and analysis was equally strong, but manifested quite differently, on the baseball blog Fire Joe Morgan. Active from 2005 until the end of the 2008 baseball season, Fire Joe Morgan was authored by a group of friends and fellow comedy writers posting under pseudonyms like "dak," "Junior," and "Ken Tremendous." In the style of FreeDarko's eponymous mission, the imperative of Fire Joe Morgan's nomenclature—to get ESPN television baseball analyst and MLB Hall of Famer Joe Morgan removed from his job—was only occasionally its focus. Instead, the site specialized in using Sabermetric analytics to satirize journalists who remained statistically ignorant or obstinate in their thinking about, and commenting on, baseball.[2] Fire Joe Morgan's website header declared itself the site "Where Bad Sports Journalism Came To Die," and, as Ken Tremendous put it, the site took "borderline-sociopathic joy [in] meticulously criticizing bad sports journalism" (2008, "Post #1377"). While the tools of Fire Joe Morgan's criticism emanated from their understanding and application of Sabermetric analytics, the bloggers' meticulousness was best represented in their use of a line-by-line comedic commentary known in internet parlance as "fisking" (Urban Dictionary 2004). The technique involves quoting a passage of an offending author's text, following it with a sentence or two of comedic rebuttal, followed by the next section of the original author's writing, then another rebuttal, and so on through the text. The effect was one of a clinical dismantling of rhetorical weakness, of scientific deconstruction of another's narrative in the name of comedy.

Though any baseball writing that exhibited "old-timey mythology and tradition and ignorance and distrust of modern analysis" was fair game, the authors of Fire Joe Morgan had noticed in particular that Michael Lewis's 2003 book about the Oakland Athletics front office, *Moneyball*, had come under fire from baseball media commentators unwilling or unable to understand the enhanced analytical methods it espoused (dak 2005, "Some Questions"). Among this group of deniers, Joe Morgan had made his distaste especially well known, loudly declaring at seemingly every available opportunity both that he had not read the book and that he was sure its findings were completely wrong: an untenable combination of claims that stoked the satirical fires of Fire Joe Morgan's stable of professional comedy writers. Though dak asserted that the site had "never been singularly devoted to picking on Joe," the obstinately anti-Sabermetric Hall of Famer proved exceptionally apt for a figurehead (2005, "Some Questions"). As Fire Joe Morgan's authors and readers would be reminded over and over again, Morgan was not particularly receptive to the notion that new ideas and modes of evaluation could or should affect the way one viewed the game. According to Morgan, baseball excellence is self-evident to those with expertise and first-hand experience. "I watch baseball every day," Morgan asserted, "[and] I have a better understanding about why things happen than the computer, because the computer only tells you what you put in it. I could make that computer say what I wanted it to say, if I put the right things in there" (quoted in Junior 2005, "Excerpt From the Previously Linked Article"). In other words, as Junior satirically put it: to determine if someone is a great player, use "good old-fashioned gut feeling [and] always, always state your opinions as incontrovertible THINGS THE WAY THEY ARE" (2007, "Someday You, Too"). The nebulous "computer" that Joe Morgan derided as easily manipulable is a threat because it calls into question this sense of the established order by producing new metrics.

Many baseball media lifers agreed with Morgan. One such writer, AOL's Jim Armstrong, asserted that Sabermetrics cannot "add to the enjoyment of the game." In his fisking of Armstrong's piece, Ken Tremendous responded with righteous indignation:

> Shut up. Seriously, man, shut the fuck up. This is like saying, "I don't like action movies, so no one can ever enjoy action movies because action movies are terrible." If you don't want to use stats, don't use them. I don't care. But for the love of goddamned God, don't tell me that statistical analysis "doesn't add up [sic] to enjoyment of the game." You are telling me that my friends and I are incapable of enjoying baseball. I promise you—I PROMISE you—I enjoy baseball. I love baseball. This is not a situation where only one kind of person can love baseball. Lots of different people can love baseball for lots of different reasons. In my case, I love baseball every bit as much as you, but—and here's the difference between you and me—I also understand it. (2008, "Heady Days")

Despite Tremendous's fury, the FJM crew responded more often with humor rather than anger. And, as it turned out, making the site's readers laugh at the technophobic and anti-intellectual voices in baseball media proved to be a quite effective means of advocating for statistical awareness. The folksy tropes of baseball wisdom, like the espousal of a player's "intangible" qualities, the belief that certain hitters are particularly "clutch," or the notion that greatness can be measured by "memorable moments," might seem truthy and harmless when taken at face value. Satirized by Junior, dak, and Ken Tremendous, however, these same tropes are revealed to be seriously wrongheaded. Take for example, this typical line of argument from Joe Morgan, as fisked by Junior:

> [Joe Morgan:] Stats don't tell you about heart, determination and mental attitude.
> [Junior:] Or grit, hustle and calm eyes. No, unfortunately, statistics just tell you how good a player is at avoiding making outs while playing baseball. Information that is essentially useless in talent evaluation. When I'm building a team, I want a bunch of inspi-

rational stories. A team of Rudys, or Air Buds. Yeah. I'll call them the Los Angeles Air Buds.

[Morgan:] I have heard there are teams that think they can look at a stat sheet and tell you if a guy can play. I don't agree.

[Junior:] The operative words here are "can play." Can a guy play if he OPSes 1.200 for a whole season for the Portland (Maine) Sea Dogs, or WHIPs 0.79 for the Portland (Oregon) Beavers? I would be inclined to say yes, the likelihood is very high that these guys can play. In fact, I would feel much more confident about these fellows than, say, a guy I saw for three days go 8–12 with a couple of home runs and a real sweet swing.

[Morgan:] I never would have gotten a chance to play if someone had just looked at me on paper. I got a chance and it paid off.

[Junior:] For the last time, Joe: *you had great statistics*. Because you were great at playing baseball. *In spite of* your underwhelming physical appearance. I don't know how to be more emphatic about this. I'm already writing in choppy sentence. Fragments. (2006, "JoeChat?" emphasis in original)

Addressing Joe directly in "responding" to text produced in an earlier chat, Junior pointed out not only that the baseball Hall of Famer was reproducing a melodramatic narrative trope about effort and attitude, but that he did so because he perceived his own narrative to have followed that same formula. Yet the Joe Morgan baseball narrative was always determined by statistical effectiveness. Morgan just refused to recognize that fact because he did not understand, or could not personally account for, the measures of that effectiveness. This kind of solipsism was not exclusive to media members like Morgan who are former players. Take Jon Heyman's argument about Hall of Fame evaluation, as fisked by Junior:

[Jon Heyman:] Enshrinement in Cooperstown shouldn't be about numbers.

[Junior:] It should be about guessing. Waving your hands in the air and shouting baseball players' names. Loud. Getting piss-drunk on Schlitzes, beating up some Finnish guy for looking gay, putting more Schlitzes in your gut and then using that gut to remember who was great. Because who remembers better, guts or numbers? Guts. Guts remember.

[Heyman:] If anyone thinks so, let's trash tradition and have a computer select the honorees.

[Junior:] You know who a computer would probably pick? All of his computer friends. Hope you like a Hall of Fame full of Commodore 64's, ENIACS and vacuum tubes, you number-loving asshole.

[Heyman:] The Hall of Fame should be about who starred and who dominated. And about who made an impact. It should be about greatness.

[Junior:] And how do we determine these things? Simple. Jon Heyman's brain matter. It's a little-known fact, but Jon Heyman's brain matter has been scientifically determined to be the most infallible substance on the planet Earth. Jon Heyman's brain matter has retained every scrap of information it has ever received through Jon Heyman's sensory organs. Jon Heyman's brain matter can tell you the number of hairs on the skin of a Lhasa Apso Jon Heyman's eyes saw in 1974, though of course it would prefer not to, because that would be a number, and numbers are insignificant to Jon Heyman's brain matter. Jon Heyman's brain matter specializes in the recognition of domination, star power, impact and greatness. It does not need numbers to aid it. It simply knows. We must trust it. (2007, "Jack and Bert")

Junior's humorous responses to Heyman's notion that "greatness" is not measured by numbers were hyperbolic in their satire, to be sure. But they effectively highlighted the fact that Heyman's is an argument for solipsistic subjective evaluation that prioritizes the men doing the selecting over those who are selected for the Hall of Fame. The reflexive recognition of which is, at its base, the larger problem with "computers" and other statistical boogeymen for Heyman and the other journalists satirized by Fire Joe Morgan. In effect, such "new" thinking forced baseball writers to not merely consider the *what* of the baseball game in front of them, but *how* they consider it and represent it in writing. It forced them to consider that baseball is not self-evident and its traditional representation is not necessarily mimetic of some baseline "reality" of the game.

The same could be said for sports fans—traditional modes of team attachment do not necessarily represent the baseline "reality" of their practices of self-identification. When it comes to understanding both baseball and its fans, then, the authors of Fire Joe Morgan presented a narrative framework distinct from that which would subsume them by convention or "common sense." As Garry Crawford argues, "rather than being understood as an imagined community, [internet fans] need to be viewed as a *community of imagination*" (2004, 144). Advocating for statistical analytics via satirical narratives and largely foregoing team identification, Fire Joe Morgan's fan community was based in just such imaginative boundary-breaking. Though Ken Tremendous, Junior, and dak were, in fact, self-identified Boston Red Sox fans, the site was decidedly not oriented around that allegiance. There can be no better evidence of this than the fact that the site regularly defended Alex Rodriguez, a member of the rival New York Yankees, against critics by citing his superlative stats. Instead of forming a team-based community, the authors of Fire Joe Morgan and its dedicated readers were baseball fans united in journalist anti-fandom. As fan studies scholar Jonathan Gray has argued, "hate or dislike of a text can be just as powerful as can a strong and admiring, affective relationship with a text, and they can . . . serve just as powerfully to unite and sustain a community or subculture" (2005, 841). Deriving pleasure from their dislike of analytically deficient journalists via sarcasm, Fire Joe Morgan used comedic narratives to construct community boundaries without regard to, or interest in, the conventional definitions used to describe sports fans. "Snark," that acerbic irreverence in which many internet communities traffic, became the site's calling card, attracting fellow fans interested in calling attention to the failures they perceived in the way professional journalists handle the metatextual corpus of baseball, and suggesting alternative approaches.

Though Jessica Luther could be funny in her blog posts, sarcasm was not her preferred rhetorical means of calling for change. Like FreeDarko and Fire Joe Morgan, the blog name Power Forward was an imperative— reflecting Luther's desire "to move the discussion about sports forward in a meaningful way" as well as indicating her preferred position on the basketball court (2014, "About"). Active from 2012 to 2014, Power Forward's focus was not on a particular sport, as with FreeDarko or Fire Joe Morgan, but on recontextualizing the mainstream media discussion of sports and athletes from Luther's feminist, social justice–oriented perspective. Powering forward, then, concerned not just "the momentum of moving forward [but] the forceful act of powering through the muck to create that forward motion" (Luther 2014, email message to the author). Variously addressing sports leagues, the sports media, and her fellow sports fans, Luther called them out for their perpetuation of, or silent complicity in, injustices based on gender, sexuality, or race. Her training as a historian had made her "sensitive . . . to narratives, [to] whose story gets told and why, whose story we'll probably never know, whose story we aren't even trying to tell or whose story we often refuse to acknowledge" (Luther 2014, email message to the author). Applying that sensitivity in an athletic context in her writing on Power Forward, Luther recognized that to grasp the depth and complexity of sports' fundamental narrativity, we must pay attention to the stories that aren't being told or amplified by media attention, and ask why not.

Where FreeDarko and Fire Joe Morgan creatively recontextualized fan attachment through aesthetics and analytics, Jessica Luther's Power Forward did its recontextualizing by embracing the distinctiveness and political will of groundbreaking athletes, many of them in individual sports, like tennis, rather than team-based leagues. In doing so, Luther largely transcended the communal frameworks for understanding sports fandom theorized by Wann and others, and naturally considered her fandom on terms that had much more in common with the individualized interactions of media fans. Consequently, Luther's connections to Serena Williams and Brittney Griner weren't otherwise based on conventional social motives for fan attachment such as geography or family. Instead, as she put in an interview with David J. Leonard for The Feminist Wire, "I admire any athlete who goes against the stereotypes of athletes" (quoted in Leonard 2014). Williams and Griner go against such stereotypes with regard to both who they are and the unapologetic way they comport themselves. As a result, their narratives are often handled by the media and fans alike in awkward or inconsiderate ways.

It is with regard to this treatment that Luther was particularly attentive to each on Power Forward.

Serena Williams has been a dominant competitor on the women's tennis tour since her debut in the mid-1990s, and is considered by some to be the greatest women's tennis player of all time. All the same, as Luther put it, because Williams is African American and tennis is "a predominantly white sport, [Williams's] not-white body has endured an endless amount of scrutiny" (2012, "Serena Williams is Not a Costume"). This scrutiny comes from fans, commentators, and sometimes even her fellow players. In a post titled "Serena Williams is Not a Costume," Luther took to task fellow players—in particular Caroline Wozniacki—for stunts in which Williams's body was mimicked, ostensibly in the name of comedy and couched in personal friendship.

Via a series of links, Luther cited the history of racism and body shaming that Serena has been subject to throughout her career, and asserted that

> when Wozniacki decided to "impersonate" Serena by adding towels to her breasts and butt, she wasn't doing so inside of a vacuum where all of this hatred doesn't exist. [One can't ignore that] the body you are mimicking has been the target of vitriol and judgment for years and even more so when you are white and much of that vitriol and judgment of the person's body that you are mimicking has been racist. Serena Williams' body is not a costume for another tennis player, especially a white tennis player, to put on and use for laughs when they feel like it.
>
> If Wozniacki had chosen instead to paint her face black in order to impersonate Williams, would we be questioning if this type of display is racist? (2014, "Serena Williams is Not a Costume")

Attentive to the larger body of rhetoric surrounding Williams's muscular frame and its connection to the denigration of black bodies that pervades much sports discourse, Luther echoed Susan Birrell and Mary McDonald's notion that "structures of dominance expressed around . . . the power lines of race, class, gender, and sexuality . . . do not work independently and thus cannot be understood in isolation from one another" (2000, 4). Luther thus rejected the supposedly exculpatory notion that Wozniacki's actions may have been acceptable to Williams because the two women are friends: "As much as people want so desperately to divorce the imitations of Serena's body from the long history of violence, ownership, disparagement, sexualization, and co-opting of black women's bodies, you can't do it. Stop trying" (2012, "Serena Williams is Not a Costume, Part 2"). For Luther, no incident can be isolated from the broader discourse. Williams's mistreatment necessarily exemplifies systemic injustice.

Luther was also careful to note that *all* women's tennis players must grapple with the notion that "athleticism and femininity [are] mutually exclusive despite piles of evidence to the contrary" (2012, "Serena Williams is Not a Costume, Part 2"). In a sports media landscape that largely dismisses women as a niche audience, female athletes are often treated as sexualized objects, if they are treated at all. For a fellow women's tennis player implicitly to endorse that mode of public perception is to do all women athletes a disservice. Reading her favorite tennis player, Serena Williams, with an eye to larger narratives and the power structures through which Williams's public persona is mediated, Luther demonstrated that her fandom was about more than vicarious association with on-court excellence. Through Williams, Luther could champion a counternarrative breaking from the stereotypes of the sexualized woman athlete, and advocate for a sporting future in which Williams's narrative is not automatically defined by stereotypes and systemic racism.

Luther's connection to women's basketball superstar Brittney Griner was similarly predicated on resistance, though with regard to a separate set of stereotypes. Griner is a 6'8" center who was one of the most dominant players in college basketball history and the No. 1 pick in the 2013 WNBA draft. She was so dominant as a collegiate player, in fact, that for some she called into question the separation of genders in upper-level basketball. In the most famous instance, Mark Cuban, franchise owner of the NBA's Dallas Mavericks, asserted that he would like her to try out for his team. Naturally there were plenty of arguments against the notion that Griner should try out, both of the misogynistic type and of the sort that argued, as ESPN's Kate Fagan put it, that "constant comparisons do little more than reinforce the notion that the women are somehow second-class players, instead of world-class athletes in their own right" (quoted in Luther 2013, "On Brittney Griner").

On Power Forward, Luther took a different tack. Agreeing with Fagan that it is "unfair to put Griner's accomplishments up against the men's," she nevertheless disagreed with the notion "that people don't implicitly measure her against her male counterparts all the time" (Luther 2013, "On Brittney Griner"). As for the notion that such a tryout would be a demeaning "spectacle," Luther broke the fourth wall to emphasize that the media itself bears responsibility for such an outcome:

> This is the point where I look directly at the camera and speak to the sports journalists out there who write about these things:
> *clears throat*
> If you are in the sports media and you're worried the sports media will handle Griner's tryout poorly, then choose to handle it well.
> If you are in the sports media and you're worried the sports media will spotlight her sex and gender over her skill, then choose to only spotlight Griner's skill. (2013, "On Brittney Griner")

Furthermore, since comparison is inevitable, Luther argued that media should "focus on . . . the systemic differences in how boys and girls and eventually men and women are treated across the board that leads to major differences in the level of physicality and the play of the game, differences that make a comparison between Griner and male centers in the NBA unfair" (2013, "On Brittney Griner"). In other words, as with the Serena Williams body-shaming incident, Luther argued that we cannot divorce the exceptional individual from the larger discourse—the discussion as to whether Griner should play with men should always also be a discussion about why men and women are separated in the first place, and consider the ramifications of that separation. This argument, in turn, led Luther to construct counterfactual narratives for Griner and other exceptional woman athletes:

> What I like to imagine is what Brittney Griner would be like today if teams had been separated by skill level and not gender or sex. What if, regardless if you call yourself a "girl" or "boy," you received the best coaching, the most resources, and the biggest cultural support because you were simply the best at what you do in the game you play? Would Abby Wambach be starting on the soccer field next to

Landon Donovan? Would Serena Williams be plowing over Roger Federer the way she regularly does over every woman she plays? (2013, "On Brittney Griner")

Though Luther didn't elaborate further on these imagined narratives, they point to another reason that Griner's excellence, like Williams's, fostered her fan affiliation beyond titles won or awards received. Transcendent athletes like Griner and Williams call into question the conventional notion that women athletes are second-tier competitors. By doing so they exposed the systemic inequalities that normalize or essentialize this second-tier status as based in gender physiology.

Even as she called into question gender-based stereotypes, Brittney Griner also appealed to Luther because of the way she chooses to talk about her sexuality. Asked by *Sports Illustrated* about why it was that American men's sports had so few openly gay players when the WNBA had been welcoming LGBTQ athletes since the league's inception in 1997, Griner said,

> I really couldn't give an answer on why that's so different. Being one that's out, it's just being who you are. Again, like I said, just be who you are. Don't worry about what other people are going to say, because they're always going to say something, but, if you're just true to yourself, let that shine through. Don't hide who you really are. (Quoted in Luther 2013, "Brittney Griner: 'Being One That's Out'")

Griner's statement about tolerance and being true to her own sexual identity was rather innocuous, but it was treated as a bombshell because, to that point, Griner herself had never "come out" in a public forum. Subsequent stories on ESPN.com and other sites that proclaimed she had done precisely that revealed their inability to understand LGBTQ identity beyond the construct of "the closet." "The media is bad about talking about a person who is openly gay and who does not consider themselves having ever been in the closet," wrote Luther:

> This is really a symptom of the heterosexist way in which our entire society talks about people's sexual lives: one is assumed to be heterosexual unless they choose to indicate otherwise (an incredibly flat way to talk about sexuality). As many people have said eloquently

before, because of this assumption, someone who is not heterosexual has to constantly "come out" to people throughout their life even if they, like Griner, don't consider themselves "in." (2013, "The Heteronormativity").

Nonchalantly talking about her sexuality in a public forum was not a mode of revelation for Griner because in her mind there was nothing to reveal. That the mainstream sports media could only understand it as a revelation speaks to their inadequacies, and Luther eagerly pointed them out. That said, beyond conceptual errors and few headlines, most media seemed to move on from Griner's non-announcement announcement rather quickly.

By contrast, when NBA veteran Jason Collins chose to "come out," the news was considered so significant that it was featured on the cover of *Sports Illustrated*. Given the pervasive legacy of homophobia still present in men's sports, this was understandable, but as Luther argued in an article for *The Atlantic* titled "The WNBA Can Teach Male Athletes About Coming Out and Being Allies" (2013), Griner's non-announcement is the model of sexual identification we should strive for—for the sake of athletes, media, and fans alike. Much like Serena Williams, then, Griner is a favorite athlete for Luther because she calls into question the established thinking and stale tropes of sports narratives just by being herself. In a manner rather similar to the reorientation of fandom espoused by the writers of FreeDarko and Fire Joe Morgan, then, Luther's prioritization of her connection to individual athletes demonstrated that the enjoyment of sports fandom can lie in critically questioning and reconceptualizing the very notion of team-based affiliation. In rejecting the teams they might otherwise have been expected to follow on account of geography or familial ties, the authors of FreeDarko, Fire Joe Morgan, and Power Forward developed a distinct approach to fan writing that earned them recognition, devoted followers, and professional opportunities to write about sports (and many other subjects). They demonstrated not only that a broader range of discourses can inform individual sports fans' modes of attachment to their preferred texts, but that web-based mediation of such unconventional approaches can foster the formation of alternative imagined communities.

Narrative Reconceptualization

As I've argued throughout this book, sporting events often seem to hide their status as narratives in plain sight. On one hand, this has something to do with the necessary open-endedness of competition as the foundational element of the narrative construct. Since no one has determined the winner and loser before any given sporting contest, the event seems "real," not story-based. Just as significant in determining the seeming anti-narrativity of sporting events, however, is the fact that the statistical metrics used to provide context rely on quantitative data. Databases often seem to be "natural enemies" of narrative, doing "battle" with stories by implicitly asserting their superiority as quantitative entities (Hayles 2012, 173). Nevertheless, as Gerald Early argues in *A Level Playing Field*, "sports uniquely combine certainty (statistics and data) and uncertainty (the fact that the outcome of sporting contests can never be consistently predicted, as sports unfold live and with no preset ending) into a heroic narrative of action" (2011, 21). These seemingly oppositional forces of under- and over-determination balance each other out to create narratives that consumers around the world crave. Unlike Early, however, most of those consumers *don't recognize* what they're consuming as narratives. The reason for that, I argue, is that the "heroic narrative of action" for every single sporting event, at least as represented in popular media, is always just that: a "heroic narrative of action," every single time. In popular parlance, this rote story is called the "recap," and it inevitably relates the same narrative touchstones (score, statistics, attendance) and is predicated on the ultimate designation of "winners" and "losers." The vagaries of how the participants assume these designations matter, of course, but given the competitive stakes on which athletic contests are premised, mainstream media accounts inevitably tailor their recaps to not only accommodate but emphasize the binaristic designations assigned at its conclusion. This mode of accounting for what happened in a sporting event thus relies on a specific teleology—masked by the purported objectivity of journalistic methods—and has become so ingrained in media sport representation that it is invisible to most fans. The history of a sporting event may not be literally written by the winners, but it is determined by their victory. Compared to the narratives preferred by fans of popular media genres like crime drama and science fiction, this narrative formula can seem overly shallow and restrictive of fans' appropriative authorial possibilities.

In contrast with the conventional sports recap model, FreeDarko, Fire Joe Morgan, and Power Forward represent the dynamic critical thinking that the sports blogosphere can foster because they overtly treat sports as complex narratives. In different contexts and in very different ways, all three blogs recognize the narrative bases of their preferred sports and criticize the way the sports media represents those narratives as mimetic or uncomplicated. Reconceptualizing sports narratives on their own terms, the three blogs demonstrate the capacity of the sports fan—like any critical reader—to bring to a narrative as much meaning as they take from it.

The most notable and subversive manifestation of FreeDarko's Liberated Fandom that the plasticity of digital mediation enabled came in its attention to narrative. Rather than "watch to see who wins," as Shoals put it: "I'm going to take stock of whether the game has style. . . . I reserve the right to enjoy a basketball game, no matter how unimportant it may be—and dismiss them even if there's a ton of invested value in the outcome" (2008, "State of Fiery Heaven Address"). On the surface, this mindset could seem to deemphasize narratives altogether, but its aesthetic priorities did not stifle them. Instead it allowed Shoals and his compatriots to account for the games that drew their interest on terms beyond competition. Rather than recount a game's leading scorers, key competitive moments, and ramifications for a given team's pursuit of a championship, FreeDarko's authors could manifest their investment by weaving broader-reaching narratives than the results-oriented model allows. This freed them to synthesize Gilbert Arenas's on-court abilities and his outsized off-court persona; to notice tendencies and weave narratives about the relationships between coaches and sideline reporters; to imagine counterfactuals in which players did not merely switch teams, but play without regard to traditional notions of position; to attempt to represent the aesthetic resonances between basketball and hip-hop without collapsing them into to broad-based essentialisms like those that link baseball and American pastoral nationalism, for example. As Chris Ryan put it, Free-Darko taught readers "to see stories and narratives everywhere, even if they were just products of [our] imagination. And it taught . . . that all those stories and narratives mattered; as much, if not more, than the one being told on the court" (quoted in Shoals 2011, "The Day Never Ended"). In effect, FreeDarko's liberated fans imagined non- or even anti-teleological narratives, bases for fan association distinct from those documented in game recaps and mass-media narratives.

FreeDarko's reconceptualization of the NBA's narrative structures was also rooted in an emphasis on aesthetics in determining the fan-authors' interest. Six months into publishing the site, Bethlehem Shoals exclaimed "THIS IS A LEAGUE OF STYLE!" (2005, "Free Drafto, Pt. 5"). Style, the defining criterion of what makes a player worth adopting under the terms of Liberated Fandom, connoted a transgressive aesthetics of player performance that realized FreeDarko's avant-garde ideals. This could mean playing basketball at a tempo out of sync with the norm (a la the mid-2000s Phoenix Suns), or possessing skills not normally associated with a particular position or body type (a la Kevin Durant), or merely playing the game with unconventional joie de vivre (a la Gilbert Arenas). However manifested, the aesthetic that FreeDarko celebrated was not style-for-style's sake—as might be seen in a slam-dunk contest—but *competitive* style, the "joyous extension of playing your ass off," at once both "wild and determined" (Shoals 2005, "Alone With My Notes," 2007, "Plants Are Not Small Trees"). In effect, style not only contributes to but in fact determines on-court excellence. It is not mere window-dressing but "the 'how' of substance . . . a means of highlighting his approach to the game, of making it explicit and feared" (Shoals 2007, "Amphibians on Dry Land").

Given the site's proclivity to critical analysis—born, at least in part, from the graduate school experiences of many of the contributors—FreeDarko wasn't content merely to proclaim and celebrate style, however. Instead the collective sought to understand its exhibition amid a larger media narrative that praised a highly managed game of "fundamentals" and "teamwork" above the bombastic and highly individualized expression of stylish players. Shoals quickly identified player psychology as a connecting characteristic, asserting that "most of our favorite NBA stars are presumed to be people whose inner lives consist of some degree of complexity" (2006, "A Complicated Game"). At once a recognition that basketball players are real humans whose life experiences inescapably affect who they are as players and an affirmation that complex characters make the NBA-as-narrative worth reading, the psychological aspect of style furthers that "part of FreeDarko's immortal credo [which] holds that aesthetic discovery is its own kind of drama" (Shoals 2006, "Between Fists and Speckles"). In effect, the fact that those players whose playing abilities astonish the fans also seem to be the ones with compelling personalities and personal histories only confirms the necessity of Liberated Fandom—of choosing those players that command our attention, not merely those assigned to us by local allegiance or club affiliation.

The notion that style is based in hyper-individuality also led FreeDarko to explore the collective bureaucratic structures of basketball. Not only do the competitive imperatives and team-first constructs of organized basketball run counter to an ethos of individuality, but the professional sport's "corporate environment of control and management . . . [is] fundamentally at odds with freedom, not matter what we may say about style" (Shoals 2008, "Strength For Everyone!"). This corporate structure serves traditional fandom, making players into "pawns in the team narrative" (Shoals 2007, "The Mind's Lungless Ankle"). Such team narratives, like melodramatic literary narratives, rely on staid formulas of personal sacrifice and make performers beholden to conventional roles. Against these tropes, a player with style, like LeBron James, "creates an airlock of suspended disbelief around everything he does" (Shoals 2006, "Strength Begat Mind"). To put it in the terms of media fandom, these transcendent players defy canonicity by their very nature—practically begging to be rewritten in new and creative ways by fans.

Players who exhibit such "overwhelming and almost problematic idiosyncrasy" in their style affect the Liberated Fan in the vein of Rita Felski's doubly conscious reader—making her utterly enchanted, rapt with attention, and yet aware that these players always "contain contradictions" (Shoals 2007, "All Breath in Angles," 2008, "Our Kind of Scraping"). They force the fan-reader to recognize that, beneath their enchanting brilliance, these players construct narratives that demand critical analysis. "Basketball is not jazz," the members of the collective proclaimed, but like jazz, the wordless beauty of basketball performance seemed to the authors of FreeDarko to contain narratives unavailable to the uncritical consumer (Shoals 2008, "SEE, BASKETBALL IS NOT JAZZ"). Himself a former music critic, Shoals credited famed music writers "Greil Marcus and Francis Davis [for teaching me] how to get inside music and pull a larger story out of it. That's pretty much all I've ever tried to do with sports—do more than scratch the surface or stop at 'sports is sports and it's beautiful'" (2014, email message to the author). For FreeDarko, the beauty of basketball was not mere facade, but an important signifier of its underlying narrative complexity.

In addition to a consideration of the interrelation between aesthetics and narrative, the idiosyncratic basketball expression of players with style led the collective to question the conventions of basketball strategy. In particular, FreeDarko reconsidered positionality in basketball, asking why the game traditionally features a point guard, shooting guard, small forward, power forward, and center, each with prescribed skills and at least partially defined body types. Players with style subverted these archetypes, leading FreeDarko to foment what they called "The Positional Revolution." The site celebrated "centers [that] have become play-making assist-guys in the post, . . . power forwards [that] have become obsessed with the three-ball, and point guards [that] have become shoot-first dynamos" (Dr. Lawyer IndianChief 2006, "Am I My Brother's Brother?"). Like the notion that individual players' stylistic idiosyncrasies could determine individual fans' investment in sports narratives, the shock to the system provided by players with skills not associated with their prescribed place on the court fit FreeDarko's (and especially Bethlehem Shoals's) revolutionary inclination. Take the example of Amare Stoudemire, who, Shoals asserted, "exists to subvert the game, to overwhelm it into accommodating him, to avoid the role of center because of the baggage that comes with technicality" (2005, "Artestifyin' Vol. 1"). Adopting the avant-garde's language of "provocation, extremity, defiance . . . the annihilation of logic, reason and all systems," Shoals saw Stoudemire's extreme basketball abilities as annihilating the limitations imposed by the NBA's positional logic (Felski 2008, 108).

But Stoudemire was far from the only player to disrupt traditional ideas about positionality on the basketball court. As apositional, "antifoundational" players like LeBron James and Rajon Rondo flourished, representing the "known busting apart at the seams" as they excelled and eventually won championships, Shoals et al.'s avant-garde instincts with regard to player preference began to be incorporated into the logic of the game (Shoals 2010, "Ask Me About the Baptist"). More than mere vindication of FreeDarko's aesthetic intuition, these successes also augured something odd for a narrative-oriented blog: the "Positional Revolution" became an accepted term in broader basketball discourse and analysis. In 2011 Shoals wrote that "it appears the Positional Revolution has gone mainstream, and I've been left behind" ("Ain't No Use"). Analysts of all stripes—of journalistic (Cavan 2014), fannish (Mieuli 2012), and even those with NBA organizational credentials ("Running The Break" 2013)—began to use the term, often without reference to its origins on FreeDarko. As Shoals had predicted in 2007, the Positional Revolution's "inflamed individual [had been] transubstantiated into a form of basketball logic" ("In The Land of Spiny Columns"). But it was no longer avant-garde, or even radical. "Basically, [positional] categories must wither and die," Shoals summed it up matter-of-factly, "and instead you get [on-court] heuristic groupings that vary depending on situations" (2011, "Ain't No Use"). If your center can distribute the ball, your need for a pass-first point guard is lessened. The stylistic resonance of that scenario may still be potent, but its competitive logic is ordinary and incorporated into the on court strategy of NBA teams.

If we think about the Positional Revolution as a kind of rebellion against canonical notions of literary genre, then its strategic incorporation into the game represents a realization of a kind of postmodernism—a fluid blurring of aesthetic forms that endorses dynamism as the truest possible mode of representation. If the liberated fan informs his sense of identity in a different way by taking an active role in reading the NBA as narrative, and stylish players can be said to provide the individual textual basis of that autobiographical association, then the realized Positional Revolution represents the formal context (or lack of firm context) in which that process of identification can come to its fullest fruition. In such an environment, the notion that the NBA is a serial narrative—one ripe for active fan reading and rewriting—is not only apparent, but eminent. In this sense, the Positional Revolution never left FreeDarko behind—it made basketball strategy FreeDarko-an such that Liberated Fandom is more potent than ever. Reconceptualizing NBA narratives both aesthetically and strategically, FreeDarko demonstrated that dynamic critical readings can impact sports narratives beyond the fan communities that originate and propagate them.

While FreeDarko unabashedly embraced narrative reconceptualization as a way for readers to draw new meaning from the purportedly limited corpus of outcomes and meanings present in sporting events, Fire Joe Morgan was considerably more hesitant. In fact, based on their often aggressive deconstruction of journalists' narratives, it might seem as if primary authors Ken Tremendous, Junior, and dak sought to limit the range of narrative possibilities drawn from baseball games. In a 2005 fisking of Mike Lupica's column, Junior took a step back from his specific ridicule of New York's self-proclaimed "premier sports columnist" to make a larger point about sports media: "nearly every sportswriter and commentator wants to make a neat little narrative out of every single thing that happens in sports. Often these cute fables reinforce virtues like resilience, harmony, hard work, and effort. Often they're bullshit" (2005, "More New York Stupidity"). On the surface, Junior's assertion seems anti-creative, suggesting that journalists with the wrong narrative imperatives should have their "bullshit" voices dampened. Yet in calling attention to the neatness and cuteness of the "fables," Junior effectively argues that bad sports writers allow traditional, easy narratives built on clichéd notions of "resilience, harmony, hard work, and effort" to *limit* the wider range of narratives they might construct from a given play, game, or season. The problem isn't the narratives themselves, but that they are made "neat" and "little" instead of smart and open to new ideas.

For example, when MLB.com's Tom Singer praised Ichiro Suzuki, a noted singles hitter, by asserting that "there's a good reason baseball is called a game of inches, not a game of 400 feet," Junior sarcastically retorted, "Yes, I agree. We should allow the cliché 'Baseball is a game of inches' to determine what works and doesn't work in the game. It's fortunate the song 'Take Me Out To The Ballgame' includes the lyric 'One, two, three strikes you're out at the old ballgame' because if it said four, we would have to change gameplay accordingly" (2007, "These Poor Unfamous Men"). In deriding cliché and purple prose alike, Fire Joe Morgan's fan-authors functioned much like the suspicious readers of literary criticism, who read from "poses of analytical detachment, critical vigilance, [and] guarded suspicion" (Felski 2008, 2). Ken Tremendous even recognized himself as such, writing of one deconstruction of a Joe Morgan chat transcript that "it's only for people who are really into a like New Critical-style close-reading of Joe's off-the-cuff babble" (2007, "Apologies in Advance"). This suspicious readerly stance did serve the critical agendas of statistical advocacy and anti-technophobia that inaugurated the site. But it was always also inextricable from the creative process by which FJM produced its own satirical narratives. In critiquing sports narratives in the name of comedy, then, Ken Tremendous, dak, and Junior also inevitably produced them. As Katherine Hayles has argued, rather than "natural enemies," "narrative and database are more appropriately seen as *natural symbionts*. . . . If narrative often dissolves into database, . . . database catalyzes and indeed demands narrative's reappearance as soon as meaning and interpretation are required" (2012, 176). To explain what the numbers that emerge from a spreadsheet mean, even the Sabermetricians need stories.

Fire Joe Morgan's stories took many forms. The most prevalent was the narrative that Michael Schur fashioned for his nom de plume, "Ken Tremendous." Claiming to be a "mild-mannered Pension Fund Monitor for Fremulon Insurance, based in Partridge, KS,[3] who copies dumb articles about baseball and adds snarky comments," Ken Tremendous often prefaced his "snarky comments" with details about his purported life and travels (2007, "Missed Connections"). These details gave the character a stable identity, which, in turn, allowed Schur to assume a narrative continuity for Ken Tremendous across a series of posts. This was most evident when critiquing "JoeChats," the ESPN online fan exchanges with Joe Morgan that Schur/Tremendous fisked after the fact. Writing the chatters' questions, Morgan's posted answers, and Tremendous's commentary as dramatic dialogue, Schur was able to not only satirize Morgan's obvious rhetorical and analytical deficiencies, but also relate them to the baseball analyst's prior answers *and* Tremendous's prior responses. The effect was one of an ongoing play spread out over many acts, in which Tremendous, the unheard gadfly, presented a kind of memoir of his time with Joe Morgan, professional baseball commentator and statistical ignoramus.

While the JoeChat dialogues may have constituted the site's most prevalent narrative, Fire Joe Morgan was also chockablock with smaller, more pointed satires. Occasionally these satires would riff on canonical litera-ture to humorous effect. Take, for example, Ken Tremendous's response to Joe Morgan's claim that "you can't compare things with statistics":

> [Ken Tremendous:] My point is: you can't compare things with statistics. Think about that, people. "You can't compare things with statistics."
>
> Exactly what, one might be tempted to ask, as one's hands were shaking so badly one would think one had just survived an assassi-nation attempt, might one use to compare things? Metaphor? How about the infallible human memory? Or perhaps poesy?
>
> *Much have I traveled, in realms of gold*
> *And many goodly states and kingdoms seen*
> *Round many Western Islands have I been,*
> *And I have observed some stuff about some shortstops*
> *Bill Hall did not have a monster year*
> *Derek Jeter has a calmer set of eyes*
> *David Eckstein is super clutch*
> *Please don't show me statistics that disprove my observations*
> (2007, "Joe Wants to Chat," emphasis in original)

Adapting John Keats's poem "On First Looking into Chapman's Homer" as a sort of punch line (Keats 1816), Tremendous makes a point about the absurdity of Joe Morgan's claim that one "can't compare things with statistics" while transposing baseball players onto a piece of literature that was itself an homage to an earlier work (2007, "Joe Wants to Chat"). No matter the reader's depth of literary knowledge, however, the satiri-cal humor is evident. Though Tremendous's basic frustration—the fact that Joe Morgan, baseball expert, will not entertain the idea that his gut reactions to particular players are not infallible measures of their effec-tiveness—is not necessarily very funny, the literary tableau amplifies the absurdity of the situation to humorous effect.

But most of the satirical narratives the Fire Joe Morgan authors created were not so self-consciously literary in their orientation. Many merely poked fun at the media's inclination to follow an established pattern in writing about certain athletes by taking that pattern to extremes. Others satirized the self-seriousness with which columnists propagated thinly evidenced communal belief-based narratives of "curses" and "jinxes" in a bald attempt to capitalize on the fame of prior incarnations. The most prominent example of this was the so-called curse that supposedly afflicted the Red Sox and their fans from 1918 to 2004. In response to just such an example, Ken Tremendous (himself an admitted Red Sox fan) wrote that

> I really don't want to be a killjoy. I like the humanistic element of baseball fandom. I often do not move from my seat if the Red Sox have a rally going. But: and this is key: I do not actually believe that my actions affect those of the players on the field. How is it possible for me to differentiate between superstition and the actual doings of men I have never met? Because—and this is my secret—I am a sentient human. (2007, "Apologies in Advance")

Juxtaposing the "humanistic element of baseball fandom," by which he seems to mean superstitious practices, with the "sentient human" who understands that those practices do not actually affect the game in question, Tremendous ostensibly imposed a narrative hierarchy based on logic and reason. What happens on the field, as measured and represented by Sabermetric analytics, represents reality. What happens in his living room, enjoyable though it might be, is a peripheral narrative. But such a juxtaposition belies the fact that Fire Joe Morgan demonstrated, in its own comedic conceit, that the "humanistic element" of such peripheral narratives facilitates our attachment to the baseball action we "sentient humans" recognize as real. Baseball's on-field narratives, however metricized, aren't worth anything unless reading them has value to the readers. Journalists often do the work of translating baseball narratives quite poorly, at least in part because they don't understand how to analyze the game statistically. Fire Joe Morgan's reconceptualizations of those bad narratives did more than demonstrate how they might be told using statistically sound reasoning, however. They also showed, via the creativity of their satirical narratives, how vital the "humanistic element" could be.

Unlike the authors of FreeDarko and Fire Joe Morgan, Jessica Luther was never particularly invested in expressing her own creativity on Power Forward. Instead, she focused on recognizing sports narratives as such, and reconceptualizing how they might be written by a mainstream sports media less beholden to conventions that privilege sport's power brokers.

"Sports are ONLY narratives," she told me, "and how we tell those stories matter" (Luther 2014, email message to the author). That attention to narratives took on particular resonance when Luther considered the way the media treats cases of sexual assault in college football.

In the blog's second post, titled "Predictable," Luther considered the praise then being lavished on Penn State head coach Bill O'Brien, the man who took over in the wake of the Jerry Sandusky child sex-abuse scandal. The problem with such praise, for Luther, didn't have anything to do with O'Brien himself. Rather, she wrote:

> I have a problem with the National Sportscasters and Sportswriters in the US participating in a redemption narrative for PSU so quickly after Sandusky's crimes were publicly declared and the coverup [sic] by [then–Head Coach Joe] Paterno and PSU bigwigs was uncovered. I have a problem with our unending desire for a "redemption" narrative generally. (2012, "Predictable")

These redemption narratives "equate 'success' with 'atonement'" such that media and fans assuage their implicit guilt about the football culture that facilitated and covered up Sandusky's heinous crimes by celebrating it in another way (Solomon quoted in Luther 2012, "Predictable"). Resigned to the notion that such a redemption narrative "has always been inevitable," Luther nevertheless wondered why its inexorable march so quickly and decisively stifled necessary attention to the power structures that enabled Sandusky's years of abuse:

> Can't we have even a little room to criticize the machine that caused all of that? Don't people see that if we don't criticize that we are just all actively participating once more in the very circumstances that created the culture at PSU? . . . The redemption narrative around O'Brien and the PSU football program doesn't exist in some kind of vacuum divorced from the scandal that led to O'Brien's hiring and, I reiterate, the need for redemption in the first place. At least some people at PSU would like to move on. Sports media certainly wants to move on. How predictable. (2012, "Predictable")

Despite demonstrating her proclivity to read sports on narrative terms and voicing her related desire that myopic fans and media look beyond the immediate crimes and/or football capacities of the individuals in front of them and interrogate the larger systems at play, Luther herself seemed ready to move on, if exasperatedly. But in 2013, as Luther began to note a burgeoning series of sexual assault cases filed against college football players that were inadequately covered by media and ignored or minimized by fans, questions closely related to those raised in her "Predictable" post kept recurring. Why was the redemption narrative so pervasive? Why were the victims of sexual assault so often erased or stigmatized? Why weren't college coaches held accountable for the rape culture pervasive in their locker rooms?

But perhaps the most troubling recurring question for Luther was: "Where is the media?" By way of example, she conducted a simple search for "rape" on ESPN.com and returned 762 items. "Sexual assault" yielded 775, with 314 popping up for "domestic violence." Was this a large number? "[It] seemed like a lot to me until I searched 'concussions,'" Luther wrote. "Concussions" returned 5,018 results. "Brittney Griner" returned 1,163 hits (2013, "The Reductions of Penn State Sanctions"). Concerned by this relative lack of attention, Luther began keeping her own list tracking sexual assault cases involving NCAA athletes, with links to whatever media coverage she could find for each case. From time to time, she published updated versions of this list on Power Forward. Certain cases, such as those involving the football teams at Vanderbilt, the U.S. Naval Academy, the University of Montana, and BYU, were chronicled in stand-alone posts on her site. Though her freelancing career for sites like Sports on Earth and VICE Sports was also propelled by this research, Luther's reportorial writing style retained the dampening trappings of journalistic objectivity. On Power Forward, by contrast, Luther could analyze *and* rage against the system. "I am SO CONFUSED as to why this isn't bigger news?" she wrote of the Vanderbilt case, which involved the gang rape of an unconscious victim: "If you were upset about Steubenville, why aren't you LIVID about this? Come on. COME ON" (2013, "The Vanderbilt Rape Case"). Likewise, on Power Forward, Luther could exhort that

we—all of us as a society—need to do better by rape victims. Because until we do better on teaching enthusiastic consent, making sure everyone understands what rape actually is, who normally perpetrates it, how victims often respond, etc., we will find ourselves right back here again. Probably sooner and more often than we really want to admit. (2013, "Going Into the Jameis Winston Press Conference")

And she could remind again that athletes benefit "from our society's often devastating desire to see redemption in almost every sports story, its endless need to focus attention and praise on such stories, no matter at whose expense that narrative comes" (Luther 2014, "On Bill O'Brien"). For, at its base, the problem is one of narrative: "we are supposed to see athletes as the protagonists in their own story" (Luther 2013, "How You Talk About Domestic Violence"). Media and fans alike find it all too difficult to recontextualize the stars of on-field hero narratives on the basis off-field actions, no matter how unacceptable the latter may be.

Luther could relate to this difficulty herself when it came to the rape allegations levied against Florida State quarterback and 2013 Heisman Trophy winner Jameis Winston. In an article for Sports on Earth titled "The Hazy Middle," Luther provided a first-person narrative of her lifelong affinity for Florida State football. She was, she wrote,

> born with garnet and gold blood. Both of my parents graduated from Florida State. Growing up, I spent Saturday afternoons in the autumn watching FSU football, either sitting next to my dad in front of a TV or in the stands of Doak Campbell Stadium. When it came time for me to go to college, I only applied to one school. And during the four years I was at Florida State, I went to every home game, sweating in the blistering heat of an early season 11 a.m. start or freezing cold during mid-November rivalry games against Florida. One summer, as an orientation leader, it was my distinct honor to teach the incoming class the words to the fight song. (Luther 2013, "The Hazy Middle")

So ingrained in Florida State's football culture, Luther describes looking past previous (non-assault-related) scandals embroiling Seminole players, and eagerly rooting on Winston when he joined the team in 2012: "I was a fan." But when "news broke in November [2013] that Winston had allegedly committed a sexual assault in December 2012," her view changed (2013, "The Hazy Middle"). Suddenly Luther—like football fans at Vanderbilt, Penn State, and all the programs on her list—had to reconcile her feelings about her favorite football team to her feelings about sexual violence and systemic inequality. "I do not know what to think," Luther admitted after reading Florida state attorney Willy Meggs's report about his decision not to charge Winston:

> I am not a person who can operate in some neutral space where I put aside the many women in my life who have been assaulted, plenty of them failed by the police who should be protecting them, and many whose communities did not believe them. . . .
>
> There will be people who think I should, somehow, be able to turn off my brain or compartmentalize my knowledge. I simply cannot, though a part of me wishes I could watch the game detached from all of this. The FSU fan in me is desperate to feel the high of cheering on my team as it fights to be national champions. I think back to my 1999–2000 self, a student who paid little attention to the details of off-field problems and focused on the play on the field. Ignorance, as they say, is bliss.
>
> I bleed garnet and gold, but that blood now flows into a brain that is no longer ignorant nor blissful. And all of it together makes my heart hurt. (2013, "The Hazy Middle")

Grappling with this poisonous complication to her own football hero narrative, Luther was left without easy answers. Inclined as she was to believe the alleged victim, she declared that "we will never know what happened. There is no way to ever know. The sad part is that because we do such a piss-poor job actually teaching what enthusiastic consent is in our society—especially to boys, Winston may truly believe he did not rape her while she truly believes that he did" (Luther 2013, "Going Into the Jameis Winston Press Conference"). And regardless of Winston's guilt or innocence, Luther was cognizant of the fact that, when it comes to athletes accused of sexual assault, "black men are overrepresented" and that Americans "have such a long, messed up, racialized way in which we talk and think about crime, especially that of sexual assault" (2014, "About UT Football"). A case like Winston's was, for Luther, "the hazy middle . . . solid gray with no hope of ever becoming clearly black and white" (2013, "The Hazy Middle").

One of the main reasons the sports media under-examines sexual assault, it would seem, has to do with this haziness: sexual assault narratives are difficult to pin down. Unlike traditional sports narratives, which quantify actions and use the final score to reduce the end result to a binary outcome, these contentious human stories are fraught with uncertainty, unreliability, and inconvenient truths. Nobody wins. Luther, to her credit, pursued them despite their disconcerting narrative incoherence, first on Power Forward and then in the book project that became *Unsportsmanlike Conduct: College Football and the Politics of Rape* (Luther 2016). In doing so, as in her writing about Serena Williams and Brittney Griner, Luther argued that media and fans alike should look beyond the particulars of the incidents and think systemically:

> It is hard to imagine a sports media that does not always focus on the athlete. But it is an intriguing idea, a goal to work towards perhaps. Because, in the end, de-centering the athlete is not only more fair to alleged victims, it is more fair to the players, as it draws attention away from the individual and instead forces us to interrogate the system itself. (2014, "Who We Talk About")

In other words, to really get at the root of what is going on in sexual assault cases in college football, we need to examine the broader hypermasculine, misogynist atmosphere that pervades football culture, and indeed much of the larger sports landscape, college and professional. We need to remove ourselves as readers from the "heroic narrative of action," at least for a while, and consider the human costs of producing those narratives (Early 2011, 21). For Luther, then, reconceptualizing sports narratives means not only reconsidering how we draw stories from the on-field action, but also reexamining who those stories affect and who they serve.

Though narrative structures are endemic to sports, on the rare occasions that they are explicitly recognized as such in sports media, they are usually presented as forced ascriptions of fiction or bias. Rather than representing the truth or reality of a situation, these artificial "narratives" are said to propagate vendettas or appeal to lowest common denominators in pursuit of readers or ratings. Addressing arguments in this vein by sports journalists, literary critic and basketball philosopher Yago Colás affirmed that

> there is no such thing as a narrative free zone where truth lives. . . . What we need in order to overpower the influence of *bad* narratives

(which is to say, narratives that advance descriptions of reality we find impractical or, worse, contrary to our practical purposes in the world) is *more and better narratives* (not appeals to some illusion of "reality" or "facts" or "truth" we imagine we may access free of the irritation of noisy narrative interference). And we need these better narratives, whether they be grounded in science, statistics, philosophy, emotion, intuition, imagination or aesthetics. (2014, "For More, And Better, Sports Narratives," emphasis in original)

For their part, the authors of FreeDarko, Fire Joe Morgan, and Power Forward provided those more and better narratives (and collectively cover all of the areas of knowledge production floated by Colás). In doing so, they affirmed the capacity of fans not merely to read from, but to write onto the metatextual corpus of sport in a manner that can benefit athletes, journalists, and fellow fans alike. Furthermore, in doing so successfully online, they demonstrated the web's capacity to provide a platform for such narrative innovations, to legitimize them and extend their range such that their metatextual work gains recognition and influence.

Identity Politics

The expanded narrative landscape fostered in online fan expression has ramifications that extend beyond the mere representation and recreation of the games themselves, however. The individual fan's search for an identity mediated by sports narratives is an even more complicated endeavor in a digital landscape. Cornel Sandvoss asserts that "the relative number of identity and political discourses surrounding a particular athlete has increased, whereas their intersubjective signification value both within such discourses and processes of social structuration has decreased" (2012, 178). Thus, where star athletes were once thought to represent singular, easily identifiable themes like "the founding myth of the nation" to broad fan communities, "contemporary athletes have largely ceased to denote any such specific discourses and, hence, incorporate potentially any number of discourses and forms of individual appropriation in self-reflective reading formations" (Sandvoss 2012, 178). Though it seems to me that Sandvoss mischaracterizes pre-internet sports fan signification as monolithic, his assertion does reflect the fact that more-diverse modes of meaning-making and self-articulation are evident online, simply because they are so easily communicated. The attendant notion that the "intersubjective signification value" of these "identity and political discourses" is lessened is more problematic to me, however, because it equates volume with importance (Sandvoss 2012, 178). The voice of the monolith—whether it is real or merely represented as such by mainstream media—should never be heard alone. One of the primary strengths of the open-access nature of the blogosphere and other online writing spaces (like those that host fanfiction) is that they provide a platform for "identity and political discourses" that would otherwise be ignored or marginalized.

For their part, FreeDarko, Fire Joe Morgan, and Power Forward each recognized, in one way or another, the significance and interconnectedness of "identity and political discourses" in reading sports narratives. This attention to identity politics meant examining the larger power structures in which fans operate, as well as the related extent to which demographics inform their privilege as fans. With the exception of FreeDarko's "Brown Recluse Esq." and Fire Joe Morgan's "Junior," who are Asian American, all of the major contributors to the three blogs are white. Only Jessica Luther, sole author of Power Forward, is a woman. None of the fan-authors openly identified as anything other than heterosexual. The ramifications of the privilege reflected in those demographic details were not lost on the authors, especially because many of the athletes they cheered for were of different races, genders, or sexual orientations. Like the fan-authors of the basketball memoirs I examined in chapter 3 of this book, the authors of FreeDarko, Fire Joe Morgan, and Power Forward grappled with the social stratifications that structure spectator sports and American society at large. In doing so, unlike Scott Raab, David Shields, and Bill Simmons, the bloggers were able to articulate anti-racist and anti-misogynistic possibilities so that demographic differences between fans and players do not define their relationship. They demonstrated that athletes and their sporting exploits are narrative entities whose reception and appropriation by fans need not reproduce social inequalities.

As a self-proclaimed "hip-hop-reared blog" that was informed by the cultural expressions of African Americans both on and off the basketball court, FreeDarko was attuned to matters of race and racial difference from the start (Shoals 2005, "Come Back Strong"). And though Bethlehem Shoals proclaimed that he did not purposefully "racialize style," it was notable that almost all of the players said to exhibit "style" were African American (2006, "Call it Pyrite"). Since the vast majority of the players in the NBA are African Americans, one might be tempted to attribute this tendency to mere probability. But the FreeDarko collective itself did not accept this explanation, and, as a general rule, the site never shied away from talking about race. Instead, FreeDarko recognized the "Style vs. Fundamentals debate [as] the long-form narrative of race and basketball in America" (Shoals 2006, "Snack of Fair Demons"). Players praised by media for their fundamentals, said to play "within the system" or with particular intelligence, are almost always white. Meanwhile, players with FreeDarko's notion of style—who transcended or undermined the terms of such systematic forms of basketball with "shocks" or "sudden leaps" of transformative ability—were almost always African American (Shoals 2009, "Safe to Say"). Were they able to perform in this way because of their race? FreeDarko rejected any simplistic notion of causation, but recognized, via William C. Rhoden's taxonomy of "black athletic style" in *Forty Million Dollar Slaves* (2006), that the difficulties facing African American men in this country could—in highly individualized ways—affect the on-court manifestation of their basketball abilities. Each player's style "is a function of his personality," Shoals wrote, and "there exists a similar bond between personality and biography" (2008, "My Interview with Nets Rookie Anthony Randolph"). Beating incredible odds not merely by becoming professional athletes but also by navigating an American social landscape structured with bias against them, black players often have dramatic life stories. Since style is an exercise in "personalized basketball storytelling," it would follow that, at least to some degree, their on-court stories would be similarly dynamic (Shoals 2007, "The Mind's Lungless Ankle").

Still, the primary authors of FreeDarko were careful to recognize the limitations of their ability to speak on matters of racial inequality. As Shoals wrote,

> We at FreeDarko are not exactly in a position to speak authoritatively about race in the NBA. Some of us are pretty dark, several of us could

get away with claiming non-white when we take standardized tests, and (here it comes) I can always mouth "Holocaust" if you want to call me out on my people's place in the big book of discrimination. But on the real, I'm not black, none of our contributors are, and I'd just as soon defer to African-Americans in the league when it comes to deciding what they think might stink of Grand Wizardry. (2005, "Just Remember Who Said It")

Despite this assertion, Shoals and Co. couldn't ultimately leave the conversation about race to African American players themselves. In the NBA's "war between corporate interests and African-American aesthetics," the players are implicitly, if not explicitly, discouraged from speaking out (Shoals 2005, "Amare Who?"). And in the wake of Hurricane Katrina, the inequalities it laid bare, and the NBA players' response to it, the authors of FreeDarko had to admit, as Brown Recluse, Esq. put it, that "race is never too far from our minds and hearts" (2006, "Happy Birthday to Us"). In addition to the site's consideration of Katrina, race "also provided a lens through which we've viewed such [NBA] topics as the age limit and the new dress code" (Recluse, Esq. 2006, "Happy Birthday to Us"). Occasionally carried out in stand-alone posts that bore the titular prefix "Racial Semiotics," the work of discussing race was taken seriously even as it was constantly incorporated into the discussions surrounding *the site's* conceptual innovations like the Positional Revolution. "No sport more accurately represents the contemporary question of race in America than this treasured diversion of ours," Shoals asserted, adding that "the NBA offers no easy answers, no fixed categories, and no clear sense of direction. I'm not here to insult anyone's intelligence, but this ambiguity, coupled with the haunting possibility of socio-cultural landmines, pretty much mirrors American attitudes on race" (2006, "The Crown Is Dead").

Whether discussing the discriminatory business practices of Donald Sterling, the racist connotations of the word "thug" as they pertained to polarizing players like Allen Iverson and Ron Artest, or the meaning of Jeremy Lin, FreeDarko continually asserted that just having the conversation was important, because, as Shoals wrote, "fans are not particularly inclined to rock the boat these days, since most sports fans are aware of athletes, not socio-culturally constituted public figures. When things are going well, no one wants to talk about race, especially if it can be kept out of the basketball conversation entirely" (2006, "The Unfortunate Moss"). But considerations of race and the NBA should also affect more than just the basketball conversation, contributor ForeversBurns argued: "Black cultural norms and white fear of them sorely needs intelligent discussion in this country and . . . the NBA provides a forum large enough for everyone to hear it" (2007, "Harvest Moon"). Rather than merely a mode of escape or distraction, basketball's popular position as an entertainment product makes it an even more potent forum for racial considerations.

Even so, Shoals was careful to point out that while the NBA, its players, and fans reflect many American racial issues, they do not usually affect the larger politics of race in this country. Contrary to the Jackie Robinson-mediated notion that sports is a kind of forerunning influence on social justice, as Shoals puts it, "sports can have political undertones and associations, but rarely lead the way" (2007, "Look Down That Lonesome Road"). When fans closely read the NBA narrative, in other words, they can see racial misunderstanding and implicit bias everywhere in it. As with any text, those readings matter, and sharing them in pursuit of a more inclusive, informed, racially aware culture is important. That does not mean that the players can be expected to advance the politics fans prefer, or even express any politics. Fans can mythologize and celebrate players, but they must always remember that they are people, too: much as the league, teams, or corporate sponsors might attempt to influence them, the players author themselves. "You can read the world onto the NBA," Shoals wrote, "but you can't read the NBA back onto the world" (2007, "FreeDarko Book Club #2"). Writing long before the NFL's Colin Kaepernick took a knee and started a protest movement, before Donald Trump became president and fanned the flames of bigotry, Shoals and company could not have envisioned how much prominence athletes, and particularly black athletes, would assume in our political discourse beginning in 2016. Still, FreeDarko recognized the players' personhood and political potential a decade beforehand.

Politically aware as they were, the authors of FreeDarko were nevertheless made to wonder if being any kind of fan of the NBA could have pernicious effects for African Americans. These worries came to a head when Shoals—then a graduate student at the University of Texas—was tasked with reading the work of John Hoberman, a professor at UT and author of *Darwin's Athletes*. As Shoals aptly summarized it, in *Darwin's Athletes*, Hoberman's

> basic argument . . . goes like this: mythologizing sports leads to a gross over-estimation of their societal worth, and ignores the pernicious effect the have had on the black community. Kids want to be athletes, who ultimately are not that special or interesting and are stuck in a white-controlled business venture. Few of them will get to become one of the pros they emulate, so they'll have effectively forfeited their future. Compounding the problem are black intellectuals, who see sports as a meaningful cultural contribution. Comparing sports to jazz is an example of this. Seeing sports as a meaningful vanguard of racial harmony is another; this is also a tactic employed by white liberals who like their politics anthemic. (2007, "FreeDarko Book Club #2")

Reading *Darwin's Athletes* effectively threatened FreeDarko by calling into question the site's social responsibility: the practice of amplifying and analyzing NBA narratives about black athletes, Hoberman's book argues, is damaging to regular, non-professional-athlete African Americans. Shoals countered by reaffirming the utility of self-reflective, racially aware conversation in and of itself: "our political usefulness comes in our insistence that, through the NBA, we can be compelled to frankly discuss race," he wrote, adding that "there are forms of myth-making that can serve a political purpose without offering a false hope or loopy directive" (2007, "FreeDarko Book Club #2").[4]

In many ways, Shoals's defense of basketball fandom resonates with Italo Calvino's notion that reading literature makes us "aware of the disease of our hidden motives," and as such provides a "way of starting to invent a new way of being" (1987, 100). If communal discourse on race like FreeDarko's can help the NBA's fan-readers do the same, then it can effect political change on an individual basis. Insofar as FreeDarko had the capacity to make readers such as Will Leitch "realize the power of caring this much, of thinking this hard, and investing this much" (quoted in Shoals 2011, "The Day Never Ended"), it could help them recognize that while Allen Iverson might not be "poor, or discriminated against in any spine-sharding way, . . . what we see, and the way its dealt with by media and the fans, is certainly an effective metaphor for situation he would face if he didn't ball" (2007, "FreeDarko Book Club #2"). That said, what the readers bring to such an exercise matters as much as what the NBA text itself represents: for those seeking purportedly "post-racial" entertainment, the NBA as a commercial entity is more than happy to oblige. When it came to "Racial Semiotics," as with many things FreeDarko, one thus had to choose to "define [oneself] against 'the basketball industry'" to recognize those politically-useful forms of mythmaking (Shoals 2007, "On The Eve of Pricey Incursion"). The site's self-consciously "liberated" brand of fan identity and its racially aware politics were inextricable.

Compared to FreeDarko, Fire Joe Morgan's consideration of race seemed less urgent and existentially determining. This was the natural result of the fact that player demographics were invisible to the statistical metrics they championed. But the journalists that Fire Joe Morgan lampooned were certainly not free from bias, however, and one particular storyline—or set of descriptors, really—seemed based in something more insidious than mere hewing to rhetorical formulas or cutting narrative corners. These descriptors, of the "throwback" "lunchpail" player who played with particular "grit," "hustle," or "scrappiness" were frequently used by writers and commentators operating in a nostalgic mode. The Fire Joe Morgan crew naturally balked, as these designations are basically impossible to quantify. But they also objected for another reason: in assessing the notion that particular players could represent some historically determined measure of effort, the writers of Fire Joe Morgan noticed that the players described in this way were almost always white. "No minority players [are] ever called 'throwbacks' or praised for their 'grit' and 'hustle' and 'old-school'-ness," wrote Ken Tremendous; "It is one of the oddest things. No Dominican players, no Afro-Am players, not even the odd Curacaoian" (2007 "Someday You, Too"). It was as if baseball writers, in asserting that extra effort was somehow evocative of a nostalgic pseudo-history, could not see beyond the color line imposed by Major League Baseball from the 1880s until 1947, ignored or disregarded the Negro Leagues, *and* were incapable of making interracial comparisons between modern MLB players of color and their white forbears from baseball's "Golden Age." In the writings of baseball journalists, it seemed, the virtues of "hustle" were still segregated.

The paragon of "the scrappiness racism that pervades baseball commentary" as delineated by Fire Joe Morgan was the 5′7″, 175lb. shortstop of the 2006 St. Louis Cardinals, David Eckstein (Murbles 2005, "As a GM"). Eckstein was a journeyman known for his bunting ability whose performance in the 2006 postseason helped St. Louis make an improbable run to the World Series title (for which he was named the Series' Most Valuable Player). The media covering the playoffs fell in love with the diminutive player, smothering him with praise that, as Fire Joe Morgan's crew was quick to point out, was disproportionate to his impact. Occasionally, Fire Joe Morgan highlighted the flawed strategic thinking inherent in this praise, like that of a *New York Times* article asserting that "although St. Louis is still best known for Albert Pujols's 450-foot home runs, Eckstein's 10-foot bunts can be just as productive" (Tremendous 2006, "Has Anyone Heard"). More often, however, they focused on mocking the rhetoric of "scrappiness," as Junior did in fisking the *St. Louis Post-Dispatch*:

> [Post-Dispatch:] Never one to shy from taking the extra base-in fact, it's in the dna of his grit-Cardinals shortstop David Eckstein did something unusual in the ninth inning as he rounded second base. He stopped.
>
> [Junior:] Now we know: David Eckstein's grit can reproduce. Look for David's awkwardly titled autobiography, *The DNA of My Grit*, ghostwritten by Buzz Bissinger and printed with ink produced from David's own blood, sweat, and tears. (2006, "Lede-Writing School)

Highlighting the incongruity between the scientific precision of "DNA" and the nostalgic gauziness of a player's "grit," Junior satirically amplified this tension by connecting the language of scrappiness—"blood, sweat, and tears"—to that of the reproduction of sportswriting itself. The nonsensical notion that bodily fluids could be used as ink is no more ridiculous, Junior suggested, than the notion that Eckstein is genetically predisposed to play harder. What's more, such a notion of "grit" as a biologically determined inclination to hard work, contextualized by its almost exclusive application to undersized white players like Eckstein, is effectively a linguistic assertion of baseball-based white supremacy.

Though they did not usually connect his "hustle" to his genes, many similar articles used effusive, racially coded language in praising Eckstein despite his apparent physical limitations and lackluster statistics. By the end of the 2006 season, the Fire Joe Morgan crew had come across so many such articles that they began forgoing thorough fiskings. Instead, they merely linked to each article and provided a list of its most objectionable descriptors. Concerned that they not be perceived as "haters," the Fire Joe Morgan authors reminded readers that their jokes at Eckstein's expense were not ad hominem: "we . . . do not hate David Eckstein. What we hate is bad sports journalism. . . . Apparently, nothing brings out the cliché machines faster than a small man who plays sports" (Tremendous 2006, "Eckstein Round Up"). But they also could not entirely limit their criticism of the "scrappiness racism" that surrounded Eckstein to the media members propagating it (Murbles 2005, "As a GM"). Major League Baseball and its fans also eagerly endorsed the notion that Eckstein incarnated a vintage, racially coded bootstraps ethos that would suggest that effort conquers all. To wit, Eckstein easily won the 2006 Holiday Inn "Look Again Player of the Year" award. Junior fisked the award description by providing his "translation" of its verbiage:

> Behind every great team on the diamond, lurking in the shadow of baseball superstars, live the role players who sacrifice for their team in often unrecognized effort. Which of these role players' best deserves recognition for their contributions as the Holiday Inn Look Again Player of the Year? . . .

> Behind all the great colored and Latino or whatever the fuck players who are actually good at baseball, in the deep dark shadow-realm of guys who only make $3 to 8 million dollars a year, live the role players whose jobs are so torturous and awful that other grown humans pay to see them and applaud when they walk into their offices. White, tiny, albino, and white, these Ecksteins, proto-Ecksteins, and mega-Ecksteins need more love from crappy budget-priced motel chains and you, the paying fan. Which of these Ecksteins is the Eckiest? The answer: David Eckstein. (2006, "The David Eckstein Memorial")

Consequently listing "David Eckstein's name and the names of the guys who will lose to David Eckstein," Junior sarcastically asked about the list of thirty names: "Notice anything? Yep, two non-whiteys. White people: role players who are always sacrificing for the glory of the non-whites" (2006, "The David Eckstein Memorial"). Pointing out the overwhelming whiteness of role players eligible for the award, Junior satirically framed this disproportion on the terms of reverse racism, whereby white people suppose that minorities have an advantage over them because of compensation for past disadvantage. In such a rhetorical economy of false self-victimization, the notion that "gritty" players like Eckstein are popular because they "are always sacrificing for the glory of the non-whites" makes sense. His timely performance amplified by the postseason spotlight, Eckstein had become the preeminent icon of "scrappiness," but the racial connotations of who is or is not a "role player" were extended league-wide and, in this case, reified by fan voting. In challenging the language of "hustle" and "grit" and pointing out its unbearable whiteness, then, the ramifications of Fire Joe Morgan's close reading in the name of comedy reached well beyond David Eckstein and the individual propagators of "Bad Sports Journalism." It addressed the legacies of U.S. racism, the related danger of nostalgia, and their influence on the very language with which "America's Pastime" was considered in the broadest discourse. Though Fire Joe Morgan's consideration of race was certainly less self-reflective than FreeDarko's, the FJM authors effectively recognized the eminently quotidian nature of systemic inequality, and pointed out that something as simple as close reading could be used to expose it.

Where FreeDarko and Fire Joe Morgan primarily attended to matters of race and fandom, Power Forward's politics were usually oriented to issues of gender inequity. In particular, given Jessica Luther's primary understanding that sports are narratives and that "how we tell those stories matter," her focus on gender inequity often considered the many ways in which sports media narratives disregarded women fans such as herself (2014, email message to the author). For example, "during the Olympics," Luther wrote of the 2012 Summer Games, "we get to watch all sorts of women play all sorts of sports. That is no small deal" (2012, "The Double-Edged Sword"). Unlike much of the rest of the modern American sportscape, in which "men are the assumed participants unless otherwise specified," at the Olympics "'men's' is not the default" (Luther 2012, "The

Double-Edged Sword"). These women's events get roughly equivalent billing, and ratings to match: a circumstance unequaled in other spectator sports contexts. Why? Because, as Luther put it, "the Olympics is an event predicated on nationalism, a manufactured collective 'us'" (2012, "The Double-Edged Sword"). So long as the women's competitors wear flags on their uniforms, they are placed under the "metaphorical umbrella" of national collective identity (2012, "The Double-Edged Sword"). Jingoism, in this case, serves to draw women athletes into the sphere of interest and relevance to millions of sports consumers who would normally ignore or stigmatize them.

Even under the "metaphorical umbrella," however, these women athletes are covered by the same sports media that is largely inconsiderate to them in other contexts. Documenting numerous instances of this insensitivity in coverage surrounding the 2012 games, Luther demonstrated that the enhanced coverage of women's Olympic athletes was a "double-edged sword" both "awesome and . . . maddening" (2012, "The Double-Edged Sword"). Between Olympics, however, the sword predominantly cuts the maddening way, and Luther frequently took it upon herself to criticize the "DudeBro Sports Media" for its gender bias and essentialism (2013, "DudeBro Sports Media"). "It's not simply that misogyny exists," Luther wrote, "it's that it is specifically hellish within sports culture and the media plays a significant role in that" (2013, "On Brittney Griner").

How is this sports media misogyny manifested, beyond the mere fact of the relative lack of coverage for women's sports? In seemingly ordinary conversations like the one in which ESPN *SportsCenter* anchor John Anderson analogized "Wes Welker going from catching footballs from Tom Brady to catching footballs from Peyton Manning as 'sort of like Leo DiCaprio trading a Victoria Secret model for a *Sports Illustrated* model'" (2013, "Catching Footballs"). To many—maybe even most—heterosexual men accustomed to their hegemony in American sports culture, the notion that, as the title of Luther's post put it, "Catching Footballs Is Just Like Trading Women" may seem utterly unremarkable. But for Luther, "as a woman and a huge sports fan and spectator, [it is representative of the way in which] the sports media is ALWAYS there to remind me with casual, everyday sexism, that I am NOT the intended audience for their programs and their clever quips" (2013, "Catching Footballs"). Like the inclusion of cheerleaders on football sidelines, such "everyday sexism" normalizes the notion that women are "images/accessories" and drives away many women from potential interest in spectator sports (2013, "Why Ladies Nights").

This kind of quotidian objectification thus also buttresses the

> popular cultural narrative that women, as a group, don't really like sports or are ignorant of how sports are played [which itself could be thought of as] a self-fulfilling prophecy: girls aren't taught about sports or encouraged to enjoy them because people assume that the girls don't want to know. But we live in a post-Title IX world. [To quote journalist] Lindsey Adler . . . 'We are not rare.'" (Luther 2014, "Charlie Strong's UT Women's Football Camp").

The statistics cited by Adler and others about sports consumption back this up: despite the pervasive misogyny around them, more than one in three self-identifying sports fans is a woman, and leagues like the NFL largely have women to thank for recent expansions in their consumer base (Chemi 2014). Luther noted, however, that rather than adopting more-inclusive discourse, the major sports leagues have largely responded to the expanded role of women sports fans by sectioning them off as a "special" interest. Hosting "Ladies Nights" and marketing pink merchandise on and off the field, the sports industry communicates that "for one night/month we will focus on women and include them in our club" and implicitly denies the fact that "women are in the club all the time, they just aren't acknowledged as such. I just wish (and wish and wish and wish) that we could start from a place where men and women are both seen as normal fans of the sport. If pink = women, what do the other colors mean the rest of the time?" (Luther 2013, "About the Oregon Ducks' Pink Uniforms"). Asserting that all sports narratives are for all women all of the time, Luther rebuked the implicit gender segregation of sports fans by sports leagues. But this is not merely a matter to be handled by the teams and their marketing departments: Luther imagined and demanded a gender equitable sports media to match, and she aspired to make herself a part of it.

Because "sports media sucks for women," Luther embraced the notion on Power Forward and in her freelance work that she is a member of the "rebel media" (2014, "Weeping for Sports Media"). She aimed, as she put it, to "operate outside of the standard journalistic structures that often demand that people not offend people by talking about the problems they see" (Luther 2013, "On Brittney Griner"). Uncompromised by the commercial partnerships of an entity like ESPN, Luther was able to set her own freelance agenda. Even as a free agent, however, Luther noted that she has had to ask herself whether the price of tolerating misogyny was worth publication:

> I've written at sports sites that have their own section just to show off boobs. And publishing in those spaces always leads to me questioning what I am doing: "Do I publish at the sports place that has the boobs stuff and get my stuff at least near to that? Or do I avoid it all together because the very rape culture I'm trying to discuss is just being propped up right over there next to my words?" I feel constantly pulled between these two questions and angry that these are questions I even have to ask . . . . Sure sex sells. And sports media makes bank off that . . . But this is the sports media you want to be a part of? This is the sports media you are happy to do? Objectifying women for some fucking clicks on your SUPPOSED SPORTS SITE? (2014, "Weeping for Sports Media")

Publishing work about rape culture in sports next to pictures of minimally-attired women may further her professional goals, but the price of having the journalistic medium undermine her message led Luther to question a system that would require such a sacrifice. Envisioning and demanding a sports media landscape that not only transmits but affirms feminist politics, Luther reaffirmed her role as a woman, fan, and writer unwilling to compromise any single aspect of her identity to accommodate another. As she told The Feminist Wire, "I am a feminist sports fan. I am a feminist anything. That's a hat I can't take off." As such, it is her mission to continually remind: "I am here! Women are here!" (quoted in Leonard 2014).

On one hand, Luther's fan critique of gender and sports media is distinct from FreeDarko and Fire Joe Morgan's considerations of race because, as a woman, she is a member of the disadvantaged group whose status she interrogates. The white male heterosexism inherent in most sports media narratives affects her directly, not just the athletes she follows.

On the other hand, given her professional identity as a journalist, Luther has put herself in a position to work within that media to affect change. Regardless of any additional influence her professional status may afford her, however, the fact that Luther was able to gain such professional status by asserting the inherent politics of her fan identity on Power Forward speaks to the additional agency afforded fans by web-mediated expression. "Women are here" indeed, and blogs like Power Forward allow such women to assert their presence, and their politics, to a much broader audience of fellow fans, male and female.

Expanding on his notion that the discursive framing of athletes has diversified to the point of incoherence, Cornel Sandvoss concludes that contemporary athletes have become "constantly adaptable spaces of discourse that correspond with changing sociocultural conditions as well as agency within them" (2012, 179). For the European sociologist, the athletes' status as "flexible vessel[s] of identity" for fans renders a "diminishing role [for such] athletes as authors of their public persona" (Sandvoss 2012, 179, 182). But such assertions effectively represent for sports narratives what literary critics call "the intentional fallacy." Sports stars partially author the narratives in which they participate, but they do not determine their meaning in that narrative's interpretation. That has always been the fan-readers' role, and such fan-readers have always done so in diverse and politically distinct ways. The difference is that earlier incarnations of sporting mass media did not effectively communicate the wide range of those interpretations to, or among, distinct social groupings of fans. FreeDarko, Fire Joe Morgan, and Power Forward counter Sandvoss's notion that an increasing number of discourses of fan signification is to the athletes' detriment. These blogs demonstrate the capacities of fans to consider identity politics as a determining influence on their modes of interpreting sports narratives, and therein, on their consideration of athletes. While such self-aware considerations of how fan consumption affects the mediation of athletes may represent the exception, rather than the rule, their very presence shows the importance of the blogosphere in allowing fans to communicate nuanced interpretations beyond the "singular, easily-identifiable themes" ascribed to athletes by mass media (Sandvoss 2012, 178).

In a larger sense, what FreeDarko, Fire Joe Morgan, and Power Forward did—in rethinking sports fan attachment, reconceptualizing the structures and emphases of sports' narrativity, and reexamining the stakes of sports' identity politics—was emphasize and extend the intertextual potential of sports narratives. Far from marginal, sports narratives can powerfully inform and influence the way fans make sense of the world, and to pretend they are isolated from our larger concerns about politics, aesthetics, and culture—as some fans and media are wont to do as part of a "stick to sports" mentality—is reductive and dishonest. But intertextuality is not an innovation of the internet era. It is "not new," asserted Patrick O'Donnell and Robert Con Davis in their 1989 compendium *Intertextuality and Contemporary American Fiction*. Rather, intertextuality "is the oldest troping we know, the most ancient textual (con)figuration" (xiii). As poststructuralist literary critics recognized, texts are always relational—all writing, at least implicitly, references other texts. All the same, as Linda Hutcheon and other critics of postmodernism realized, the authorial ethos of referentiality has changed over time, ensuring that "intertextuality in postmodern art both provides and undermines context" (Hutcheon 1989, 8). Intertextual reference, in other words, can be used to not merely to communicate, but to interrogate the very basis of communication.

Framed in this way, we might think of mainstream sports news websites like ESPN.com and SI.com, which include hyperlinks, images, and embedded video in their textual coverage, as using internet tools to provide conventional contexts for sports narratives. For example, a typical game recap might have links to player biographies and statistics, a photo gallery of the game, and video of an analyst describing the contest's significance and determining factors. By contrast, FreeDarko, Fire Joe Morgan, and Power Forward used those same internet tools to extend, or even undermine, contexts. They self-consciously juxtaposed ideas and stories not commonly associated with sports narratives in order to gain a greater purchase on how those narratives might be better understood. This could mean (de)contextualizing a sports narrative by discussing hip-hop and Hegel, referencing Oedipus or jurisprudence, including photos of political revolutionaries and videos of jazz performance, or embedding a Twitter conversation about feminism in a blog post. Far from forced, this mode of comparative media generation was effective in part because it was natural.

In the information-intensive environment of the internet (and especially in light of social media), users are perpetually "hyper-reading": "filtering by keywords, skimming, hyperlinking, . . . juxtaposing, as when several open windows allow one to read across several texts, and scanning, as when one reads rapidly through a blog to identify items of interest" (Hayles 2012, 61). These blogs co-evolved with the metatextual architecture of web-based narratives so that they not only had the capacity to connect disparate cultural forms and intellectual contexts, but also internalized the inclination to do so.

Distinct as FreeDarko, Fire Joe Morgan, and Power Forward's incarnations of intertextuality may have been, each naturally extended and undermined contexts for sports narratives in ways that would have seemed unprecedented or exceptional in the pre-internet era. And in doing this intertextual work, the three blogs were not ostracized or ignored, but in fact developed devoted readerships that functioned as fan communities of their own. For thousands of fan-readers, finding fellow fans who thought about sports narratives beyond the confines of the play-by-play, postgame recap, and television talking heads was a revelation and a reassurance. In writing their own literature of sports experience and expressing it online, then, FreeDarko, Fire Joe Morgan, and Power Forward not only reoriented what it means to be a fan through their selection of words, images, and video, but fostered the reimagined communities that grew up around their texts. They exemplify Paul Booth and Lucy Bennett's assertion that "fans are a compelling, ever-changing audience with multiple layers that are often more dimensional than the overarching and limited ways they have been historically represented in media and popular culture" (2016, 1).

EPILOGUE
Feminist Rewritings of Sports Fan Culture

> As a woman who writes and talks about baseball, I know there's
> always a man at the ready to tell you that you got it wrong.
>
> STACEY MAY FOWLES, *Baseball Life Advice*[1]

As conventional wisdom would suggest, and much of my analysis in this
book has demonstrated, sports fandom is often hierarchizing; along lines
of gender, sex, and race, normative sports culture too often works as a tool
of oppression meant to preserve the entitlement and empowerment of
the white heterosexual men who still wield disproportionate authority in
American society writ large. However, as the examination of self-reflective
fan accounts contained herein has also demonstrated, sports fan culture
should not be construed as static, monolithic, or uncreative. The potential
for alternative narratives that remake or reshape fans' understanding
of their role such that they subvert or reconceptualize that hierarchical
structure is always present, and never more palpable than in electronically
mediated contexts. And yet, especially since the rise of Trumpism, it would
be naïve and irresponsible to suggest that those very same electronically
mediated spaces—particularly social media platforms like Twitter and
Facebook—are not all-too-often repurposed to further oppressive, hate-
ful, and even violent ideologies. Self-reflective fan authorship and the
creative possibilities fostered by online spaces is not enough to liberate
sports fandom from its oppressive cultural underpinnings. For that, we
need feminism.

In concluding *The I in Team: Sports Fandom and the Reproduction of
Identity*, Erin C. Tarver provides a history of feminist critiques of sport

and sporting cultures, and comes to the conclusion that feminist thinkers have been too quick to write off sports as *inherently* masculinist. To "accept [this premise] without question," she writes, "is to reproduce a problematically reductive view of [sports fandom], which accepts the very normative framework it seeks to criticize. Women's sports fandom may not by 'typical,' but this is precisely the point. Women fans and fans of women's sports *do* fandom in ways that give us reason to hope that for sports fans, all may not yet be lost."[2] Indeed, all is not lost: rather, as Tarver demonstrates in examining fan cultures like the "LeBron James Grandmothers Fan Club" and the WNBA's LGBTQ fan community (the league's core fan base), there is plenty being gained. And when it comes to prominent narrative representations of woman fan authors operating in a feminist authorial mode, there is no better recent example than Stacey May Fowles and her memoir, *Baseball Life Advice: Loving the Game that Saved Me.*

Born from the archives of Fowles's regularly published "Tiny Letter," an email-based online writing platform not dissimilar in form and function from the blogs examined in the last chapter, *Baseball Life Advice* is a collection of essays that convey both what the game means to the author and, crucially, what it *could mean* to many more people if its fan culture can be detoxified—eliminating the vestiges of misogyny and homophobia that still linger (or thrive). Using Fowles's work as a road map, I conclude this book on a hopeful note and imagine how sports fandom can arrive at a more inclusive future. Tracing four main themes from Fowles's work—community, gender, violence, and narrativity—I demonstrate the means by which sports fandom, for all the flaws in the mainstream manifestation that dominates the public imagination, remains at its core a mode of identity construction with empowering possibilities that are inclusive and accessible to all.

Part of what makes Fowles's fan narrative so dynamic and effective is that she would seem (and is often seen as) an outsider to baseball culture: not only is she a woman (never—as Jessica Luther argues persuasively—the presumed audience for spectator sports), she is also a Canadian obsessive of America's "national pastime." Furthermore, as a survivor of an abusive relationship, Fowles recognizes her particular sensitivity to the ways in which male athletes' domestic abuses are brushed aside or ignored by fans prioritizing on-the-field excellence over off-the-field malfeasance. Yet for all these obstacles to her meaningful attachment to the game, Fowles finds in baseball a mode of self-discovery that invigorates and provides insight into her identity. Even in spite of the misogynist confrontation and denigration she faces in online spaces, she is committed to making baseball fandom a more inclusive space for women.

Fowles is not shy about the fact that "baseball is one of those things I was never told I should love. It wasn't passed down to me like some sacred family heirloom, and I didn't take it up because of a desperate need to fit in." Rather, she asserts, "I chose it for myself," despite the fact "that I was largely discouraged from loving this pastime and culture—built for men and boys, fathers and sons—that's not always welcoming of my gender."[3] Rather than a birthright, "baseball fan" is for Fowles a consciously assumed mantle of identity, and her sense of its positive possibilities is based on her pride in overcoming obstacles: baseball "made itself hard to love and I embraced it anyway. Because of that, it belongs to me in a way nothing else does."[4] This formulation of possession reverses the usual terms of belonging: Fowles has agency over baseball, rather than belonging to the game, or her team, the Toronto Blue Jays. Instead of being "told what we want and will enjoy," Fowles asserts the right of female sports fans to "articulate it ourselves."[5] Her feminism powers her understanding that "every fan's personal experience of the game is different, regardless of gender, and the stereotypes we reinforce only limit and harm the overall community."[6]

Crucially, Fowles's inherent sense of agency in identification as a baseball fan emboldens her to encourage others (particularly other women) to make similarly empowering decisions. In a chapter titled "All Aboard the Bandwagon," she admits to getting "overly excited . . . about being a part of someone's very first baseball outing. That's largely because I want them to love the game experience as much as I do . . . to enjoy every last minute of those nine innings."[7] She also espouses an aggressively anti-hierarchical stance on the practice of "gatekeeping," by which "real" fans, who are almost always men, presume their authority to mark other would-be fans (often women, or other men perceived to be insufficiently knowledgeable) as unworthy of the mantle. "There is absolutely nothing wrong with jumping on a sports-fandom bandwagon," Fowles writes, "and anyone who says otherwise hates joy. . . . Gatekeeping is never admirable, and what defines a 'real fan' could possibly be one of the most boring topics of conversation in the world. . . . Lifelong adherents of the Church of Baseball know that it makes good sense to encourage as many devotees as possible."[8] Embracing a flexible, self-determined basis for fan identification even as she invokes the ubiquitous religious analogy (one that would seem to at least partly undermine her anti-hierarchical stance), Fowles recognizes—as Andrei Markovits and Emily Albertson did in *Sportista*,[9] their study of female fandom—that gatekeeping is a practice of preserving power based on gender distinctions, of ensuring "the inherent loneliness of being a female fan."[10]

By purposely resisting these masculinist exclusionary practices, and fostering an inclusionary practice of welcoming new fans of both genders, Fowles demonstrates that, as Tarver puts it,

> women tend to know sports fandom as a means of social bonding, as a set of practices that increase feelings of love, connection, and community. Whereas men know the details of the histories of the games, which they take to be the crux of fandom, women often recognize the larger set of social practices—the rituals, the traditions, the means of cultivating family and group identity—as meaningful, and perhaps as the underlying reason for participating in the spectacle of the games at all.[11]

Women like Fowles, in other words, get that the community of sports fandom is not a tertiary benefit, but rather the prime reason to identify with a sports team, player, or league. In this, they are fundamentally similar to the online media fan communities and fanfiction writing groups, often predominately made up of women, that espouse an ethics of fandom based on mutual support and community-building. As Fowles bluntly puts it, "those who refuse to actively foster a welcoming environment at the ballpark and within sports culture are on the wrong side of history."[12] But she is clear-eyed about the fact that her vision for and practice of sports fandom face an uphill battle: "as a woman who writes and talks about baseball, I know there's always a man at the ready to tell you that you got it wrong. There's always someone at the ballpark eager to test your knowledge, your fandom, your passion, and your right to be there."[13]

Gender powers gatekeeping because, per Tarver, "to trivialize fandom by making it feminine" constitutes an existential threat to the "homosocial and hypermasculine" proxy benefits that many men perceive.[14] So whether they articulate it explicitly or not, community matters to male fans, too. Their "hatred of newcomers," Fowles reflects, is indicative of their "fear of losing power, and reveals an anxiety around who gets to define sports culture and how it is discussed."[15] Being demeaned by threatened male fans, in the stands and online, takes its toll on her, Fowles admits, asserting that such "harassment has tainted the enthusiasm I once had for being a part of the sports community."[16] And yet she refuses to back down, to yield an inch to those hostile men who would have her take her writing talents elsewhere. Feminism accounts for this tenacity, to be sure, but Fowles also reaffirms the things that brought her to baseball stadiums in the first place: "During every high-intensity play, pitch or at-bat, I cry, and I squirm, and I yell full-throated without fear of who hears me. I am raw, vulnerable, and unashamed. I am my most authentic self."[17] Fowles understands that not only is she an important part of baseball and its culture, baseball has become an important part of her. To allow herself to be driven out of the game would be to tantamount to a betrayal of her "most authentic self."

Insofar as feminist fans like Fowles can push for inclusivity in community formation in the stands, however, they must also grapple with the ramifications of the parallel hypermasculine culture surrounding the players in the men's professional leagues that dominate the most mass-mediated sports. This male bravado influences fan perceptions of the players' capacities for camaraderie, emotional expression, and violence. One such manifestation is baseball's assortment of "unwritten rules," a collection of purportedly ironclad codes indicating appropriate behavior on a baseball diamond, and which mete out violent retribution—in the form of fastballs or fisticuffs—for perceived indiscretions. Fowles writes back against this culture, and fan endorsement of it:

> *Don't be openly proud of your accomplishments lest ye get hit in the ribs and punched squarely in the jaw, little one.* What kind of deranged, destructive viewpoint is that? When baseball disputes happen, we're expected to take a side—brand one team or player evil, the other

good, and then fight it out viciously among the fanbases. We fail to foster any productive dialogue or nuance, nor do we understand how ingrained systems of institutional violence just beget more violence, and that a "pound of flesh" pitch is a sanctioned first step toward a punch in the face. We watch as high-profile commentators [claim] that this is just the way it's supposed to be, and everyone involved is simply a puppet in baseball's grand, mythical stage play.[18]

Rather than merely dispute the appropriateness of violent retribution for an in-game spirit of fun and fair play, as many others have done, Fowles highlights the toxic ramifications that unquestioned acceptance of these "ingrained systems of institutional violence" must have far beyond the field. The potential for "productive dialogue and [appreciation of] nuance" aren't merely benefits of a self-reflective fan identity, then, they are necessary measures of improvement for the culture of these sports themselves.[19] To those who might question Fowles's standing to call for such careful consideration and reform of such "traditional" sporting institutions and cultures, she defiantly proclaims: "this is my game as much as it is the game of those who view it through [a] fetishized, old-school, lens. I am allowed to object to escalating (and sometimes illegal) aggressive acts, sanctioned or otherwise. . . . The fact is, when violence is promoted as an appropriate dispute resolution in sports, that concept can bleed into all areas of our lives, with dire results."[20] The question as to whether athletes can rightly be considered "role models" is one debated by sports philosophers like Tarver and Randolph Feezell, but Fowles's point is well-taken regardless. The normalization of violence in conflict resolution transcends the ludic frame of these games and inevitably influences broader cultural norms. "I came to baseball fandom precisely because it offered me a shelter from the ubiquity of violence," Fowles asserts, "and I am allowed to express my disappointment when aggression rears its ugly head in this place where I've found refuge."[21]

But the gendered expectations for athletes when it comes to their capacity for violence are not merely a matter of their in-stadium conduct. They also extend to such athletes' off-the-field behavior, and this is a particular concern for Fowles when it comes to domestic abuse. Beginning her chapter on the subject, "Moving Forward Without Forgetting: Major League Baseball and Domestic Violence," with a personal narrative of her own recuperative efforts in the wake of abuse, Fowles then relates the case of José Reyes, a one-time Toronto Blue Jay, who was suspended by MLB after allegedly grabbing his wife, Katherine Ramirez, by the throat and shoving her into a sliding-glass door. Fowles asserts that "for those of us who have endured abuse at the hands of someone we loved and trusted, the discussion around [Reyes and other athletes accused of abuse] is not an abstract baseball debate, or some logic puzzle to be solved. It's more like opening an old wound that will never completely heal."[22] The trauma Fowles and millions of other women have suffered is not resolvable in the matter of wins and losses, nor is it measurable like statistics. It cannot be subtracted from a roster or rendered harmless by allegations recanted or charges dropped. In the case of Jose Reyes, the conviction never came "even though, in coded language, he has taken some ownership of the incident, and offered a lacklustre public apology for it at least twice."[23] While asserting that Ramirez's decision to drop the charges was a "personal choice . . . that was hers alone to make—just like forgiveness is hers alone to give," Fowles aims to complicate public discourse around "the kind of reception a player deserves post-suspension, and the flawed narrative of a 'triumph over adversity' that is being written about Reyes's return to the Mets."[24] Since Reyes previously played for the Blue Jays, Fowles

> can understand the challenge of reconciling the likeable, jovial face of Reyes, and the talent he displays on-field, with the reality of what he has done. I cheered exuberantly for him during the two and a half years he was on "my team." . . . Yet none of those prior warm feelings negate the alleged act of violence he committed. Those seeming opposites can exist in the same person—and very often, they do. Abusers can be "nice, likeable guys." Those of us who have been abused, or have witnessed abuse, understand all too well that nice guys hurt women all the time . . . that's exactly the kind of person you allow to get close enough to hurt you.[25]

Refuting any "satisfying, tidy resolution" of the type that many fans crave, one that would allow them to pretend that nothing happened and go on cheering for their favorite athletes after allegations of abuse, Fowles proclaims that "our team loyalties, and our desire to be comfortable watching the game, don't supersede the violation of another human being."[26] Though a lack of criminal charges or publicly visible evidence often means that athletes accused of violence against family members and intimate partners are allowed to return to prominence in the sports in which they excel—furthering the psychic toll for many victims—there is opportunity in the unresolvable situation: "If [sports leagues] seek to benefit from [an alleged abuser's] athletic skill, they have to accept valid criticism and take responsibility for what he has done—for what he has the capacity to do. Fans should also continuously hold these institutions, and the outlets that cover them, accountable, because if not us, who will?"[27] Though their own traumatic experiences may incline domestic abuse victims to silence as a mode of self-preservation, Fowles encourages them, and all fans who would hold baseball to a higher standard, to speak out: to help make the game's on- and off-the-field cultures of masculinist violence a thing of the past. Accountability begins at the home field, Fowles implies, not because fans *should be* responsible for holding their favorite teams accountable to standards of nonviolence and inclusivity, but because they recognize their fan identification provides them an opportunity. Rather than allow "racism, homophobia, sexism, DUIs, domestic abuse, physical violence, sexual assault, gambling, [and] drugs [to be] cloaked . . . by our fandom," Fowles asks that fans use their platform to call for justice and reform.[28]

Yet Fowles's encouragement of fan engagement is informed by more than her obvious desire to inculcate the anti-hierarchical intersectional feminist politics needed to transform baseball culture. It is also premised on her conceptualization of fan behavior on narrative terms. Fowles points out that despite fans' often obsessive association with athletes, "we often know so little about the players we come to love. We are rarely privy to their belief systems, or the way they treat the people in their lives. But we form a connection to athletes in much the same way we come to adore the characters in our favourite books. We revel in the feelings they conjure, and enjoy what our love for them reveals about ourselves."[29] Like many of the other fans and scholars examined in this book, Fowles self-consciously recognizes that her affiliation with real athletes is based on premises both fictional and personal. But she also takes this conceptualization one step further—beyond the mere recognition of the readerly basis of her fandom—to claim an interpersonal obligation to function as a *critical* reader. "Though the theatre of it all understandably entertains and amuses," Fowles asserts, "it shouldn't be remotely controversial to suggest that every plot point in the narrative . . . is worthy of our critique."[30] Reading sport isn't just something fans can and should do for personal fulfillment, but also a form of labor that can be directed to improve the games themselves. As Fowles recognizes, part and parcel of this critical mindset is an attendant widening of fan-readers' readerly purview. It is not merely the game on the field that should concern or motivate fans—the narrative landscape extends in every direction that these athlete-characters tread. Like literary critics, fans are capable—and encouraged, per Fowles—to analyze much more than the ostensible plot. And like athletes themselves, many of whom have been emboldened to speak out against injustice in the age of Trump, fans should never "stick to sports." Mass-mediated athletics are not an island of distraction: they are integrally interwoven into every aspect of fans' lives.

In many ways, *Baseball Life Advice* is the culmination of the creative and critical possibilities for self-reflective fan narratives that I have analyzed in this book. Fowles's memoir, though available in print, builds on the intertextual richness of web-based exchanges, without ignoring the ugliness that is also present in online spaces. Her self-conception as a fan is fundamentally rooted in a readerly perspective, alive to an understanding of athletes as flexible, fictional characters while always also recognizing that they are real people outside her fannish appropriations. And—perhaps most vitally—as a feminist fan unafraid to share her own traumas and attempt to build a better, more egalitarian baseball culture, Fowles is dedicated to expanding the progressive possibilities for fandom: to fighting and writing back against those heterosexual white men who would suggest that the game is ineluctably grounded in a retrograde, violent, misogynist politics that preserves their power. She provides hope that progress toward a more inclusive sports culture, though not inevitable, is possible—and premised on fans' understanding of the way they behave on narrative terms. Though every fan may be to some degree "average" and "unbeautiful," as David Foster Wallace cynically suggests, one wonders whether the "techne" that he sees in athletic genius—"mastery of craft [that] facilitate[s] a communion with the gods themselves"—might also be available to those attempting to "see, articulate, and animate the gift we are denied."[31] If so, while no fan may have achieved "techne," it seems to me that fans like Fowles are getting closer to it than Wallace ever imagined possible.

NOTES

Preface

1. Bixby, "Trump on Colin Kaepernick," https://www.theguardian.com/sorts/2016/aug/29/donald-trump-colin-kaepernick-national-anthem-protest.
2. Graham, "Donald Trump blasts," https://www.theguardian.com/sports/2017/sep/22/donald-trump-nfl-national-anthem-protest.
3. See, in particular, Schilling, "The 'Stick to Sports' Era Is Over" and Curtis, "The End of 'Stick to Sports,'" https://bleacherreport.com/articles/2735321-stick-to-sports-anthem-protest-interviews and https://www.theringer.com/2017/1/30/16046088/sportswriters-media-donald-trump-politics-a8b332bc48cf.
4. Wallace, "How Tracy Austin Broke My Heart," 143.

Introduction

1. Wallace, "How Tracy Austin Broke My Heart," 142–43.
2. Wallace, "How Tracy Austin Broke My Heart," 142.
3. Wallace, "How Tracy Austin Broke My Heart," 141, 143.
4. Wallace, "How Tracy Austin Broke My Heart," 155.
5. Wallace, "How Tracy Austin Broke My Heart," 155.
6. Wallace, "How Tracy Austin Broke My Heart," 142.
7. Before I go much further, I should articulate exactly what I mean by "fans." I share with Wallace a relative disinterest in drawing firm distinctions between "fans" and "spectators." Some scholars, such as psychologist Daniel Wann and his co-authors in *Sports Fans: The Psychology and Social Impact of Spectators*, have attempted to differentiate between "fans [as] individuals who are interested in and follow a sport, team, and/or athlete . . . [and] spectators . . . who actively witness a sporting event in person or through some form of media" (Wann et al. 2). In other words, fans *like* sports, and spectators *watch* them. Wann and company recognize, of course, that most fans are also frequent spectators, but they want to create a separate category for those who

watch sports with little interest in emotionally or analytically internalizing the proceedings. But Wallace's notion that "we spectators . . . see, articulate, and animate" sports complicates Wann's attempt at differentiation by emphasizing that the categorization of a spectator or fan cannot be static: each individual possesses a range of levels of engagement that can change at any moment (155). Like Wallace and literary theorist-cum-Stanford sports fan Hans Ulrich Gumbrecht, I position sports engagement on a wide "spectrum" of behavior that includes rote observation, analytical focus, and emotional outburst (Gumbrecht 221), and I thus consider "fan" and "spectator" as fluid assignations rather than concrete ones. Within the temporal boundaries of a single sporting event, a fan's level of investment can change drastically. And even those who dislike sports immensely can be said to have an emotional reaction to the games. Philosopher Erin C. Tarver's "broad definition of 'sports fan,' which is characterized by a combination of *care* (that is emotional investment) and *practice* (that is, some form of active engagement with the sport one watches)" (10–11), is closest to my own. Rather than rigidly define its limits, I use the term "fan" loosely to refer to anyone consuming (or "reading") sports.

The ramifications of this indistinction are significant. Foremost, it allows me to emphasize that the self-reflective engagements of the sports fans depicted in the texts I examine, while exceptional in some respects, are located on a common spectrum of fan behavior. Insofar as these fans are distinct from "average" fans, they are so as a matter of degree, not kind. To better understand what I mean, we might translate Wallace's description of fan actions into influential fan theorist John Fiske's terms for fan productivity: "semiotic," "enunciative," and "textual" (37, 39). "To see" sports is to participate in semiotic production (Wallace 155), to create meaning from sporting stimuli, and thus, as fellow fan theorist Cornel Sandvoss paraphrases it, to operate "on an intrapersonal level" (29). All spectators must do this, no matter their perceived or stated disinterest. Enunciative productivity, or the ability "to articulate" sports (Wallace 155), involves communicating that meaning-making to others. It encapsulates the "social interaction" of fandom, however informal (Sandvoss 29). Textual productivity, or the ability "to animate" sports (Wallace 155), is to create something new from sports narrative and the fan's experience with it; necessarily "manifested concretely," such texts can take the form of visual art, recorded audio, or writing (Sandvoss 29).

8. Tarver, *The I in Team*, 151.
9. Birrell and McDonald, *Reading Sport*, 10.
10. Birrell and McDonald, *Reading Sport*, 11.

11. Birrell and McDonald, *Reading Sport*, 11.
12. For a classic academic formulation of fans as a mob, see David P. Barash's 2009 essay in the *Chronicle of Higher Education*, "The Roar of the Crowd." https://www.cronicle.com/article/The-Roar-of-the-Crowd/32744.
13. Wallace, "How Tracy Austin Broke My Heart," 142.
14. Eakin, *Living Autobiographically*, x.
15. Perinbanayagam, *Games and Sports in Everyday Life*, 24, 29.
16. Busse, "Beyond Mary Sue," 168.
17. Jenkins, *Textual Poachers*, 19.
18. Ford, "I was Stabbed," 35.
19. Ford, "I was Stabbed," 35.
20. Sandvoss, *Fans*, 8.
21. Schimmel et al., "Keep Your Fans to Yourself," 589.
22. Bennett and Booth, "Introduction," in *Seeing Fans*, 9fn.
23. Sandvoss, *A Game of Two Halves*.
24. Kirkpatrick, "Hero-Fans," 128.
25. Though fans read and write sports the world over, I restrict this study to American sports in order to better understand the culturally distinct, if hardly unique, circumstances surrounding them. I also limit my project temporally, examining cultural texts published between 1950 and the present. This periodization is imposed to reflect the immense influence of television on fandom, which complicates the reception of athletic performance by both facilitating the fans' self-identification with particular teams and athletes and by undermining their sense of the competition's "liveness." Contributing to what Philip Auslander calls the "diminution of previous distinctions between the live and the mediatized," television furthers the cultural "blending of real and fabricated situations" (*Liveness* 7, 33). In light of this experiential blending, this book necessarily grapples with postmodernism's "new and historically original dilemma, one that involves our insertion as individual subjects into a multidimensional set of radically discontinuous realities," as Fredric Jameson famously put it (*Postmodernism* 413). Jameson's sense of radical discontinuity amid the overlapping, mass-mediated experiential modes that blur reality and fiction is particularly relevant to my project because fan renarrativizations are predicated on the translation of "live" bodily performance into terms of personal significance through the application of fictive—even if culturally accepted—interpretive stakes. The "real" terms on which sporting events are conducted allows for a purported clarity in their interpretation that belies their narrative construction and protects their validity as legitimate objects of

interest from those who would debase popular fictions. Founded on a kind of hyperreality, spectator sports can thus be considered postmodern narratives, and fans their multidimensional readers.

26. Hutcheon, "Historiographic Metafiction," 3.
27. Exley, *A Fan's Notes*, 76.
28. Felski, *Uses of Literature*, 74.
29. Felski, *Uses of Literature*, 76.
30. Pascal, *Design and Truth in Autobiography*, 5.
31. Leonard, *After Artest: The NBA and the Assault on Blackness*, 11.
32. The ethics of constructing fan narratives about living people is a subject of concern among media fans as well, when it comes to the genre of "real person" fanfiction, and real person "slash"—in which two people, usually of the same gender, are depicted in an often graphic sexual relationship—in particular.
33. Hills, "Afterword," 271.
34. Fowles, *Baseball Life Advice*, 9.
35. Fowles, *Baseball Life Advice*, 180.
36. Wallace, "How Tracy Austin Broke My Heart," 143.
37. Wallace, "How Tracy Austin Broke My Heart," 143.
38. Wallace, "How Tracy Austin Broke My Heart," 153, 155.
39. Wallace, "How Tracy Austin Broke My Heart," 143, 142–43.

1. So We Fabricate

1. Giamatti, "Take Time for Paradise," 80.
2. Morris, *Making the Team*, 3.
3. Morris, *Making the Team*, 6.
4. Later, in 2001, it would be published as a novella by Scribner. Because the text of the novella is identical to that of the *Underworld* prologue, I will refer only to the *Harpers* version (referred to as "Pafko") and *Underworld* in this chapter.
5. DeLillo, "The Power of History."
6. DeLillo, "The Power of History."
7. DeLillo, "The Power of History."
8. DeLillo, "The Power of History."
9. DeLillo, "The Power of History."
10. Hutcheon, "Historiographic Metafiction," 4.
11. Fitzpatrick, "The Unmaking of History," 151.
12. Fitzpatrick, "The Unmaking of History," 151.
13. Fitzpatrick, "The Unmaking of History," 151.

14. Eakin, *How Our Lives Became Stories*, 100.

15. Coover quoted in Gado, *First Person*, 152.

16. Giamatti, *Take Time for Paradise*, 38.

17. Coover, *The Universal Baseball Association*, 212.

18. DeLillo, "The Power of History."

19. DeLillo, "The Power of History."

20. DeLillo, *Underworld*, 11.

21. Duvall, *Don DeLillo's Underworld: A Reader's Guide*, 29.

22. DeLillo, *Underworld*, 14.

23. DeLillo, *Underworld*, 20.

24. Hutcheon, *A Poetics of Postmodernism*, xii.

25. Hutcheon, "Historiographic Metafiction," 5.

26. DeLillo, "The Power of History," 62.

27. DeLillo, *Underworld*, 31.

28. DeLillo, *Underworld*, 31.

29. DeLillo, "Pafko at the Wall," 48.

30. Duvall, "Baseball As Aesthetic Ideology," 288.

31. DeLillo, *Underworld*, 33.

32. DeLillo, "Pafko at the Wall," 50.

33. DeLillo, *Underworld*, 33.

34. Hutcheon, *Poetics of Postmodernism*, 114.

35. DeLillo, "Pafko at the Wall," 48.

36. DeLillo, *Underworld*, 45, 44.

37. DeLillo, *Underworld*, 45.

38. DeLillo, *Underworld*, 49.

39. DeLillo, *Underworld*, 49.

40. DeLillo, *Underworld*, 52.

41. DeLillo, *Underworld*, 52, 56.

42. DeLillo, "Pafko at the Wall," 68.

43. Duvall, "Baseball As Aesthetic Ideology," 287.

44. DeLillo, *Underworld*, 57.

45. Greiner, "Sustaining Power of Myth," 107.

46. Duvall, *Don DeLillo's Underworld: A Reader's Guide*, 29.

47. DeLillo, *Underworld*, 14.

48. DeLillo, "The Power of History."

49. Mullins, "Objects & Outliers," 283.

50. Hutcheon, *The Poetics of Postmodernism*, 230.

51. DeLillo, *Underworld*, 11.

52. Duvall, *Don DeLillo's Underworld: A Reader's Guide*, 29.

53. Hutcheon, "Historiographic Metafiction," 6.

54. DeLillo, *Underworld*, 14, 15.

55. DeLillo, *Underworld*, 34, 34-35, 26.

56. DeLillo, *Underworld*, 15.

57. DeLillo, *Underworld*, 15-16.

58. Duvall "Baseball As Aesthetic Ideology," 301.

59. Duvall, "Baseball As Aesthetic Ideology," 301.

60. Duvall, "Baseball As Aesthetic Ideology," 304.

61. DeLillo, *Underworld*, 15-16.

62. DeLillo, *Underworld*, 25.

63. DeLillo, *Underworld*, 26.

64. DeLillo, "Pafko at the Wall," 44.

65. DeLillo, *Underworld*, 26.

66. Hutcheon quoted in Fitzpatrick, "The Unmaking of History," 151.

67. DeLillo, *Underworld*, 27.

68. DeLillo, *Underworld*, 27.

69. DeLillo, "Pafko at the Wall," 44.

70. DeLillo, *Underworld*, 36.

71. DeLillo, *Underworld*, 36.

72. DeLillo, "The Power of History."

73. DeLillo, *Underworld*, 36.

74. DeLillo, *Underworld*, 42.

75. DeLillo, *Underworld*, 43.

76. DeLillo, *Underworld*, 43.

77. Fitzpatrick, "The Unmaking of History," 150.

78. DeLillo, *Underworld*, 36.

79. DeLillo, *Underworld*, 60.

80. DeLillo, *Underworld*, 60.

81. DeLillo, *Underworld*, 60.

82. Greiner, "Sustaining Power of Myth," 105.

83. DeLillo, *Underworld*, 17.

84. DeLillo, *Underworld*, 17.

85. DeLillo, "Pafko at the Wall," 39.

86. DeLillo, *Underworld*, 29.

87. DeLillo, *Underworld*, 17.

88. DeLillo, *Underworld*, 28.

89. DeLillo, *Underworld*, 44-45.

90. DeLillo, *Underworld*, 39, 50.
91. Greiner, "Sustaining Power of Myth," 107.
92. DeLillo, *Underworld*, 28.
93. DeLillo, *Underworld*, 50.
94. DeLillo, *Underworld*, 50.
95. DeLillo, *Underworld*, 50.
96. Hutcheon, *Poetics of Postmodernism*, 20.
97. Hutcheon, *Poetics of Postmodernism*, 133.
98. Parrish, "From Hoover's FBI to Eisenstein's *Unterwelt*," 707.
99. Parrish, "From Hoover's FBI to Eisenstein's *Unterwelt*," 707.
100. DeLillo, *Underworld*, 51.
101. DeLillo, "The Power of History."
102. Coover quoted in Gado, *First Person*, 152.
103. Busse, "Beyond Mary Sue," 168.
104. A perfect game is twenty-seven outs recorded by a pitcher without allowing a hit, walk, or error.
105. Giamatti, *Take Time for Paradise*, 33.
106. Coover, *The Universal Baseball Association*, 40.
107. Coover, *The Universal Baseball Association*, 135.
108. Caldwell Jr., "Of Hobby Horses, Baseball, and Narrative," 164.
109. DeLillo, *Underworld*, 25.
110. Punday, "Creative Accounting," 119.
111. Punday, "Creative Accounting," 124.
112. DeLillo, *Underworld*, 11.
113. Coover, *The Universal Baseball Association*, 3.
114. Coover, *The Universal Baseball Association*, 3.
115. Coover, *The Universal Baseball Association*, 35.
116. Coover, *The Universal Baseball Association*, 129.
117. Coover, *The Universal Baseball Association*, 129.
118. Coover, *The Universal Baseball Association*, 129, 3.
119. Coover, *The Universal Baseball Association*, 129.
120. Coover, *The Universal Baseball Association*, 141.
121. Mount, "Are the Green Fields Gone?" 72.
122. Frisch, "Self-Definition and Redefinition in the New World," 18.
123. Coover, *The Universal Baseball Association*, 142.
124. Coover, *The Universal Baseball Association*, 143.
125. Coover, *The Universal Baseball Association*, 160.
126. Coover, *The Universal Baseball Association*, 160.

127. Coover, *The Universal Baseball Association*, 48.

128. Coover, *The Universal Baseball Association*, 25.

129. DeLillo, *Underworld*, 27.

130. Coover, *The Universal Baseball Association*, 29.

131. Coover, *The Universal Baseball Association*, 175.

132. Coover, *The Universal Baseball Association*, 85.

133. Coover, *The Universal Baseball Association*, 85.

134. Coover, *The Universal Baseball Association*, 101.

135. Coover, *The Universal Baseball Association*, 40.

136. Coover, *The Universal Baseball Association*, 176.

137. Coover, *The Universal Baseball Association*, 179.

138. Coover, *The Universal Baseball Association*, 183.

139. Coover, *The Universal Baseball Association*, 185.

140. Coover, *The Universal Baseball Association*, 199.

141. DeLillo, *Underworld*, 27.

142. Coover, *The Universal Baseball Association*, 16.

143. Coover, *The Universal Baseball Association*, 166.

144. Coover, *The Universal Baseball Association*, 45.

145. Coover, *The Universal Baseball Association*, 55.

146. DeLillo, "The Power of History."

147. Miguel-Alfonso, "Mimesis and Self-Consciousness," 94.

148. Coover, *The Universal Baseball Association*, 152.

149. Per critic Richard Alan Schwartz in "Postmodernist Baseball," "Einstein repeatedly asserted that he refused to believe that 'God plays dice with the universe.' [Perhaps] Coover, prompted by this statement, set out to depict such a world in the form of a sophisticated baseball game played with dice" (138).

150. DeLillo, "The Power of History."

151. Coover, *The Universal Baseball Association*, 49.

152. Wineapple, "Robert Coover's Playing Fields," 71.

153. Coover, *The Universal Baseball Association*, 131, 49.

154. Coover, *The Universal Baseball Association*, 130.

155. Coover, *The Universal Baseball Association*, 49.

156. Coover, *The Universal Baseball Association*, 95, 67.

157. Wineapple, "Robert Coover's Playing Fields," 71.

158. Coover, *The Universal Baseball Association*, 242.

159. Coover, *The Universal Baseball Association*, 232.

160. DeLillo, "The Power of History."

2. It Was My Fate

1. Bloom, *The Anxiety of Influence*, 63.
2. Lasch, *The Culture of Narcissism*, 22.
3. Lasch, *The Culture of Narcissism*, 18.
4. Lasch, *The Culture of Narcissism*, 22.
5. Exley, *A Fan's Notes*, 231.
6. Lasch, *The Culture of Narcissism*, 22.
7. Exley, *A Fan's Notes*, Note to the Reader.
8. Lasch, *The Culture of Narcissism*, 19.
9. Gerdy, *Sports: The All-American Addiction*, 23.
10. Gerdy, *Sports: The All-American Addiction*, 23.
11. Barash, "The Roar of the Crowd."
12. Pomerantz, "'Silver Linings Playbook' Author Matthew Quick."
13. Quick, *The Silver Linings Playbook*, 282.
14. Crawford, *Consuming Sport*, 38.
15. Exley, *Pages from a Cold Island*, 210.
16. Yardley, *Misfit*, 143.
17. See Burke, Chabot, Parrish, and Sterling.
18. Exley, *A Fan's Notes*, 75.
19. Exley, *A Fan's Notes*, 2.
20. Exley, *A Fan's Notes*, 76, 97.
21. Exley, *A Fan's Notes*, 231.
22. Exley, *A Fan's Notes*, 232.
23. Barash, "The Roar of the Crowd."
24. Tarver, *The I in Team*, 27.
25. Exley, *A Fan's Notes*, 231.
26. Exley, *A Fan's Notes*, 41.
27. Exley, *A Fan's Notes*, 32.
28. Exley, *A Fan's Notes*, 206.
29. Exley, *A Fan's Notes*, 30, 35.
30. Exley, *A Fan's Notes*, 50.
31. Exley, *A Fan's Notes*, 2.
32. Exley, *A Fan's Notes*, Note to the Reader.
33. Yardley, *Misfit*, 133.
34. Exley, *A Fan's Notes*, 88–89.
35. Quick, *The Silver Linings Playbook*, 4.
36. Quick, *The Silver Linings Playbook*, 282.

37. Eventually, Peoples is introduced to Tiffany, a mentally-ill woman traumatized by the death of her husband. Despite his friends' encouragement, Peoples is not romantically interested in Tiffany, holding out hope that he will be able to reunite with Nikki. When Tiffany suggests that she can transmit letters to Nikki for him, however, Peoples agrees to be her partner in a dance competition in which she plans to participate as a therapeutic exercise. The connection forged in their training sessions, as well as the question of the authenticity of the letters that Peoples receives from Nikki via Tiffany, form the backbone of the novel's romantic plot.

38. Quick, *The Silver Linings Playbook*, 29.

39. Quick, *The Silver Linings Playbook*, 175.

40. Quick, *The Silver Linings Playbook*, 211.

41. Quick, *The Silver Linings Playbook*, 74.

42. Quick, *The Silver Linings Playbook*, 97.

43. Quick, *The Silver Linings Playbook*, 96.

44. Guttmann, *Sports Spectators*, 184.

45. Howard, "Social Psychology of the Spectator," 44, 46.

46. Quick, *The Silver Linings Playbook*, 97.

47. Quick, *The Silver Linings Playbook*, 12.

48. Quick, *The Silver Linings Playbook*, 13.

49. Quick, *The Silver Linings Playbook*, 161.

50. Quick, *The Silver Linings Playbook*, 161.

51. Quick, *The Silver Linings Playbook*, 103.

52. Quick, *The Silver Linings Playbook*, 106.

53. Quick, *The Silver Linings Playbook*, 108.

54. Quick, *The Silver Linings Playbook*, 107.

55. Exley, *A Fan's Notes*, 88-89.

56. Quick, *The Silver Linings Playbook*, 113.

57. Quick, *The Silver Linings Playbook*, 113.

58. Exley, *A Fan's Notes*, 346.

59. Exley, *A Fan's Notes*, 347.

60. Exley, *A Fan's Notes*, 347.

61. Exley, *A Fan's Notes*, 348, 349.

62. Exley, *A Fan's Notes*, 348.

63. Exley, *A Fan's Notes*, 348.

64. Exley, *A Fan's Notes*, 349.

65. Gifford would, ultimately, make a comeback from the injury in 1962. Exley comments on that return with interest, but also a measure of resignation that the football star's playing abilities would never be quite the same.

66. Exley, *A Fan's Notes*, 354, 356.

67. Exley, *A Fan's Notes*, 357.

68. Exley, *A Fan's Notes*, 385.

69. Exley, *A Fan's Notes*, 385.

70. Exley, *A Fan's Notes*, 76.

71. Pudaloff, "Toward a New Male Identity," 95-96.

72. Pudaloff, "Toward a New Male Identity," 96.

73. Exley, *A Fan's Notes*, 59, 35, 52.

74. Quick, *The Silver Linings Playbook*, 10.

75. Quick, *The Silver Linings Playbook*, 15.

76. Quick, *The Silver Linings Playbook*, 9.

77. Quick, *The Silver Linings Playbook*, 22.

78. Quick, *The Silver Linings Playbook*, 22.

79. Quick, *The Silver Linings Playbook*, 58.

80. Quick, *The Silver Linings Playbook*, 22.

81. Quick, *The Silver Linings Playbook*, 260.

82. Exley, *A Fan's Notes*, 76.

83. Quick, *The Silver Linings Playbook*, 260.

84. Quick, *The Silver Linings Playbook*, 217-18.

85. Quick, *The Silver Linings Playbook*, 260.

86. Quick, *The Silver Linings Playbook*, 58.

87. Quick, *The Silver Linings Playbook*, 265.

88. Quick, *The Silver Linings Playbook*, 218.

89. Exley, *A Fan's Notes*, 35.

90. Exley, *A Fan's Notes*, 149, 152.

91. Exley, *A Fan's Notes*, 240.

92. Exley, *A Fan's Notes*, 366, 367.

93. Exley, *A Fan's Notes*, 367.

94. Lasch, *The Culture of Narcissism*, 19.

95. Exley, *A Fan's Notes*, 88.

96. Exley, *A Fan's Notes*, 367.

97. Exley, *A Fan's Notes*, 367.

98. Exley, *A Fan's Notes*, 367.

99. Exley, *A Fan's Notes*, 190.

100. Exley, *A Fan's Notes*, 296.
101. Felski, *Uses of Literature*, 74.
102. Felski, *Uses of Literature*, 76.
103. Quick, *The Silver Linings Playbook*, 80, 65.
104. Exley is in fact diagnosed with schizophrenia during one of his stints in a mental institution.
105. Quick, *The Silver Linings Playbook*, 65.
106. Lasch, *The Culture of Narcissism*, 22.
107. Barash, "The Roar of the Crowd."
108. In their study of sports fans, sports psychologists Daniel Wann et al. share in this optimistic outlook regarding sports fans, citing "research [that] suggests that highly identified fans possess a healthy psychological profile" (167). These fans not only maintain that health "in light of the fact that [they] view their team's performances as a reflection of themselves" but in fact employ "a variety of tactics to protect and enhance their psychological health" in maintaining that connection (167, 169).

3. Race in the Basketball Memoir

1. Early, "A Reading of *The Greatest*," 70.
2. A few words on terminology: I mean biography, autobiography, and memoir to refer to related, but distinct generic forms. According to Paul John Eakin, "the system of classification long in place in our libraries and bibliographies posits the kinship of autobiography and biography [placing them] under the aegis of history as categories of the literature of reference . . . the theory of autobiography . . . differs from the practice of biography [such that] it has become commonplace for students of autobiography to assert that the past, the ostensible primary reference of such texts is a fiction." Meanwhile, much to Eakin's chagrin, biography "seems to have largely maintained the traditional purity of its positivistic allegiance to fact, to the past as recoverable reality," at least in the public eye (54). In contrast to the personally comprehensive and thus potentially solipsistic aspirations of autobiography, the memoir is bidirectional; "subordinated to the story of some other for whom the self serves as privileged witness," the prominence and potential unreliability of that authorial persona also separates memoir from the objective sterility of biography (Eakin, *How Our Lives Become Stories* 58). Memoir is thus both autobiographical and biographical, but it is not fully either. Derived from the French word for memory, memoir is intrinsically built on the unstable foundation that is the human recollection of past events (Couser 19).

3. Eakin, *Touching the World*, 31.

4. Yagoda, *Memoir: A History*, 7, 28.

5. Yagoda, *Memoir: A History*, 239–40.

6. Yagoda, *Memoir: A History*, 239.

7. Eakin, *Living Autobiographically*, 22.

8. Pascal, *Design and Truth in Autobiography*, 5.

9. The "Big Four" refers to the four men's team sports that collect the bulk of television and ticket revenues: MLB (Major League Baseball), NBA, NFL (National Football League), and NHL (National Hockey League).

10. The Institute for Diversity and Ethics in Sport at the University of Central Florida, in its 2013 "Racial and Gender Report Card," reports that 76.3 percent of NBA players identify as African American, 19 percent as white, 4.4 percent as Latino, and 0.2 percent as Asian. Of that same pool of players, 18.7 percent identify as "international" (Lapchick et al.).

    Meanwhile, according to a 2007 study by Scarborough Research, 64.8 percent of the NBA's American fan base identifies as white, while 28.3 percent identifies as African American, 15.7 percent as Hispanic, and 3.3 percent as Asian. Among "avid" fans, a descriptor that certainly applies to Raab, Shields, and Simmons, 78.4 percent identified as white, while just 15.7 percent identified as African American. Scarborough Sports Marketing "defines 'Avid Fans' as consumers who are 'very interested' and 'Fans' as respondents who are 'very, somewhat or a little interested' in a given sport" (*Sports Business Daily*).

11. Yagoda, *Memoir: A History*, 109.

12. Early, *A Level Playing Field*, 2–3.

13. Early, *A Level Playing Field*, 16.

14. In *A Level Playing Field*, Gerald Early further asserts that not merely sports, but "popular culture" more broadly "has been an enthralling trap from which blacks have never been able to escape with their image intact or completely under their own control" (7). However much popular culture contexts may purport fairness, the narratives produced rarely escape hegemonic biases in representation.

15. Leonard, *After Artest*, 10.

16. Leonard, *After Artest*, 6.

17. Barash, "The Roar of the Crowd."

18. Hills, *Fan Cultures*, 113.

19. Simons, *The Secret Lives of Sports Fans*, 161.

20. Dyson, *Reflecting Black*, 66.

21. Guzzio, "Courtside," 223.

22. Guzzio, "Courtside," 224.

23. Shields, *Body Politic*, 20.

24. Shields, *Black Planet*, 10, 5.

25. Shields, *Black Planet*, 5, 6.

26. Majors, "Cool Pose," 211.

27. Shields, *Black Planet*, Author's Note.

28. Public Enemy is a hip-hop group known for addressing social issues in its music. Its 1990 album, "Fear of a Black Planet," reached No. 10 on the Billboard charts.

29. Payton quoted in Shields, *Black Planet*, 10.

30. Shields, *Black Planet*, 105.

31. Shields, *Black Planet*, 146.

32. Shields, *Black Planet*, 105, 125.

33. Andrews, "The Facts of Michael Jordan's Blackness," 131.

34. Shields, *Black Planet*, 10.

35. Shields, *Black Planet*, 59.

36. Shields, *Black Planet*, 19.

37. Shields, *Black Planet*, 47.

38. Shields, *Black Planet*, 112, 28.

39. Gates quoted in Shields, *Black Planet*, 139.

40. Shields, *Black Planet*, 50–51.

41. Shields, a creative writer with an MFA from the University of Iowa, is a professor of English at the University of Washington.

42. Shields, *Black Planet*, 59–60.

43. I'm thinking here of Eve Sedgwick's classic formulation of the "crystallization of a same-sex male desire" (85) in which "the continuum of male homosocial bonds [is] brutally structured by a secularized and psychologized homophobia" (185).

44. Shields, *Black Planet*, 125.

45. Shields, *Black Planet*, 183.

46. Shields, *Black Planet*, 75.

47. The trio subsequently led the Heat to four NBA Finals and two championships.

48. Raab, *The Whore of Akron*, 59, 29.

49. Contested before the first Super Bowl, which was held in January 1967.

50. Cleveland's championship drought was forty-seven years at the time of *The Whore of Akron*'s publication in 2011. James, of course, returned to Cleveland in 2014 and led the team to its first championship in 2016. Raab quickly published the sarcastically titled *You're Welcome, Cleveland: How I Helped*

LeBron James Win a Championship and Save a City (2017), which is largely an attempt to atone for *The Whore of Akron*. While Raab's recognition of the inappropriateness of his earlier work is welcome, the sequel text is ultimately a much less evocative examination of fan identity. Pain and anger, as it does for many authors, brings out the sharpest writing in the misanthropic Raab.

51. Raab, *The Whore of Akron*, 9.
52. Raab, *The Whore of Akron*, 23.
53. Seinfeld quoted in Raab, *The Whore of Akron*, 22.
54. Gray, "New Audiences, New Textualities," 73.
55. Raab, *The Whore of Akron*, 4.
56. Raab, *The Whore of Akron*, 108.
57. Raab, *The Whore of Akron*, 5.
58. Raab, *The Whore of Akron*, 5.
59. Raab, *The Whore of Akron*, 5.
60. Raab, *The Whore of Akron*, 21.
61. Raab, *The Whore of Akron*, 91.
62. Carrington, *Race, Sport and Politics*, 88.
63. Raab, *The Whore of Akron*, 91.
64. Raab, *The Whore of Akron*, 271.
65. Raab, *The Whore of Akron*, 272.
66. Raab, *The Whore of Akron*, 273.
67. The black athlete as slave, an analogy most famously articulated by Harry Edwards in *The Revolt of the Black Athlete*, has its flaws, to be sure. But as Gerald Early astutely points out in *A Level Playing Field*, "professional sports teams operate as a cartel—that is, a group of independent entrepreneurs coming together to control an industry without giving up their independence as competitive entities. . . . The cartelization of American team sports, which so closely resembles the cartelization of the antebellum Southern planters, . . . is the strongest argument to make about slavery and sports or about sports and colonization" (207). Though Congress has only formally granted an antitrust exemption to Major League Baseball, the NBA, NFL, and NHL all effectively operate with similar monopolistic immunity. Without a viable alternative to the NBA in which to seek basketball employment (at least in the United States), James's desire to find a new employer—a right which he only gained after accruing a certain number of years' experience, as dictated by a collective bargaining agreement negotiated with said cartel by the players' union—necessitated that he leave Cleveland.
68. Simmons, *The Book of Basketball*, 4.

69. Simmons, *The Book of Basketball*, 5.
70. Simmons, *The Book of Basketball*, 5.
71. Simmons, *The Book of Basketball*, 8.
72. Simmons, *The Book of Basketball*, 537.
73. Carrington, *Race, Sport and Politics*, 175.
74. Simmons, *The Book of Basketball*, 536–37.
75. Simmons, *The Book of Basketball*, 537.
76. Simmons, *The Book of Basketball*, 375f, 376f.
77. Carrington, *Race, Sport and Politics*, 88.
78. Simmons, *The Book of Basketball*, 336, 457–58.
79. Hoberman, *Darwin's Athletes*, 34.
80. Lee, *Best Seat in the House*, 29, 40.
81. Lee, *Best Seat in the House*, 26.
82. Lee, *Best Seat in the House*, 23.
83. Lee, *Best Seat in the House*, 23.
84. Lee, *Best Seat in the House*, 40.
85. As I show in chapter 5 of this book, this notion aligns with Bethlehem Shoals of FreeDarko's idea that competitive style, or the "joyous extension of playing your ass off," is the pinnacle of attraction for the basketball fan.
86. Lee, *Best Seat in the House*, 51.
87. Lee, *Best Seat in the House*, 66.
88. Lee, *Best Seat in the House*, 62.
89. Lee, *Best Seat in the House*, 68.
90. Wideman's daughter, Jamila, was a successful Division I college player at Stanford and played four seasons in the Women's National Basketball Association (WNBA).
91. Wideman, *Hoop Roots*, 5.
92. Wideman, *Hoop Roots*, 9.
93. Wideman, *Hoop Roots*, 9.
94. Wideman, *Hoop Roots*, 11.
95. Wideman, *Hoop Roots*, 6.
96. Wideman details his relationship with Robby at length in another memoir, *Brothers and Keepers*.
97. Kalson, "Children of Promise."
98. Wideman, *Hoop Roots*, 6.
99. Shields, *Black Planet*, 75.
100. Wideman, *Hoop Roots*, 34.
101. Wideman, *Hoop Roots*, 13.

102. Wideman, *Hoop Roots*, 40.

103. Shields, *Black Planet*, 183.

104. Wideman, *Hoop Roots*, 41.

105. Wideman, *Hoop Roots*, 163–64.

106. Pearson, "Fandom in the Digital Era," 93.

107. Simmons, *The Book of Basketball*, 55.

108. Boyd, *Young, Black, Rich, and Famous*, 14.

109. Shields, *Black Planet*, 148.

110. Shields, *Black Planet*, 146.

111. Shields repeats this ventriloquism later in the memoir, when a journalist asks Payton what fellow All-Star point guard Jason Kidd said to him: "'I don't quite remember.' *It's our camaraderie, not yours*" (180).

112. Shields, *Black Planet*, 147.

113. Payton quoted in Shields, *Black Planet*, 203.

114. Shields, *Black Planet*, 203.

115. Shields, *Black Planet*, 57.

116. Raab, *The Whore of Akron*, 195.

117. Raab also interjects: "What the hell does '(pause)' mean?" (196), without providing an answer or any indication that he has found one. This is notable, given Raab's prior sexualization of LeBron, because "pause" is recognized in contemporary slang to be a less-charged synonym of "no homo," a kind of defensive assertion that the author of the preceding statement (in this case of "love" for "chef B") is not homosexual. (http://www.urbandictionary.com/define.php?term=%28pause%29).

118. Raab, *The Whore of Akron*, 195.

119. Raab, *The Whore of Akron*, 196.

120. Raab, *The Whore of Akron*, 196.

121. Raab, *The Whore of Akron*, 197.

122. Raab, *The Whore of Akron*, 199.

123. James's notion of what should offend Raab reminds again of Hoberman's conception of "the fusion of black athletes, rappers, and criminals into a single menacing figure" as representing the popular notion of "black male style" (xxviii).

124. Raab, *The Whore of Akron*, 200.

125. Andrews, "The Facts of Michael Jordan's Blackness," 125.

126. Simmons, *The Book of Basketball*, 618.

127. Dyson, *Reflecting Black*, 66.

128. Dyson, *Reflecting Black*, 72, 73.

129. Simmons, *The Book of Basketball*, 619.

130. Kimmel, *Manhood in America*, 6.

131. Simmons, *The Book of Basketball*, 619.

132. Simmons, *The Book of Basketball*, 619.

133. Shields, *Black Planet*, 125.

134. Simmons, *The Book of Basketball*, 620.

135. Andrews, "The Facts of Michael Jordan's Blackness," 137, 135-36.

136. Simmons, *The Book of Basketball*, 621.

137. Simmons, *The Book of Basketball*, 621.

138. Simmons, *The Book of Basketball*, 621.

139. Lane, *Under the Boards*, 65-66.

140. Lane, *Under the Boards*, 66.

141. Eakin, *Touching the World*, 31.

142. Shields, *Black Planet*, 43.

143. Shields, *Black Planet*, 43.

144. Auslander, *Liveness*, 33.

145. Ford, "I Was Stabbed," 35.

146. Iser, "The Reading Process," 56-57.

147. Raab, *The Whore of Akron*, 174. Raab's quote also reminds, of course, of the opening paragraph of Ralph Ellison's *Invisible Man* (1952), in which the narrator asserts that he is invisible "because people refuse to see me . . . it is as though I have been surrounded by mirrors of hard, distorting glass. When they approach me they see only my surroundings, themselves or figments of their imagination, indeed, everything and anything except me" (3). When looking at African American NBA players, Raab, like Shields and Simmons, seems to see only himself, or—as I have argued—figments of his imagination and its preferred basketball narrative.

148. Lee, *Best Seat in the House*, 94, 87.

149. Lee, *Best Seat in the House*, 18.

150. Lee, *Best Seat in the House*, 4.

151. Lee, *Best Seat in the House*, 141.

152. Lee, *Best Seat in the House*, 142.

153. Lee, *Best Seat in the House*, 211.

154. Lee, *Best Seat in the House*, 212.

155. Lee, *Best Seat in the House*, 213.

156. Lee, *Best Seat in the House*, 213.

157. Lee, *Best Seat in the House*, 214.

158. Lee, *Best Seat in the House*, 217, 218, 222.

159. "Pacers vs Knicks : le KKK et l'Indiana." *YouTube*, January 18, 2018.

160. Lee, *Best Seat in the House*, 225.

161. Pearson, "Fandom in the Digital Era," 93.

162. Lee, *Best Seat in the House*, 238.

163. Lee, *Best Seat in the House*, 272, 307.

164. Rhoden, *Forty Million Dollar Slaves*.

165. Omar—like Wideman's brother, Robby, and son, Jacob—found himself in violent circumstances while navigating the limited pathways available to black men living in poverty. Wideman laments that "Omar wasn't going to be one of the lucky ones who survived the terrible winnowing, who might evolve terms less self-destructive than those he and his peers had invented to love themselves" (44).

166. Wideman, *Hoop Roots*, 39-40.

167. Wideman, *Hoop Roots*, 40.

168. Wideman, *Hoop Roots*, 40.

169. Wideman, *Hoop Roots*, 41.

170. Wideman, *Hoop Roots*, 41.

171. Guzzio, "Courtside," 223.

172. Wideman, *Hoop Roots*, 42.

173. Wideman, *Hoop Roots*, 51.

174. Wideman, *Hoop Roots*, 51-52.

175. For more on the epistemological consequences of the formalized, officiated game for how we understand basketball, see Yago Colás's *Ball Don't Lie: Myth, Genealogy, and Invention in the Cultures of Basketball*.

176. Wideman, *Hoop Roots*, 53-54.

177. Wideman, *Hoop Roots*, 56, 164.

178. Guzzio, "Courtside," 224.

179. Wideman, *Hoop Roots*, 11.

180. Wideman, *Hoop Roots*, 12, 49.

181. Wideman, *Hoop Roots*, 13.

182. Wideman, *Hoop Roots*, 183-84.

183. Wideman, *Hoop Roots*, 234.

184. Sandvoss, "From National Hero to Liquid Star," 189.

185. Mostly, this distrust stems from an incident in which James wore a Yankees cap to a Cleveland-New York playoff baseball game (10). Characteristically, Raab's subsequent condemnation is posited in sexual terms: "His vast sense of childish entitlement seemed to speak louder every season. But, lord, the sex was fine" (9).

186. Lee, *Best Seat in the House*, 63.

187. Eakin, *Fictions in Autobiography*, 227.

188. Shields, *Black Planet*, 145.

189. Wideman, *Hoop Roots*, 10.

190. Simmons, *The Book of Basketball*, 407.

191. Simmons, *The Book of Basketball*, 24.

192. Early, *A Level Playing Field*, 138.

193. Freeman, *Rewriting the Self*, 18.

194. Shields, *Black Planet*, 152.

195. Shields, *Black Planet*, 152.

196. Couser, *Memoir: An Introduction*, 14.

197. Eakin, *Ethics of Life Writing*, 6.

198. Eakin, *Living Autobiographically*, 22.

199. Eakin, *The Ethics of Life Writing*, 14.

200. Leonard, *After Artest*, 11.

4. A Problem with Me and Women

1. Kimmel, Manhood in America, 246.

2. Bennett and Booth, "Introduction," 2.

3. Bennett and Booth, "Introduction," 2–3.

4. Baker, *Contesting Identities*, 2.

5. Baker, *Contesting Identities*, 62.

6. Baker, *Contesting Identities*, 3.

7. Stanfill, "Straighten Up and Fly White," 187.

8. Baker, *Contesting Identities*, 4.

9. Stanfill, "Straighten Up and Fly White," 190.

10. Benshoff and Griffin, *America on Film*, 260.

11. "The Fan," *The Numbers*.

12. Dyer quoted in Baker, *Contesting Identities*, 13.

13. *The Fan*. Directed by Tony Scott, 1:20.

14. *The Fan*. Directed by Tony Scott, 1:25.

15. Stanfill, "Straighten Up and Fly White," 191.

16. Jenkins, *Textual Poachers*, 10.

17. Kibby, "Nostalgia for the Masculine," 17.

18. Leonard, "'Is This Heaven?' White Sporting Masculinities," 167.

19. Leonard, "'Is This Heaven?' White Sporting Masculinities," 170.

20. Braudy, *The Frenzy of Renown*, 590.

21. Nylund, *Beer, Babes, and Balls*, 2.

22. *Big Fan*. Directed by Robert D. Siegel, 1:50.

23. Benshoff and Griffin, *America on Film*, 300.

24. *Fever Pitch*. Directed by Peter Farrelly and Bobby Farrelly, 4:00.

25. *Fever Pitch*. Directed by Peter Farrelly and Bobby Farrelly, 11:00.

26. *Fever Pitch*. Directed by Peter Farrelly and Bobby Farrelly, 9:00, 18:00.

27. *Fever Pitch*. Directed by Peter Farrelly and Bobby Farrelly, 20:00.

28. *Fever Pitch*. Directed by Peter Farrelly and Bobby Farrelly, 9:00.

29. Stanfill, "Straighten Up and Fly White," 194.

30. Quick, *The Silver Linings Playbook*, 96.

31. Quick, *The Silver Linings Playbook*, 97, 123.

32. Kibby, "Nostalgia for the Masculine," 17.

33. *Silver Linings Playbook*. Directed by David O. Russell, 12:20.

34. Stanfill, "Straighten Up and Fly White," 195.

35. *The Fan*. Directed by Tony Scott, 6:45, 23:30, 33:00.

36. Kibby, "Nostalgia for the Masculine," 17.

37. *The Fan*. Directed by Tony Scott, 42:00.

38. Wallace, "How Tracy Austin Broke My Heart," 143.

39. *The Fan*. Directed by Tony Scott, 1:11:00.

40. *The Fan*. Directed by Tony Scott, 1:16:00.

41. *The Fan*. Directed by Tony Scott, 1:17:00.

42. Pudaloff, "Toward a New Male Identity," 108.

43. *Big Fan*. Directed by Robert D. Siegel, 5:00.

44. Stanfill, "Straighten Up and Fly White," 192.

45. *Big Fan*. Directed by Robert D. Siegel, 15:45.

46. Kibby, "Nostalgia for the Masculine," 18.

47. *Big Fan*. Directed by Robert D. Siegel, 30:10.

48. *Big Fan*. Directed by Robert D. Siegel, 31:15.

49. *Big Fan*. Directed by Robert D. Siegel, 57:00.

50. *Big Fan*. Directed by Robert D. Siegel, 57:20.

51. Baker, *Contesting Identities*, 11.

52. *Big Fan*. Directed by Robert D. Siegel, 1:04:00.

53. *Big Fan*. Directed by Robert D. Siegel, 1:05:20.

54. Benshoff and Griffin, *America on Film*, 300.

55. *Fever Pitch*. Directed by Peter Farrelly and Bobby Farrelly, 1:07:00.

56. *Fever Pitch*. Directed by Peter Farrelly and Bobby Farrelly, 33:00.

57. *Fever Pitch*. Directed by Peter Farrelly and Bobby Farrelly, 33:00.

58. *Fever Pitch*. Directed by Peter Farrelly and Bobby Farrelly, 1:00:00.

59. *Fever Pitch*. Directed by Peter Farrelly and Bobby Farrelly, 45:00.

60. *Fever Pitch*. Directed by Peter Farrelly and Bobby Farrelly, 28:00.

61. *Fever Pitch*. Directed by Peter Farrelly and Bobby Farrelly, 1:13:00.

62. *Fever Pitch*. Directed by Peter Farrelly and Bobby Farrelly, 1:04:00.

63. *Fever Pitch*. Directed by Peter Farrelly and Bobby Farrelly, 28:00.

64. *Fever Pitch*. Directed by Peter Farrelly and Bobby Farrelly, 1:23:00.

65. The implicit queerness of Ben's fandom is also rendered through homophobic humor related to his homosocial bonds with his male friends. To wit, when Ben goes into a deep depression after Lindsay breaks up with him—manifested in his repeatedly watching the Red Sox traumatic loss in Game 6 of the 1986 World Series—three of his friends intervene. Entering his darkened and pizza-box-strewn apartment, they lift Ben's limp body from his recliner and drag him to the bathroom to clean him up. As they wash Ben in the shower, he asks "Not to pry . . . but why are you shaving my balls?" (1:18). The lewd humor is meant to discomfit the reader as to the appropriateness of male-male fan friendships, and to imply that homosocial bonds are always also (stigmatized) homosexual ones.

66. *Silver Linings Playbook*. Directed by David O. Russell, 29:40.

67. *The Fan*. Directed by Tony Scott, 1:23:00.

68. Kibby, "Nostalgia for the Masculine," 17.

69. Leonard, "'Is This Heaven?' White Sporting Masculinities," 188.

70. *The Fan*. Directed by Tony Scott, 1:31:40.

71. Though slavery is never mentioned explicitly, it is invoked when, joking with his supervisor early in the film, Renard speaks in stereotypical dialect and calls his boss "massa."

72. Carrington, *Race, Sport and Politics*, 175.

73. Andrews, "The Facts of Michael Jordan's Blackness," 177, 179.

74. As Mel Stanfill has pointed out, these things are commonly interrelated, such that "fandom . . . is understood to entail deviance from normative gender and sexuality, and behaving in such a way 'diminishes the value' of fans' whiteness" (188).

75. Carrington, *Race, Sport and Politics*, 88.

76. *Big Fan*. Directed by Robert D. Siegel, 57:35.

77. *Big Fan*. Directed by Robert D. Siegel, 1:00:40.

78. *Big Fan*. Directed by Robert D. Siegel, 1:15:00.

79. *Big Fan*. Directed by Robert D. Siegel, 1:18:35.

80. *Big Fan*. Directed by Robert D. Siegel, 1:19:50.

81. *Big Fan*. Directed by Robert D. Siegel, 1:23:30.

82. *Big Fan*. Directed by Robert D. Siegel, 1:24:05.

83. *Big Fan*. Directed by Robert D. Siegel, 1:25:00.
84. *Fever Pitch*. Directed by Peter Farrelly and Bobby Farrelly, 40:00.
85. Benshoff and Griffin, *America on Film*, 53.
86. Russell, *Second Wind*, 183.
87. Stanfill, "Straighten Up and Fly White," 193–94.
88. *Silver Linings Playbook*. Directed by David O. Russell, 1:12:25.
89. In the film the song is Stevie Wonder's "My Cherie Amour," while in the novel it is "Songbird" by Kenny G. It triggers Pat because it was the song playing when he caught his wife in flagrante delicto.
90. *Silver Linings Playbook*. Directed by David O. Russell, 22:20.
91. Quick, *The Silver Linings Playbook*, 161.
92. *Fever Pitch*. Directed by Peter Farrelly and Bobby Farrelly, 42:00.
93. Stanfill, "Straighten Up and Fly White," 195.
94. Hills, "Afterword," 271.
95. Austin, "How Tracy Austin Broke My Heart," 155.

5. Reimagined Communities

1. In *How We Think: Digital Media and Contemporary Technogenesis* (2012), N. Katherine Hayles redefines the anthropological term "technogenesis"—the idea that "humans and technics have coevolved together"—for the internet era (10). Arguing that digital media provide more than a new outlet for human expression and analysis, Hayles posits that they affect and in fact develop the way we think. Enhanced connectivity plays a major role in this development, of course, but so does self-reflection, allowing digitally mediated writers to reach both outward—beyond the conventional limitations of geography and print culture—and inward—toward a better understanding of the motivations and practices that constitute digital selfhood. Hayles provides a critical background upon which I position the fan blogger as a multivarious reader and self-reflective writer whose mode of expression is not merely influenced by, but inextricable from, digital connectivity.
2. "Sabermetrics," a word first coined by onetime security guard-cum-baseball analytics whiz Bill James, refers to the advanced statistical methods fomented by the members of SABR, the Society for American Baseball Research.
3. Partridge KS is the hometown of Ortho Stice, a character from David Foster Wallace's *Infinite Jest* (1996), a novel for which Schur proclaimed his affinity (Trump, "We Didn't Know What The F— We Were Doing").
4. Shoals's counter-argument evokes Ben Carrington's in *Race, Sport and Politics: The Sporting Black Diaspora*, when he writes: "[Hoberman's] argu-

ment ends up replacing one exaggerated and naïve paradigm, namely that sport erases racism and racial discourse through inter-racial contact, with its conceptual opposite, namely that sport can *only* reproduce dominant racial ideologies and relatedly that black subjects who engage in sport are, in effect, racial cultural dupes. Hoberman's provocative account is partial and in the end a distortion of the totality of both the black experience in sport and the ideological effects of that engagement. The intellectual task of understanding the relationship between sport, race and politics is in fact much more difficult and complex than these rather hyperbolic interventions would suggest" (2010, 174).

Epilogue

1. Fowles, *Baseball Life Advice*, 133.
2. Tarver, *The I in Team*, 173.
3. Fowles, *Baseball Life Advice*, 9.
4. Fowles, *Baseball Life Advice*, 9.
5. Fowles, *Baseball Life Advice*, 44.
6. Fowles, *Baseball Life Advice*, 52.
7. Fowles, *Baseball Life Advice*, 149.
8. Fowles, *Baseball Life Advice*, 152.
9. Markovits and Albertson, *Sportista*.
10. Fowles, *Baseball Life Advice*, 153.
11. Tarver, *The I in Team*, 178.
12. Fowles, *Baseball Life Advice*, 139.
13. Fowles, *Baseball Life Advice*, 133.
14. Tarver, *The I in Team*, 178.
15. Fowles, *Baseball Life Advice*, 154.
16. Fowles, *Baseball Life Advice*, 187.
17. Fowles, *Baseball Life Advice*, 270.
18. Fowles, *Baseball Life Advice*, 159–60.
19. Fowles, *Baseball Life Advice*, 160.
20. Fowles, *Baseball Life Advice*, 160–61.
21. Fowles, *Baseball Life Advice*, 161.
22. Fowles, *Baseball Life Advice*, 105.
23. Fowles, *Baseball Life Advice*, 105.
24. Fowles, *Baseball Life Advice*, 106, 108–9.
25. Fowles, *Baseball Life Advice*, 109.
26. Fowles, *Baseball Life Advice*, 112, 110.

27. Fowles, *Baseball Life Advice*, 110.
28. Fowles, *Baseball Life Advice*, 208–9.
29. Fowles, *Baseball Life Advice*, 180.
30. Fowles, *Baseball Life Advice*, 162.
31. Fowles, *Baseball Life Advice*, 150, 155.

BIBLIOGRAPHY

Abercrombie, Nicholas, and Brian Longhurst. *Audiences: A Sociological Theory of Performance and Imagination*. London: Sage, 1998.

Abraham, Peter. *The Fan*. 1995. New York: Ballantine, 2002.

Andrews, David L. "The Facts of Michael Jordan's Blackness: Excavating a Floating Racial Signifier." In *Michael Jordan, Inc.: Corporate Sport, Media Culture, and Late Modern America*, edited by David L. Andrews, 107–52. Albany NY: SUNY Press, 2001.

Auslander, Philip. *Liveness: Performance in a Mediatized Culture*. 2nd ed. London: Routledge, 2008.

Austin, Tracy. *Beyond Center Court: My Story*. New York: William Morrow, 1992.

Baker, Aaron. *Contesting Identities: Sports in American Film*. Chicago: University of Illinois Press, 2003.

Barash, David P. "The Roar of the Crowd." *The Chronicle of Higher Education*. Last modified March 20, 2009. https://www.chronicle.com/article/The-Roar-of-the-Crowd/32744.

Bennett, Lucy, and Paul Booth. "Introduction: Seeing Fans." In *Seeing Fans: Representations of Fandom in Media and Popular Culture*, edited by Lucy Bennett and Paul Booth, 1–9. New York: Bloomsbury, 2016.

Benshoff, Harry M., and Sean Griffin. *America on Film: Representing Race, Class, Gender, and Sexuality at the Movies*. 2nd ed. New York: Wiley-Blackwell, 2009.

Big Fan, directed by Robert D. Siegel. Los Angeles: First Independent Pictures, 2009.

Billings, Andrew C., and Heather Hundley. "Examining Identity in Sports Media." In *Examining Identity in Sports Media*, edited by Heather Hundley and Andrew C. Billings, 1–16. Los Angeles: Sage, 2010.

Birrell, Susan, and Mary G. McDonald. "Reading Sport, Articulating Power Lines: An Introduction." In *Reading Sport: Critical Essays on Power and Representation*, edited by Susan Birrell and Mary G. McDonald, 3–13. Boston: Northeastern University Press, 2000.

Bloom, Harold. *The Anxiety of Influence: A Theory of Poetry*. 1973. 2nd ed. New York: Oxford University Press, 1997.

Boyd, Todd. *Young, Black, Rich, and Famous: The Rise of the NBA, the Hip Hop Invasion, and the Transformation of American Culture*. New York: Doubleday, 2003.

Braudy, Leo. *The Frenzy of Renown: Fame & Its History*. Oxford UK: Oxford University Press, 1986.

Burke, William. "Football, Literature, Culture." *Southwest Review* 60, no. 1 (1975): 391–98.

Burns, Forevers. "Harvest Moon Shining Down from the Sky." FreeDarko. Last modified January 23, 2007. http://freedarko.blogspot.com/2007/01/harvest -moon-shining-down-from-sky.html.

Busse, Kristina. "Beyond Mary Sue: Fan Representation and Complex Negotiation of Gendered Identity." In *Seeing Fans: Representations of Fandom in Media and Popular Culture*, edited by Lucy Bennett and Paul Booth, 159–68. New York: Bloomsbury, 2016.

Caldwell Jr., Roy C. "Of Hobby Horses, Baseball, and Narrative: Coover's *Universal Baseball Association*." *Modern Fiction Studies* 33, no. 1 (1987): 161–71.

Calvino, Italo. *The Uses of Literature*. 1986. New York: Harcourt, 1987.

Carrington, Ben. *Race, Sport and Politics: The Sporting Black Diaspora*. Los Angeles: Sage, 2010.

Cavan, Jim. "What Will Be the NBA's Next Great Positional Revolution?" Bleacher Report. Last modified August 26, 2014. http://bleacherreport.com/articles/2177219.

Chabot, C. Barry. "The Alternative Vision of Frederick Exley's *A Fan's Notes*." *Critique: Studies in Modern Fiction* 19, no. 1 (1977): 87–100.

Chemi, Eric. "The NFL Is Growing Only Because of Women." *Bloomberg Business*. Last modified September 26, 2014. https://www.bloomberg.com/news/articles /2014-09-26/the-nfl-is-growing-only-because-of-female-fans.

Cohan, Noah. "Baseball Fan Behavior as Postmodern Praxis in Don DeLillo's *Underworld*." *Aethlon* 32.2 (2015): 37–56.

———. "New Media, Old Methods: Archiving and Close Reading the Sports Blog." *Journal of Sport History* 44, no. 2 (2017): 275–86.

———. "Rewriting Sport and Self: Fan Self-Reflexivity and Bill Simmons's *The Book of Basketball*." *Popular Communication* 11, no. 2 (2013): 130–45.

Colás, Yago. *Ball Don't Lie: Myth, Genealogy, and Invention in the Cultures of Basketball*. Philadelphia: Temple University Press, 2016.

———. "For More, and Better, Sports Narratives." Between the Lines. Last accessed November 22, 2014. http://yagocolas.com/index.php/2014/11/22/for-more-and -better-sports-narratives/.

Coover, Robert. "Robert Coover." By Frank Gado. In *First Person: Conversations on Writers & Writing*, 142–59. Schenectady NY: Union College Press, 1973.

———. *The Universal Baseball Association, Inc., J. Henry Waugh, Prop.* 1968. New York: Penguin, 1971.

Couser, G. Thomas. *Memoir: An Introduction.* Oxford UK: Oxford University Press, 2012.

Crawford, Garry. *Consuming Sport: Fans, Sport, and Culture.* London: Routledge, 2004.

dak [Dave King]. "Some Questions and Some Answers." Fire Joe Morgan. Last modified April 20, 2005. http://www.firejoemorgan.com/2005/04/some-questions -and-some-answers.html.

Daniels, Phil. "Derrick Rose and the Danger of Sports Narratives." The Cauldron. Accessed March 23, 2015 (site discontinued).

DeLillo, Don. "Director's Cut: Q&A with Don DeLillo." By Rafe Bartholomew. Grantland. Last modified October 12, 2011. http://grantland.com/features/qa -don-delillo/.

———. "Pafko at the Wall." *Harper's Magazine*, October 1992.

———. "The Power of History." *New York Times Book Review*, September 7, 1997.

———. *Underworld.* New York: Simon & Schuster, 1997.

Dewey, Joseph. "A Gathering under Words: An Introduction." In *Underwords: Perspectives on Don DeLillo's Underworld*, edited by Joseph Dewey, Steven G. Kellman, and Irving Malin, 9–19. Newark DE: University of Delaware Press, 2002.

Duvall, John. "Baseball as Aesthetic Ideology: Cold War History, Race, and DeLillo's 'Pafko at the Wall.'" *Modern Fiction Studies* 41, no. 2 (1995): 285–313.

———. *Don DeLillo's Underworld: A Reader's Guide.* New York: Continuum, 2002.

Dyson, Michael Eric. *Reflecting Black: African-American Cultural Criticism.* Minneapolis: University of Minnesota Press, 1993.

Eakin, Paul John. *Fictions in Autobiography.* Princeton NJ: Princeton University Press, 1985.

———. *How Our Lives Become Stories: Making Selves.* Ithaca NY: Cornell University Press, 1999.

———. *Living Autobiographically: How We Create Identity in Narrative.* Ithaca NY: Cornell University Press, 2008.

———. *Touching the World: Reference in Autobiography.* Princeton NJ: Princeton University Press, 1992.

Early, Gerald. *A Level Playing Field.* Cambridge MA: Harvard University Press, 2011.

———. "Some Preposterous Propositions from the Heroic Life of Muhammad Ali: A Reading of *The Greatest: My Own Story*." In *Muhammad Ali: The People's Champ*, edited by Elliot Gorn, 70–87. Urbana: University of Illinois Press, 1995.

Edwards, Harry. *The Revolt of the Black Athlete*. New York: Free Press, 1969.

Ellison, Ralph. *Invisible Man*. 1952. New York: Random House, 1995.

emynd. "Off the Head like Decapitation." FreeDarko.com. Last modified March 13, 2006. http://freedarko.blogspot.com/2006/03/off-head-like-decapitation.html.

——. "The Heart of a Perpetual Loser." FreeDarko.com. Last modified February 23, 2006. http://freedarko.blogspot.com/2006/02/heart-of-perpetual-loser.html.

Evans, David H. "Taking Out the Trash: Don DeLillo's Underworld, Liquid Modernity, and the End of Garbage." *Cambridge Quarterly* 35, no. 2 (2006): 103–32.

Exley, Frederick. *A Fan's Notes*. 1968. New York: Random House, 1988.

——. *Last Notes from Home*. 1988. New York: Random House, 1990.

——. *Pages from a Cold Island*. 1974. New York: Random House, 1988.

"The Fan (1996)." The Numbers: Where Data and the Movie Business Meet. Accessed January 11, 2018. https://www.the-numbers.com/movie/Fan-The #tab=summary.

The Fan, directed by Tony Scott. Culver City CA: Tri-Star Pictures, 1996.

A Fan's Notes, directed by Eric Till. North York ON: Warner Brothers Canada, 1972.

Felski, Rita. "After Suspicion." *Profession* (2009): 28–35.

——. *Uses of Literature*. Malden MA: Blackwell, 2008.

Fever Pitch, directed by Peter Farrelly and Bobby Farrelly. Los Angeles: 20th Century Fox, 2005.

Fiske, John. "The Cultural Economy of Fandom." In *The Adoring Audience: Fan Culture and Popular Media*, edited by Lisa A. Lewis, 30–49. New York: Routledge, 1992.

"Fisking." UrbanDictionary.com. Accessed September 1, 2014. https://www .urbandictionary.com/define.php?term=Fisking.

Fitzgerald, F. Scott. *The Great Gatsby*. 1925. New York: Scribner, 2004.

Fitzpatrick, Kathleen. "The Unmaking of History: Baseball, Cold War, and *Underworld*." In *Underwords: Perspectives on Don DeLillo's Underworld*, edited by Joseph Dewey, Steven G. Kellman, and Irving Malin, 144–60. Newark: University of Delaware Press, 2002.

Ford, Sam. "'I Was Stabbed 21 Times by Crazy Fans': Pro Wrestling and Popular Concerns with Immersive Story Worlds." In *Seeing Fans: Representations of Fandom in Media and Popular Culture*, edited by Lucy Bennett and Paul Booth, 33–43. New York: Bloomsbury, 2016.

Fowles, Stacey May. *Baseball Life Advice: Loving the Game that Saved Me*. Toronto: McClelland & Stewart, 2017.

Freeman, Mark. *Rewriting the Self: History, Memory, Narrative*. New York: Routledge, 1993.

Frisch, Mark F. "Self-Definition and Redefinition in the New World: Coover's *The Universal Baseball Association* and Borges." *Confluencia* 4, no. 2 (1989): 13-20.

Gerdy, John R. *Sports: The All-American Addiction.* Jackson: University of Mississippi Press, 2002.

Giamatti, A. Bartlett, *Take Time for Paradise: Americans and Their Games.* New York: Summit Books, 1989.

"Gilbert Arenas Career Mix HD." YouTube. Last modified June 16, 2015. https://www.youtube.com/watch?v=JAY7rbo7RD4.

Gladwell, Malcolm. Foreword. In *The Book of Basketball,* by Bill Simmons, ix-xi. New York: ESPN Books, 2009.

The Godfather, directed by Francis Ford Coppola. Hollywood CA: Paramount, 1972.

Gray, Jonathan. "Antifandom and the Moral Text: Television without Pity and Textual Dislike." *American Behavioral Scientist* 48 (2005): 840-58.

———. "New Audiences, New Textualities: Anti-Fans and Non-Fans." *International Journal of Cultural Studies* 6, no. 1 (2003): 64-81.

Greiner, Donald J. "Don DeLillo, John Updike, and the Sustaining Power of Myth." In *Underwords: Perspectives on Don DeLillo's Underworld,* edited by Joseph Dewey, Steven G. Kellman, and Irving Malin, 103-13. Newark: University of Delaware Press, 2002.

Gumbrecht, Hans Ulrich. *In Praise of Athletic Beauty.* Cambridge MA: Belknap, 2006.

Guttmann, Allen. *Sports Spectators.* New York: Columbia University Press, 1986.

Guzzio, Tracie Church. "Courtside: Race and Basketball in the Works of John Edgar Wideman." In *In the Game: Race, Identity, and Sports in the Twentieth Century,* edited by Amy Bass, 221-36. New York: Palgrave MacMillan, 2005.

Hawthorne, Nathaniel. *The Scarlet Letter.* 1850. New York: Dover, 1994.

Hayles, N. Katherine. *How We Think: Digital Media and Contemporary Technogenesis.* Chicago: University of Chicago Press, 2012.

Hemingway, Ernest. *A Farewell to Arms.* 1929. New York: Scribner, 2014.

Hill, Benjamin Mako. "Cultivated Disinterest in Professional Sports." Copyrighteous. Last modified November 23, 2012. https://mako.cc/copyrighteous/cultivated-disinterest-in-professional-sports.

Hills, Matt. "Afterword: Participating in Hybrid Media Logics?" In *Seeing Fans: Representations of Fandom in Media and Popular Culture,* edited by Lucy Bennett and Paul Booth, 267-72. New York: Bloomsbury, 2016.

———. *Fan Cultures.* London: Routledge, 2002.

Hoberman, John. *Darwin's Athletes: How Sport Has Damaged Black America and Preserved the Myth of Race.* Boston: Houghton-Mifflin, 1997.

Howard, George Elliott. "Social Psychology of the Spectator." *American Journal of Sociology* 18, no. 1 (1912): 33-50.

Hutcheon, Linda. *A Poetics of Postmodernism: History, Theory, Fiction*. New York: Routledge, 1988.

———. "Historiographic Metafiction: Parody and the Intertextuality of History." In *Intertextuality and Contemporary American Fiction*, edited by Patrick O'Donnell and Robert Con Davis, 3–32. Baltimore: Johns Hopkins University Press, 1989.

Indian Chief, Dr. Lawyer [Adam Waytz]. "Am I My Brother's Brother?" FreeDarko.com. Last modified October 12, 2006. http://freedarko.blogspot.com/2006/10/am-i-my-brothers-brother.html.

———. "Amphibians on Dry Land." FreeDarko.com. Last modified January 1, 2007. https://freedarko.blogspot.com/2007/01/amphibians-on-dry-land.html.

Iser, Wolfgang. "The Reading Process: A Phenomenological Approach." In *Reader-Response Criticism: From Formalism to Post-Structuralism*, edited by Jane P. Tompkins, 50–69. Baltimore: Johns Hopkins University Press, 1980.

Jameson, Fredric. *Postmodernism, or, the Cultural Logic of Late Capitalism*. Durham NC: Duke University Press, 1991.

Jenkins, Henry. *Textual Poachers: Television Fans & Participatory Culture*. London: Routledge, 1992.

Johnson, Derek. "Fan-tagonism: Factions, Institutions, and Constitutive Hegemonies of Fandom." In *Fandom: Identities and Communities in a Mediated World*, edited by Jonathan Gray, Cornel Sandvoss, and C. Lee Harrington, 285–300. New York: New York University Press, 2007.

Joyce, James. *A Portrait of the Artist as a Young Man*. 1916. New York: Dover, 1994.

Junior [Alan Yang]. "The David Eckstein Memorial Eckstein of the Year Award." Fire Joe Morgan. Last modified October 23, 2006. http://www.firejoemorgan.com/2006/10/david-eckstein-memorial-eckstein-of.html.

———. "Don't Forget, Experts Know Better Than You." Fire Joe Morgan. Last modified May 29, 2006. http://www.firejoemorgan.com/2006/05/dont-forget-experts-know-better-than.html.

———. "Excerpt from the Previously Linked Article." Fire Joe Morgan. Last modified July 6, 2005. http://www.firejoemorgan.com/2005/07/excerpt-from-previously-linked-article.html.

———. "Five Players You Don't Want on Your Team." Fire Joe Morgan. Last modified June 27, 2006. http://www.firejoemorgan.com/2006/06/five-players-you-dont-want-on-your.html.

———. "Jack and Bert and a Hallway Where Famous People Go." Fire Joe Morgan. Last modified December 28, 2007. http://www.firejoemorgan.com/2007/12/jack-and-bert-and-hallway-where-famous.html.

———. "JoeChat?" Fire Joe Morgan. Last modified June 9, 2006. http://www
.firejoemorgan.com/2006/06/.

———. "Lede-Writing School." Fire Joe Morgan. Last modified April 27, 2006. http://
www.firejoemorgan.com/2006/04/lede-writing-school.html.

———. "More New York Stupidity." Fire Joe Morgan. Last modified October 12,
2005. http://www.firejoemorgan.com/2005/10/more-new-york-stupidity.html.

———. "Sportswriting 101." Fire Joe Morgan. Last modified July 25, 2005. http://
www.firejoemorgan.com/2005/07/sportswriting-101.html.

———. "These Poor, Poor Unfamous Men." Fire Joe Morgan. Last modified March
13, 2007. http://www.firejoemorgan.com/2007/03/.

Kalson, Sally. "Children of Promise, Children of Pain: The Jacob Wideman Case."
Pittsburgh Post-Gazette, August 19, 1987.

"Kevin Durant Catches Fire in OKC." YouTube. Last modified October 15, 2013.
https://www.youtube.com/watch?v=yFnRMorZI-k.

Kibby, Marjorie D. "Nostalgia for the Masculine: Onward to the Past in the Sports
Films of the Eighties." *Canadian Journal of Film Studies* 7, no. 1 (1998): 16–28.

Kimmel, Michael S. *Manhood in America*. Oxford UK: Oxford University Press, 2006.

Kirkpatrick, Ellen. "Hero-Fans and Fanboy Auteurs: Reflections and Realities of
Superhero Fans." In *Seeing Fans: Representations of Fandom in Media and Popular
Culture*, edited by Lucy Bennett and Paul Booth, 127–37. New York: Blooms-
bury, 2016.

Klugman, Matthew. "'It's That Feeling Sick in My Guts That I Think I Like the
Most': Sport, Pleasure, and Embodied Suffering." In *Examining Sport Histories:
Power, Paradigms, and Reflexivity*, edited by Richard Pringle and Murray Phillips,
159–91. Morgantown WV: Fitness Information Technology, 2013.

Lane, Jeffrey. *Under the Boards: The Cultural Revolution in Basketball*. Lincoln: University of Nebraska Press, 2007.

Lapchick, Richard, et al. "The 2013 Racial and Gender Report Card: National Bas-
ketball Association." The Institute for Diversity and Ethics in Sport. Accessed
June 25, 2013. http://nebula.wsimg.com/d64d18fb8a3af0063db14e4b8b6ce4a2
?AccessKeyId=DAC3A56D8FB782449D2A&disposition=0&alloworigin=1.

Lasch, Christopher. *The Culture of Narcissism: American Life in the Age of Diminishing
Expectations*. New York: Warner Books, 1979.

Lee, Spike. *Best Seat in the House*. New York: Crown, 1997.

Leonard, David J. *After Artest: The NBA and the Assault on Blackness*. Albany NY:
SUNY Press, 2012.

———. "Feminists We Love: Jessica Luther ~ Activist, Commentator, and Change Agent." The Feminist Wire. Last modified July 4, 2014. http://www.thefeministwire.com/2014/07/jessica-luther/.

———. "'Is This Heaven?' White Sporting Masculinities and the Hollywood Imagination." In *Visual Economies of/in Motion: Sport and Film,* edited by C. Richard King and David J. Leonard, 165–91. New York: Peter Lang, 2006.

Lewis, Michael. *Moneyball.* New York: Norton, 2003.

Lowe, Zach. "Death to Ringz: Chris Paul and the NBA's Broken Narrative of Success." Grantland. Last modified November 18, 2014. http://grantland.com/the-triangle/death-to-ringz-chris-paul-and-the-nbas-broken-narrative-of-success/.

Luther, Jessica. "About." Power Forward. Accessed October 31, 2014 (site discontinued).

———. "About the Oregon Ducks' Pink Uniforms." Accessed October 31, 2014 (site discontinued).

———. "About UT Football, Sexual Assault, and Race." Power Forward. Accessed October 31, 2014 (site discontinued).

———. "Before Jason Collins, There Was Robbie Rogers, Sort of." Power Forward. Accessed October 31, 2014 (site discontinued).

———. "Brittney Griner: 'Being One That's Out, It's Just Being Who You Are.'" Power Forward. Accessed October 31, 2014 (site discontinued).

———. "Catching Footballs Is Just Like Trading Women, According to Sportscenter." Power Forward. Accessed October 31, 2014 (site discontinued).

———. "Charlie Strong's UT Women's Football Camp Gets It Right." VICE Sports. Last modified September 4, 2014. https://sports.vice.com/en_us/article/yp74xm/charlie-strongs-ut-womens-football-camp-gets-it-right.

———. "Discrimination and Assault Lawsuit against UConn Women's Basketball Coach, Geno Auriemma." Power Forward. Accessed October 31, 2014 (site discontinued).

———. "The Double-Edged Sword of Women's Visibility in the Olympics." Power Forward. Accessed October 31, 2014 (site discontinued).

———. "Dudebro Sports Media." Power Forward. Accessed October 31, 2014 (site discontinued).

———. Email interview with the author, November 13, 2014.

———. "Going into the Jameis Winston Press Conference Tomorrow . . ." Power Forward. Accessed October 31, 2014 (site discontinued).

———. "The Hazy Middle." Sports on Earth. Last modified December 18, 2013. http://www.sportsonearth.com/article/66054444/.

———. "The Heteronormativity of How the Media Talks about Sexual Identity." Power Forward. Accessed October 31, 2014 (site discontinued).

———. "How You Talk Around Domestic Violence, ESPN Style." Power Forward. Accessed October 31, 2014 (site discontinued).

———. "Jason Collins' Words, Adapted (re: Brittney Griner)." Power Forward. Accessed October 31, 2014 (site discontinued).

———. "A List of College Football Rape Cases." Power Forward. Accessed October 31, 2014 (site discontinued).

———. "The Montana University and BYU Football Rape Cases." Power Forward. Accessed October 31, 2014 (site discontinued).

———. "The Naval Academy Football Rape Cases." Power Forward. Accessed October 31, 2014 (site discontinued).

———. "On Bill O'Brien and the Benefits of Coaching at Penn State." Power Forward. Accessed October 31, 2014 (site discontinued).

———. "On Brittney Griner." Power Forward. Accessed October 31, 2014 (site discontinued).

———. "Predictable." Power Forward. Accessed October 31, 2014 (site discontinued).

———. "The Reduction of Penn State Sanctions: The Unsurprising Cowardice of the NCAA." Power Forward. Accessed October 31, 2014 (site discontinued).

———. "Serena Williams Is Not a Costume." Power Forward. Accessed October 31, 2014 (site discontinued).

———. "Serena Williams Is Not a Costume, Part 2." Power Forward. Accessed October 31, 2014 (site discontinued).

———. "The Vanderbilt Football Rape Case." Power Forward. Accessed October 31, 2014 (site discontinued).

———. "Weeping for Sports Media." Power Forward. Accessed October 31, 2014 (site discontinued).

———. "Who We Talk about When Athletes Are Accused of Sexual Assault." VICE Sports. Last modified October 14, 2014. https://sports.vice.com/en_us/article /aem9ja/who-we-talk-about-when-athletes-are-accused-of-sexual-assault.

———. "Why 'Ladies' Nights' Are Bad Short-Terms Fixes to Long-Term Problems." Power Forward. Accessed October, 31 2014 (site discontinued).

———. "The WNBA Can Teach Male Athletes about Coming Out and Being Allies." The Atlantic. Last modified April 30, 2013. https://www.theatlantic.com/sexes /archive/2013/04/the-wnba-can-teach-male-athletes-about-coming-out-and -being-allies/275414/.

Majors, Richard. "Cool Pose: Black Masculinity and Sports." In *The Masculinities Reader*, edited by Stephen M. Whitehead and Frank J. Barrett, 209–18. Cambridge UK: Polity, 2001.

Markovits, Andrei S., and Emily Albertson. *Sportista: Female Fandom in the United States*. Philadelphia: Temple University Press, 2012.

Messenger, Christian. *Sport and the Spirit of Play in American Fiction: Hawthorne to Faulkner*. New York: Columbia University Press, 1981.

———. *Sport and the Spirit of Play in Contemporary American Fiction*. New York: Columbia University Press, 1990.

Mieuli, Franklin. "The (Positionality) Revolution Will (Not) Be Televised (Due to Local Blackout)." The Diss. Last modified April 11, 2012. http://thedissnba .blogspot.com/2012/04/positionality-revolution-will-not-be.html.

Miguel-Alfonso, Ricardo. "Mimesis and Self-Consciousness in Robert Coover's *The Universal Baseball Association*." *Critique* 37, no. 2 (1996): 92–107.

Morris, Timothy. *Making the Team: The Cultural Work of Baseball Fiction*. Urbana IL: University of Illinois Press, 1997.

Mount, Nicholas J. "'Are the Green Fields Gone?' Pastoralism in the Baseball Novel." *Aethlon* 11, no. 1 (1993): 61–77.

Mullins, Matthew. "Objects & Outliers: Narrative Community in Don DeLillo's *Underworld*." *Critique* 51, no. 3 (2010): 276–92.

Murbles [Matt Murray]. "As a GM, Dennis Tuttle Makes Steve Phillips Look Like a Genius." Fire Joe Morgan. Last modified July 21, 2005. http://www.firejoemorgan .com/2005/07/.

Nylund, David. *Beer, Babes, and Balls: Masculinity and Sports Talk Radio*. Albany NY: SUNY Press, 2007.

O'Donnell, Patrick, and Robert Con Davis. "Introduction: Intertext and Contemporary American Fiction." In *Intertextuality and Contemporary American Fiction*, edited by Patrick O'Donnell and Robert Con Davis, ix–xxii. Baltimore: Johns Hopkins University Press, 1989.

Oriard, Michael. *Dreaming of Heroes: American Sports Fiction, 1868–1980*. Chicago: Nelson Hall, 1982.

———. "Muhammad Ali: The Hero in the Age of Mass Media." In *Muhammad Ali: The People's Champ*, edited by Elliot Gorn, 5–23. Urbana: University of Illinois Press, 1995.

"Pacers vs Knicks: le KKK et l'Indiana." YouTube. Last modified July 3, 2015. https:// www.youtube.com/watch?v=iOmMw13G99w.

Parrish, Timothy L. "Frederick Exley's *A Fan's Notes*: American Dreams in the Twilight of Bednarik." *Aethlon* 16, no. 2 (1999): 125–39.

———. "From Hoover's FBI to Eisenstein's *Unterwelt*: DeLillo Directs the Postmodern Novel." *Modern Fiction Studies* 45, no. 3 (1999): 696–723.

Pascal, Roy. *Design and Truth in Autobiography*. Cambridge MA: Harvard University Press, 1960.

"Pause." UrbanDictionary.com. Accessed October 12, 2013. https://www.urban dictionary.com/define.php?term=pause.

Pearson, Roberta. "Fandom in the Digital Era." *Popular Communication* 8, no. 1 (2010): 84–95.

Perinbanayagam, Robert. *Games and Sports in Everyday Life: Dialogues and Narratives of the Self*. London: Paradigm, 2006.

"Phoenix Suns-Nash & Barbosa Fast Break." YouTube. Last modified December 11, 2006. https://www.youtube.com/watch?v=g-qFRo0mpCg.

Pomerantz, Dorothy. "'Silver Linings Playbook' Author Matthew Quick on Hollywood, Happy Endings and Loving the Eagles." Forbes.com. Last modified December 27, 2012. https://www.forbes.com/sites/dorothypomerantz/2012 /12/27/silver-linings-playbook-author-matthew-quick-on-hollywood-happy -endings-and-loving-the-eagles.

"Public Enemy." Billboard.com. Accessed October 12, 2013. http://www.billboard .com/artist/354718/public-enemy/chart?f=305.

Pudaloff, Ross J. "Toward a New Male Identity: Literature and Sports." In *Jock: Sports & Male Identity*, edited by Donald F. Sabo Jr. and Ross Runfola. Edgewood Cliffs NJ: Prentice-Hall, 1980.

Punday, Daniel. "Creative Accounting: Role-Playing Games, Possible-World Theory, and the Agency of Imagination." *Poetics Today* 26, no. 1 (2005): 113–39.

Quick, Matthew. *The Silver Linings Playbook*. 2008. London: Picador, 2010.

Raab, Scott. *The Whore of Akron: One Man's Search for the Soul of LeBron James*. New York: Harper Collins, 2011.

———. *You're Welcome, Cleveland: How I Helped LeBron James Win a Championship and Save a City*. New York: Harper Collins, 2017.

Recluse, Esq., Brown [Todd Ito]. "Dropping (Three) Jewels: The FreeDarko Guide to NCAA Enlightenment." FreeDarko.com. Last modified March 15, 2007. http:// freedarko.blogspot.com/2007/03/dropping-three-jewels-freedarko-guide.html.

———. "Happy Birthday to Us: FD's Greatest Misses." FreeDarko.com. Last modified January 19, 2006. http://freedarko.blogspot.com/2006/01/happy-birthday-to -us-fds-greatest.html.

Rhoden, William C. *Forty Million Dollar Slaves*. New York: Three Rivers Press, 2006.

"Running the Break: Still Streaking." NBA.com. Last modified November 25, 2013. http://www.nba.com/blazers/news/running-break-still-streaking.

Russell, Bill. *Second Wind*. New York: Random House, 1979.

Salinger, J. D. *The Catcher in the Rye*. 1951. New York: Little Brown, 1991.

Sandvoss, Cornel. *A Game of Two Halves: Football, Television and Globalization*. London: Routledge, 2003.

———. *Fans: The Mirror of Consumption*. Cambridge UK: Polity, 2005.

———. "From National Hero to Liquid Star: Identity and Discourse in Transnational Sports Consumption." In *Bodies of Discourse: Sports Stars, Media, and the Global Public*, edited by Cornell Sandvoss, Michael Real, and Alina Bernstein, 171–92. New York: Peter Lang, 2012.

"Scarborough Research Data Examines NBA Fan Demographics." Sports Business Daily. Last modified February 13, 2007. https://www.sportsbusinessdaily.com /Daily/Issues/2007/02/13/The-Back-Of-The-Book/Scarborough-Research -Data-Examines-NBA-Fan-Demographics.aspx.

Schimmel, Kimberly S., C. Lee Harrington, and Denise D. Bielby. "Keep Your Fans to Yourself: The Disjuncture between Sport Studies' and Pop Culture Studies' Perspectives on Fandom." *Sport in Society* 10, no. 4 (2007): 580–600.

Schwartz, Richard Alan. "Postmodernist Baseball." *Modern Fiction Studies* 33, no. 1 (1987): 135–49.

Sedgwick, Eve Kosofsky. *Epistemology of the Closet*. 1990. Berkeley: University of California Press, 2008.

Shelton, Frank W. "Humor and Balance in Coover's *The Universal Baseball Association, Inc.*" *Critique: Studies in Contemporary Fiction* 17, no. 1 (1975): 78–90.

Shields, David. *Black Planet: Facing Race during an NBA Season*. 1999. Lincoln: University of Nebraska Press, 2006.

———. *Body Politic: The Great American Sports Machine*. New York: Simon and Schuster, 2004.

Shoals, Bethlehem [Nathaniel Friedman]. "Against the Endless Maze of Sport." FreeDarko.com. Last modified December 25, 2006. http://freedarko.blogspot .com/2006/12/against-endless-maze-of-sport.html.

———. "Ain't No Use Clutchin' at the Butter." FreeDarko.com. Last modified January 25, 2011. http://freedarko.blogspot.com/2011/01/aint-no-use-clutchin-at -butter.html.

———. "All New Breath in Angles." FreeDarko.com. Last modified December 20, 2007. http://freedarko.blogspot.com/2007/12/all-new-breath-in-angles.html.

———. "Alone with My Notes." FreeDarko.com. Last modified November 8, 2005. http://freedarko.blogspot.com/2005/11/alone-with-my-notes.html.

———. "Amare Who?" FreeDarko.com. Last modified December 29, 2005. http:// freedarko.blogspot.com/2005/12/amare-who.html.

———. "Artestifyin', Vol. 1." FreeDarko.com. Last modified October 13, 2005. http:// freedarko.blogspot.com/2005/10/artestifyin-vol-1.html.

———. "Ask Me about the Baptist." FreeDarko.com. Last modified June 14, 2010. http://freedarko.blogspot.com/2010/06/then-something-happened.html.

———. "Between Fists and Speckles." FreeDarko.com. Last modified November 12, 2006. http://freedarko.blogspot.com/2006/11/between-fists-and-speckles.html.

———. "Call It Pyrite, It's Shiny for a Reason." FreeDarko.com. Last modified January 18, 2006. http://freedarko.blogspot.com/2006/01/call-it-pyrite-its-shiny -for-reason.html.

———. "Come Back Strong, People of Toil and Bloodshed!!!" FreeDarko.com. Last modified December 12, 2005. http://freedarko.blogspot.com/2005/12/come -back-strong-people-of-toil-and.html.

———. "A Complicated Game for Complicated Men." FreeDarko.com. Last modified February 20, 2006. http://freedarko.blogspot.com/2006/02/complicated -game-for-complicated-men.html.

———. "The Crown Is Dead, Long Live the King." FreeDarko.com. Last modified February 14, 2006. http://freedarko.blogspot.com/2006/02/crown-is-dead -long-live-king.html.

———. "The Day Never Ended." FreeDarko.com. Last modified April 11, 2011. http:// freedarko.blogspot.com/2011/04/day-never-ended.html.

———. Email interview with the author. October 5, 2014.

———. Email interview with the author. October 6, 2014.

———. Email interview with the author. December 4, 2014.

———. "The Ever-Renewing Cauldron's Dutiful Thud." FreeDarko.com. Last modified February 28, 2006. http://freedarko.blogspot.com/2006/02/ever-renewing -cauldrons-dutiful-thud.html.

———. "FreeDarko Book Club #2: Of Frank Obsequious Necessity." FreeDarko .com. Last modified February 5, 2007. https://freedarko.blogspot.com/2007 /02/freedarko-book-club-2-of-frank-oedipal.html.

———. "FreeDrafto, Pt. 5: Sit Tightly, Then SPURN." FreeDarko.com. Last modified June 27, 2005. http://freedarko.blogspot.com/2005/06/freedrafto-pt-5-sit -tightly-then-spurn.html.

———. "In the Land of Spiny Columns." FreeDarko.com. Last modified August 19, 2007. http://freedarko.blogspot.com/2007/08/in-land-of-spiny-columns.html.

———. "Just Remember Who Said It." FreeDarko.com. Last modified April 12, 2005. http://freedarko.blogspot.com/2005/04/just-remember-who-said-it.html.

———. "Look Down That Lonesome Road." FreeDarko.com. Last modified September 30, 2007. http://freedarko.blogspot.com/2007/09/look-down-that -lonesome-road.html.

———. "The Mind's Lungless Ankle." FreeDarko.com. Last modified March 6, 2007. http://freedarko.blogspot.com/2007/03/minds-lungless-ankle.html.

———. "My Interview with Nets Rookie Anthony Randolph." FreeDarko.com. Last modified July 17, 2008. http://freedarko.blogspot.com/2008/07/my-interview -with-nets-rookie-anthony.html.

———. "On the Eve of Pricey Incursion." FreeDarko.com. Last modified January 22, 2007. http://freedarko.blogspot.com/2007/01/on-eve-of-pricey-incursion.html.

———. "Our Kind of Scraping." FreeDarko.com. Last modified August 2, 2008. http://freedarko.blogspot.com/2008/08/our-kind-of-scraping.html.

———. "Plants Are Not Small Trees." FreeDarko.com. Last modified July 11, 2007. http://freedarko.blogspot.com/2007/07/plants-are-not-small-trees.html.

———. "The Poetical Don't Last." FreeDarko.com. Last modified June 14, 2006. https://freedarko.blogspot.com/2006/06/poetical-dont-last.html.

———. "'Safe to Say, This Is What Saturday's Should've Been'-TK." FreeDarko.com. Last modified February 23, 2009. http://freedarko.blogspot.com/2009/02/safe -to-say-this-is-what-saturdays.html.

———. "Save Your Claws, Chew Angles." FreeDarko.com. Last modified November 7, 2006. http://freedarko.blogspot.com/2006/11/save-your-claws-chew -angles.html.

———. "SEE, BASKETBALL IS NOT JAZZ." FreeDarko.com. Last modified March 26, 2008. http://freedarko.blogspot.com/2008/03/basketball-is-tourist-friendly.html.

———. "Snack of Fair Demons." FreeDarko.com. Last modified September 3, 2006. http://freedarko.blogspot.com/2006/09/snack-of-fair-demons.html.

———. "State of Fiery Heaven Address." FreeDarko.com. Last modified February 14, 2008. http://freedarko.blogspot.com/2008/02/state-of-fried-heaven -address.html.

———. "Strength Begat Mind." FreeDarko.com. Last modified May 4, 2006. http:// freedarko.blogspot.com/2006/05/strength-begat-mind.html.

———. "Strength for Everyone!" FreeDarko.com. Last modified April 8, 2008. https:// freedarko.blogspot.com/2008/04/strength-for-everyone.html.

———. "Sweet Fields of Unfastened Terrain." Timothy McSweeney's Internet Tendency. Last modified October 12, 2006. https://www.mcsweeneys.net/articles /sweet-fields-of-unfastened-terrain.

———. "The Unfortunate Moss." FreeDarko.com. Last modified August 13, 2006. https://freedarko.blogspot.com/2006/08/unfortunate-moss.html.

———. "When Citizenry Got Settled Again." FreeDarko.com. Last modified April 12, 2006. http://freedarko.blogspot.com/2006/04/when-citizenry-got-settled -again.html.

———. "You Can Grade Me Shorter." FreeDarko.com. Last modified December 10, 2006. http://freedarko.blogspot.com/2006/12/you-can-grade-me-shorter.html.

Silver Linings Playbook, directed by David O. Russell. New York: Weinstein Company, 2012.

Simmons, Bill. *The Book of Basketball*. New York: ESPN Books, 2009.

Simons, Eric. *The Secret Lives of Sports Fans: The Science of Sports Obsession*. New York: Overlook Duckworth, 2013.

Smith, Patrick A. "Constructing Contemporary Utopias: Robert Coover's *The Universal Baseball Association* and the Games We Play." *Aethlon* 16, no. 1 (1998): 13–21.

Stanfill, Mel. "'Straighten Up and Fly White: Whiteness, Heteronormativity, and the Representation of Happy Endings for Fans." In *Seeing Fans: Representations of Fandom in Media and Popular Culture*, edited by Lucy Bennett and Paul Booth, 187–95. New York: Bloomsbury, 2016.

Sterling, Phillip. "Frederick Exley's *A Fan's Notes*: Football as Metaphor." *Critique: Studies in Contemporary Fiction* 22, no. 1 (1980): 39–46.

Tarver, Erin C. *The I in Team: Sports Fandom and the Reproduction of Identity*. Chicago: University of Chicago Press, 2017.

Tompkins, Jane. "An Introduction to Reader-Response Criticism." In *Reader-Response Criticism: From Formalism to Post-Structuralism*, edited by Jane P. Tompkins, ix–xxvi. Baltimore: Johns Hopkins University Press, 1980.

Tremendous, Ken [Michael Schur]. "Apologies in Advance." Fire Joe Morgan. Last modified March 27, 2007. http://www.firejoemorgan.com/2007/03/apologies-in-advance.html.

———. "Eckstein Round-Up." Fire Joe Morgan. Last modified October 31, 2006. http://www.firejoemorgan.com/2006/10/eckstein-round-up.html.

———. "Follow-Up: Joe Morgan's Epistemological Nightmare." Fire Joe Morgan. Last modified April 27, 2006. http://www.firejoemorgan.com/2006/04/follow-up-joe-morgans-epistemological.html.

———. "Has Anyone Heard of This 'Eckstein' Fellow?" Fire Joe Morgan. Last modified October 10, 2006. http://www.firejoemorgan.com/2006/10/has-anyone-heard-of-this-eckstein.html.

———. "Heady Days." Fire Joe Morgan. Last modified April 10, 2008. http://www.firejoemorgan.com/2008/04/heady-days.html.

———. "I Don't Want to Chat with Joe, As I Don't Watch Him Chat Every Day, So I Don't Want to Chat One Way or the Other." Fire Joe Morgan. Last modified April 17, 2007. http://www.firejoemorgan.com/2007/04/i-dont-want-to-chat-with-joe-as-i-dont.html.

———. "Joe Wants to Chat." Fire Joe Morgan. Last modified April 28, 2007. http://www.firejoemorgan.com/2007/04/joe-wants-to-chat.html.

———. "Missed Connections." Fire Joe Morgan. Last modified November 18, 2007. http://www.firejoemorgan.com/2007/11/missed-connections.html.

———. "Post #1377: The Relatively Short Goodbye." Fire Joe Morgan. Last modified November 13, 2008. http://www.firejoemorgan.com/2008/11/post-1377-relatively-short-goodbye.html.

———. "Someday You, Too, Could Be Drastically Overrated." Fire Joe Morgan. Last modified June 25, 2007. http://www.firejoemorgan.com/2007/06/someday-you-too-could-be-drastically.html.

Trump, Rob. "The Innate Quality to Win: Fire Joe Morgan on Fire Joe Morgan." The Classical. Last modified December 19, 2012. http://theclassical.org/articles/the-innate-quality-to-win-fire-joe-morgan-on-fire-joe-morgan.

———. "We Didn't Know What The F— We Were Doing: Fire Joe Morgan on Fire Joe Morgan." The Classical. Last modified December 17, 2012. http://theclassical.org/articles/we-didnt-know-what-the-f-we-were-doing-fire-joe-morgan-on-fire-joe-morgan.

———. "What Are We Doing Here?: Fire Joe Morgan on Fire Joe Morgan." The Classical. Last modified December 20, 2012. http://theclassical.org/articles/what-are-we-doing-here-fire-joe-morgan-on-fire-joe-morgan.

Wallace, David Foster. "Derivative Sport in Tornado Alley." In *Body Language: Writers on Sport*, edited by Gerald Early, 157–74. Saint Paul MN: Gray Wolf, 1998.

———. "Federer as Religious Experience." *New York Times: Play Magazine*. Last modified August 20, 2006. https://www.nytimes.com/2006/08/20/sports/playmagazine/20federer.html.

———. "How Tracy Austin Broke My Heart." In *Consider the Lobster and Other Essays*, 141–55. New York: Little Brown, 2006.

———. *Infinite Jest*. New York: Little Brown, 1996.

Wann, Daniel L., and Merrill J. Melnick et al. *Sports Fans: The Psychology and Social Impact of Spectators*. New York: Routledge, 2001.

Wideman, John Edgar. *Hoop Roots*. New York: Houghton Mifflin, 2001.

Wineapple, Brenda. "Robert Coover's Playing Fields." *Iowa Review* 10, no. 3 (1979): 66–74.

Yagoda, Ben. *Memoir: A History*. New York: Riverhead Books, 2009.

Yardley, Jonathan. *Misfit: The Strange Life of Frederick Exley*. New York: Random House, 1997.

INDEX

aesthetics: of athletes, 1, 63, 85, 90, 91, 156, 172, 186–88; critical distance and, 10, 70; fan judgment of, 4, 15–16, 85, 156, 171–75, 186–88; and fans as unbeautiful, 1–2, 4, 15–16, 210. *See also* blackness: style and

American identity: autobiography and, 73–74; baseball and, 17–18, 23, 28, 34, 51, 194, 202; football and, 56; meritocracy and, 18, 76, 142. *See also* blackness: basketball and; identity; racism

aspirational homosocial ventriloquism, 80, 98–115

athletes: as beautiful, 1, 63, 85, 90, 91, 156, 172, 186–88; as bodies, 3, 11, 78, 82–83, 96, 99, 104, 110–15, 143, 165–66, 172; as characters, 3, 12, 15, 44, 76, 78, 104–7, 113–14, 182, 208–9; as geniuses, 1, 2, 15, 210; as greedy, 82, 125; masculinity and, 82–83, 85–87, 89–90, 94–95, 98, 104–5, 114, 205–8; as objects, 78, 82, 90, 98, 103, 107, 113–17, 143, 166; political activism and, ix–xi, 11, 114, 164, 173–75, 189; reality of, 9, 12, 20, 76, 98, 143, 172, 208–9; women, 164–69, 194–95. *See also* domestic violence

Aufiero, Paul (character), 125–26, 133–36, 142–47, 150–51

Austin, Tracy, 1–2

authors: filmic depiction of, 121–22, 150–51; as narrators, 53–55, 57, 65, 67–68, 71, 107, 119; reception and, 11, 13, 51, 73, 198–99; self-reflection and, 19–21, 79–80, 89–90, 96, 101–3, 110, 115, 197; sports fans as, 2–8, 75–76, 93–94, 116–17, 126, 153–54, 170–85, 209, 233n1. *See also* readers

autobiography. *See under* American identity; memoir; novel

Baker, Aaron, 121, 122, 135

Barash, David P., 54, 55, 56, 58, 77, 213n12

baseball: American identity and, 17–18, 23, 28, 34, 51, 194, 202; history and, 8–9, 18–34, 37–41, 48–51, 72, 191, 204; MLB, 21, 39, 191, 193, 207; nostalgia and, 17–18, 22, 26, 34, 45, 124–26, 131, 141, 159, 191; novel and, 8–9, 17–52; pastoralism and, 17–18, 22, 42, 53, 171; statistics and, 17–19, 31, 158–63, 177–79, 191, 193, 207, 233n2; unwritten rules of, 205–6; whiteness and, 23, 26–27, 29, 191–94

253

basketball: NBA, 11, 74–119, 166–67, 169, 171–76, 186–91; playground hoop, 78–79, 93–94, 113–15; as resistance, 11, 79, 114, 173–75. *See also under* blackness

Baskett, Hank, 10, 58–59, 62, 65, 148

beauty. *See* aesthetics

Big Fan (film), 12–13, 121–23, 125–26, 133–36, 142–47, 149–51

Birrell, Susan, 3, 165

Bishop, Quantrell (character), 125, 133–35, 142–44

blackness: basketball and, 10–11, 73–119; commodification of, 79, 90, 98, 104, 109–13; masculinity and, 22–28, 82–83, 85–87, 89–91, 94–95, 98, 114, 142–44; physicality and, 78, 79, 83, 86, 90, 112–13, 148, 165–66; poverty and, 94–95, 96; self-consciousness of, 23, 26–27, 83, 88, 95–96, 142; sexualization of, 11, 78, 82–83, 85–87, 90, 98, 112–13, 142–44, 148, 165–66; style and, 92, 186–88; as threatening, 105–6, 112–13, 146, 183; white audiences and, 23, 26, 73–119, 141, 189. *See also* politics: athletes and; racism

blogs. *See* internet

Boston Red Sox, 126–28, 137–39, 147–48, 163, 179, 232n65

Brooklyn Dodgers, 24, 29, 34

Bruegel, Pieter, 36–38, 47, 48

Busse, Kristina, 5, 39

canonicity, 34, 64, 173, 175, 178

Carrington, Ben, 89, 90, 141, 143, 233n4

celebrity, 35, 53, 56–58, 65, 68, 78, 97, 107, 109–11

characters: athletes as, 3, 12, 15, 44, 76, 78, 104–7, 113–14, 182, 208–9; fans as, 9–13, 53–55, 66, 113, 121–23, 128–29, 137, 177. *See also* authors: as narrators

Colás, Yago, 184–85, 229n175

Cold War, 18–19, 23, 29, 34–38

competition. *See* sports: as competitive

consumerism. *See* fans: as consumers

Coover, Robert: *The Universal Baseball Association*, 8–9, 20–21, 39–52, 72

counternarratives, 3, 28, 38, 50, 114, 166–67, 201

crowd: adulation of, 26, 35, 36, 48, 57, 59, 63, 121, 124; anonymizing, 8, 23, 28–29, 32, 51, 60, 65, 78, 119; as mob, 26, 30, 51, 60, 61, 63, 213n12

DeLillo, Don: "Pafko at the Wall," 18, 22, 25, 26, 27, 35, 214n4; "Power of History," 18–19, 24, 28, 38, 50, 51; *Underworld*, 8–9, 18–38, 39, 51, 53, 72, 214n4

DeNiro, Robert, 123, 124, 128, 129, 140

domestic violence, 181, 182, 202, 206–8

Duvall, John, 23, 25, 26, 27, 29

Eakin, Paul John, 4, 7, 20, 73–74, 107, 118–19, 222n2. *See also* narratives: identity and

Early, Gerald, 73, 75–77, 117–18, 170, 184, 223n14, 225n67

Eckstein, David, 178, 192–94

Exley, Frederick: *A Fan's Notes*, 9–10, 53–59, 62–72, 118, 121, 145, 221n65

fame. *See* celebrity

The Fan (film), 12–13, 121–25, 131–33, 140–42, 145, 146, 149 fans: as authors, 2–8, 75–76, 93–94, 116–17, 126, 153–54, 170–85, 209, 233n1; as characters, 9–13, 53–55, 66, 113, 121–23, 128–29, 137, 177; community among, 13, 51–52, 77, 127, 147, 149, 154–56, 163, 169, 200, 203–5; as consumers, 2–5, 13, 36, 55, 78–79, 96, 98, 115–16, 120–23, 152, 170; definition of, 211n7; as economically limited, 123–30; as gatekeepers, 203–5; identity and, 4–7, 9–12, 17–21, 34, 53–69, 73–77, 83–85, 93–94, 115–19, 143, 148–49, 197–98, 202–6; idiosyncrasy of, 3, 7, 18–19, 22–24, 28, 30–31, 37, 49–50, 58, 122; as infantilized, 125, 133, 136; as isolated, 9, 38, 40, 42, 44–45, 122, 133, 204; as losers, 9, 12, 42, 122, 125, 132, 137, 147, 151; masculinity and, 12–13, 22–28, 38, 47, 104–5, 122–51, 202–5; and mental illness, 9–10, 43–47, 51–52, 53–72, 135, 148–49; as passive, 40, 54–56, 63, 79, 122, 123, 153; as pathological, 12–13, 38–39, 51, 60, 120–23, 129–30, 140–42, 150–51; as rabid, 1, 51, 53, 57, 62, 86, 118, 122; racism and, 11, 26–27, 63, 74–112, 119, 125, 140–49, 186–94; as resistant, 4, 11, 25, 38, 109, 155, 156, 171, 201, 204; as self-gratifying, 133–34; stereotypes of, 8, 9, 12, 38, 42, 54, 122, 130; subjectivity of, 8, 21, 30, 33, 40–41, 50, 70, 74, 117, 162; team affiliations and, 35, 85, 115–16, 118, 154–56, 163–64, 169, 207–8, 222n108; as uncritical, 10, 54, 55, 64, 129, 153, 157, 173; as violent, 58–63, 66, 124–25, 129–32, 141–42, 145, 149,

206–8; and whiteness, 11, 23, 26, 75–91, 95–100, 103–7, 109, 122–26, 130, 140–49, 223n10; as women, 14–15, 121, 133, 147, 166, 194–98, 201–10. *See also* crowd; homophobia; homosociality; liberated fandom; media fans; misogyny; narcissism; readers; reality: escape from; sports: as quantified

fan studies, 2, 5–6, 12, 16, 77, 116, 122, 152, 163

Farrelly, Bobby and Peter, 126, 136–37

Felski, Rita, 7, 10, 70, 157–58, 173–74, 176–77

feminism, 14, 106, 124, 126, 164–65, 197, 199, 201–10

Fever Pitch (film), 12–13, 121–23, 126–28, 136–39, 140, 147–48, 149–51

film, 12–13, 120–51

Fire Joe Morgan (blog), 13–14, 154, 158–63, 164, 169, 171, 176–79, 184–86, 191–94, 197–200

fisking, 158–59

Fitzpatrick, Kathleen, 19, 24

football: literature and, 9–10, 55, 64–67; NFL, X, 62–63, 67, 84, 135; violence of, 47, 53, 62–63, 125

Fowles, Stacey May: *Baseball Life Advice*, 14–15, 201–10

Frazier, Walt "Clyde," 92

FreeDarko (blog), 13–14, 154, 155–58, 163, 164, 169, 171–76, 179, 185–91, 194, 197, 198–200, 226n85

Gerdy, John, 54, 55, 58

Giamatti, A. Bartlett, 17, 21, 39

Gifford, Frank, 10, 54, 56–57, 58–59, 62–64, 65, 69, 71, 221n65

objectivity: of dice, 20–21, 39–40, 42, 48, 50. *See also* baseball: history and; media; reality: of lived experience

Oswalt, Patton, 125

patriarchy, 44, 123, 125, 126, 129–30, 136, 141–44, 149

Payton, Gary, 81–82, 92, 98–100, 227n111

Peoples, Pat (character), 10, 55–56, 58–62, 65–69, 70–72, 128–30, 149, 220n37

Philadelphia Eagles, 58–62, 65, 67, 128–31, 133, 140, 144–45, 148–49

players. *See* athletes

politics: athletes and, ix–xi, 11, 114, 164, 173–75, 189; sports and, ix–xi, 74, 164, 185–86, 189–91, 198–99, 208–9

positional revolution, 174–75, 188

postmodernism, 7, 8, 19, 22, 25, 28, 175, 199, 213n25

Power Forward (blog), 13–14, 154, 163–69, 171, 179–84, 185, 186, 194–200

Prynne, Hester (character), 10, 66–67

Quick, Matthew: *The Silver Linings Playbook*, 9–10, 54–56, 58–62, 64–68, 70–72, 128–29, 130, 140

Raab, Scott: *The Whore of Akron*, 11, 83–88, 90, 91, 96–98, 100–103, 106–8, 116–17, 224n50, 227n117, 229n185; *You're Welcome, Cleveland*, 224n50

racism: "colorblind" or "new," 11, 77, 81, 89, 100, 142, 191; among fans, 11, 26–27, 63, 74–112, 119, 125, 140–49, 186–94; sports as obscuring, 11, 23, 27, 76, 119. *See also* aspirational homosocial ventriloquism; blackness; whiteness

rape. *See* sexual assault

Rayburn, Bobby (character), 123, 132–33, 140–42

readerly double-consciousness. *See* Felski, Rita

readers: fan reception and, 3–7, 55–56, 72, 108, 157, 166, 173, 179–80, 189–91, 211n7; filmic depiction of, 121, 151; hyper-reading, 200, 233n1; sports fans as, x, 10–15, 28, 107, 171–72, 175–77, 198, 209, 213n25

reality: of athletes, 9, 12, 20, 76, 98, 143, 172, 208–9; as blurred, 9–10, 54–56, 64, 65, 70, 71–72, 103; escape from, ix–x, 23, 29, 41–43, 54, 56, 65, 154, 189; of historical events 18–20, 21, 24, 25, 27–28, 33, 34, 35, 50, 222n2; of lived experience, 11, 28, 39, 41–43, 64–65, 67, 69, 71–74, 107–8, 213n25; of sporting events x, 2, 9–10, 30–33, 40–41, 75–76, 107–8, 163, 170, 179. *See also* memory: and memoir; mental illness: fans and; subjectivity

Renard, Gil (character), 123–25, 131–33, 140–42, 150–51, 232n71

Robinson, Jackie, ix, 91, 189

Russell, Bill, ix, 88–89, 97, 147

Russell, David O., 128

Rutherford, Damon (character), 39, 41, 43, 45–47, 51

Sandvoss, Cornell, 5, 6, 115–16, 185–86, 198, 211n7

San Francisco Giants, 123, 131–32

Scott, Tony, 123, 132, 140–41, 145

sexism. *See* misogyny

sexual assault, 46, 131, 180–84, 197, 208

white supremacy. *See* racism

Wideman, John Edgar: *Hoop Roots*, 11, 75, 78–79, 93–96, 109, 112–15, 117, 226n90, 229n165

Williams, Serena, 164–69, 184

Winston, Jameis, 182–83

women: as athletes, 164–69, 194–95; as fans, 14–15, 121, 133, 147, 166, 194–98, 201–10. *See also* feminism; misogyny

wrestling, 5, 107

Wrightman, Ben (character), 126–28, 136–39, 147–48, 150, 151

CPSIA information can be obtained
at www.ICGtesting.com
Printed in the USA
LVHW112147160519
618183LV00004B/46/P